Literacy and the Second Language Learner

Volume 1 of
Research in Second Language Learning
Series Editor: JoAnn Hammadou Sullivan, *University of Rhode Island*

Literacy and the
Second Language Learner

Edited by

JoAnn Hammadou Sullivan

**INFORMATION AGE
PUBLISHING**

80 Mason Street
Greenwich, Connecticut 06830

ISBN: 1-930608-86-1 (paper); 1-930608-87-X (cloth)

Printed in the United States of America

CONTENTS

LIST OF CONTRIBUTORS

Cindy Brantmeier   Washington University
                             St. Louis, MO

María M. Carreira   California State University
                             Long Beach, CA

Rebecca L. Chism   Kent State University
                             Kent, OH

Andrew D. Cohen   University of Minnesota
                             Minneapolis, MN

James N. Davis   University of Arkansas
                             Fayetteville, AK

Michael E. Everson   University of Iowa
                             Iowa City, IA

Michael Fast   American Institutes for Research,
                             Washington, DC, and University of
                             Massachusetts, Amherst

Leonore Ganschow   Professor Emerita
                             Miami (OH) University

Terri Ann Gebel   University of Northern Iowa
                             Cedar Falls, IA

Rosalind Horowitz The University of Texas–San Antonio
San Antonio, TX

Ann Johns San Diego State University
San Diego, CA

John I. Liontas University of Notre Dame
Notre Dame, IN

Mary Ann Lyman-Hager San Diego State University
San Diego, CA

Honorine Nocon University of California–San Diego
San Diego, CA

Elke Schneider State University of New York at Fredonia
Fredonia, NY

Leslie L. Schrier University of Iowa
Iowa City, IA

Sufumi So Carnegie Mellon University
Pittsburgh, PA

Richard L. Sparks College of Mt. St. Joseph
Cincinnati, OH

JoAnn Hammadou Sullivan University of Rhode Island
Kingston, RI

INTRODUCTION

THE SECOND LANGUAGE EDUCATORS' CHALLENGE: LEARNING ABOUT LITERACY

JoAnn Hammadou Sullivan

INTRODUCTION

The current volume on literacy and second language learners is the beginning of a new series that will highlight cutting-edge research in the area of second language (L2) learning and teaching. The field of second language learning research has grown rapidly in recent years. Educators have become increasingly aware that pedagogical knowledge varies significantly among subject domains. This series will provide an important outlet for research that examines specifically the needs and concerns of second language learners and those who support their efforts.

UNDERSTANDING LITERACY

Literacy means many different things to different people. It is often a topic that generates strong emotional reactions and heated debates. And, as is common with an emotion-laden topic, its definition can be particularly difficult to nail down. Definitions of "literacy" vary depending on the lens of the discipline from which a person is studying it. In shaping the current volume, second or foreign language literacy was conceived at first as the ability to use text to communicate ideas in writing, understand written information and to make interpretations based upon it in a second language. It is distinct from second language proficiency, which refers to the totality of language acquisition. Several authors in the volume expand on and clarify this initial definition. Literacy in this volume is seen as a continuum, so there is no precise point at which an individual is "literate" or not. In these studies, literacy is not extended to include literacy in interpreting art, music or film, for example, as it often is today. Nor does this volume examine the ability to use and understand mathematical functions known as mathematical literacy or numeracy. In today's technological societies, the concept of literacy is typically extended to electronic texts and that will be the case here as well. In other words, this volume focuses primarily on written texts and the thinking and problem-solving processes that are involved in reading, writing, and interpreting their social and cultural contexts. The volume contains examples of important work in several second language settings—including those of foreign language learners, bilingual learners, and English as a second language learners. Educators in these overlapping fields have much to share with each other.

Graff (1994) offers us eight important lessons from history, which are a part of our legacy in the study of literacy. These eight lessons can serve as a useful backdrop for the research reported in this volume. The first lesson is that the understanding of literacy and practices of schooling are historically grounded and therefore powerfully resistant to change or reform. The second is the fundamental complexity of the topic of literacy. An historical myth is that literacy development is straightforward and simple but, when examined, we can find frequent disagreement on what literacy means, where it fits into the larger picture of communication, and the outcomes of educational interventions. Lesson three is that "no mode or means of learning is neutral" (p. 46) and therefore we need to own up to our personal perspectives when studying literacy. Lesson four is that literacy has historically played a key role in the "great divide" between haves and have nots. Lesson five is that history has shown that learning literacy is hard work and we may need to appreciate and value the individual's efforts and successes. Lesson six is that historically there have been "multiple paths of learning literacy" and the use of "an extraordinary range of instructors, institutions and other environments" (p. 49) working toward literacy goals. Lesson seven is the pervasive myth through history that learning literacy is the purview of children, not adults, and a resulting long-standing lack of opportunities to learn. Finally, lesson eight is that formal literacy learning and economic development are related, but "the nature of those connections is anything but simple, direct, unmediated" (p. 53).

Although these lessons were drawn from the history of first language (L1) literacy, they can serve as a useful setting for these studies in second language literacy too. Even though research in second language literacy has a shorter history, we can recognize these legacies also.

Literacy is an international issue with different ramifications and triggering different concerns in differing corners of the globe. The studies in this volume are all products of literacy studies done primarily in the United States and may display a slant toward the perceived needs and concerns of its educational communities as a result. Literacy policies of national or regional governments have been debated extensively in other forums and are not analyzed directly here.

This volume contains only a small segment of the possible voices and possible questions that make up the broad and complex field of second language literacy study. We do not claim to have exhausted the possible issues to study or perspectives to take. Rather, the researchers here share their current investigations into segments of the variable set of literacy processes and the textual, cognitive, or social factors that influence them. They explore how learners make use of texts, their own or others, and some of the myriad influences on those uses. Future advances in understanding literacy development will require breaking down traditional barriers among research disciplines to widen our understanding of this complex phenomenon.

REFERENCE

Graff, H.J. (1994). Literacy, myths and legacies: Lessons from the history of literacy. In L.T. Verhoeven (Ed.), *Studies in written language and literacy: Vol 1. Functional literacy: Theoretical issues and educational implications* (pp. 37-60). Amsterdam: John Benjamins.

REVIEWERS FOR VOLUME 1

Rick Donato
University of Pittsburgh

Norbert Hedderich
University of Rhode Island

Keiko Koda
Carnegie Mellon University

Scott McGinnis
National Foreign Language Center

Lee Wilberschied
University of Cincinnati

Joseph Morello
University of Rhode Island

Ann Masters Salomone
Kent State University

JoAnn Hammadou Sullivan
University of Rhode Island

Richard E. Sullivan
University of Rhode Island

CHAPTER 1

THEORETICAL DEVELOPMENTS IN READING CHINESE AND JAPANESE AS FOREIGN LANGUAGES

Michael E. Everson

ABSTRACT

During the past few decades, there has been increased research interest into how readers of languages employing non-alphabetic writing systems develop reading proficiency. Less well publicized is the research strand investigating this developmental process among foreign language learners of Chinese and Japanese, languages that are increasingly available for students in United States educational settings. This chapter will discuss some of the findings of research studies conducted among learners of these languages, and will highlight some of the theoretical frameworks used to anchor various research studies. The chapter will also discuss issues that have achieved importance for teachers of these languages, and point out research directions that seem promising for the future.

INTRODUCTION

During the past few decades, we have seen within the field of second language (L2) reading a small yet determined strand of research investigating reading in Chinese and Japanese as foreign languages (CFL/JFL). Perhaps this reflects the feeling that the 21st century will be "the Asian century," or that globalization is indeed the watchword for the world's economies. Or perhaps it is a foreshadowing of what needs to be accomplished by educational and government agencies due to our inability as a nation to meet security as well as scholarly needs in these areas (Brecht & Rivers, 2000). The small amount of research on the reading of these languages should not be surprising, given that only a small percentage of our overall national language capacity is devoted to the study of these languages. Yet, the period between 1970 and 1995 showed significant growth in these languages which now represent 6% of all student enrollments at the college level (Brod & Wells, 2000).

Despite this stability and growth in Japanese and Chinese foreign language enrollments, research conducted to understand how foreign language learners come to learn these languages is in its infancy, and is often not reported in a summative way so as to allow foreign language educators ready access. This chapter, then, will serve this purpose by investigating recent research dealing with how foreign language learners go about the task of learning to read in these languages. For this chapter, "foreign language" is defined as a second language learned in what are primarily formal, classroom settings where there is little or no environmental support outside this setting to aid in language acquisition. Given this setting, this chapter will highlight the areas of inquiry that seem to interest researchers in both these languages, discuss the findings of selected studies, and put forth suggestions for further research.

BEGINNING THE PROCESS OF LEARNING TO READ IN CFL/JFL

Researchers and teachers involved in Chinese and Japanese language instruction have always been interested in trying to qualify why these languages seem to be more difficult for Westerners to learn. Government agencies, for instance, have classified Chinese and Japanese, along with Korean and Arabic, as Category IV languages, based on the time it takes for a learner to reach a specified level of proficiency. Research from the Foreign Service Institute indicates that to reach level two proficiency (Advanced Level on the ACTFL scale) in a Category I language such as French or Spanish, students need to complete approximately 480 hours of instruction; to attain equivalent proficiency in a Category IV language requires approximately 1,320 hours. If one was to equate this to a typical program in a university setting, to reach a proficiency level of two would take approximately eight years (Walton, 1992).

Although there are a host of factors that contribute to this differential that are both linguistic and cultural in nature, researchers have cited the orthographies employed in Chinese and Japanese as significant hurdles for American learners to overcome. Chinese is considered to be a logographic script, where each character represents a word or morpheme. Unlike alphabetic scripts, Chinese characters reflect their phonology in a largely irregular and unsystematic manner, leading some to conjecture that Chinese readers are more reliant upon visual cues in reading their own script. For the American learner, the opaque sound-to-symbol correspondence inherent in Chinese means that they must learn a "helping language" that is used to acquire vocabulary from the first day of class. That is, instead of using large amounts of Chinese characters immediately, students begin to learn Chinese using romanization whereby Chinese vocabulary items are written using the Roman alphabet, with diacritical markings used to signify the tone of the character. The most common romanization system used in the United States to teach Chinese is *pinyin*, the system used in China for romanization. Eventually, the romanization is replaced by Chinese characters so that CFL students can begin to read authentic text. However, romanization stays with them throughout their language learning career as a way to mediate this problem.

Japanese, on the other hand, employs multiple scripts, thus offering a series of different challenges to American learners. Two of the scripts are syllabary systems, whereby sound maps onto the printed symbol at the syllable level. These two syllabaries also have somewhat specialized functions, with one (*hiragana*) being used primarily for function words such as case-marking particles, and the other (*katakana*) being used for borrowed words. Chinese characters, termed *kanji*, are also used in Japanese, and primarily represent content words. The three scripts are used together in authentic Japanese writing. Although there are romanization systems to represent Japanese sounds using the Roman alphabet, current pedagogy frowns upon using these systems to teach Japanese, and espouses teaching the syllabary systems immediately so that vocabulary can be delivered to students using these authentic forms. Given that the symbols for both *hiragana* and *katakana* are limited and have consistent sound to symbol correspondence, students learn vocabulary in the native script very early in their language learning experience. *Kanji* are usually introduced to the students during the first year of study, but only in amounts considered to be manageable for study purposes. The lack of apparent sound cues that make Chinese characters difficult to learn for American students of Chinese is compounded by the fact that in Japanese, *kanji* have multiple readings depending upon the context of the character's usage.

Although these orthographic considerations are the more typical issues usually pointed out by theorists and practitioners when describing the difficulties of learning to read in Chinese and Japanese, there are other factors that should be kept in mind when evaluating this research. First, it is often forgotten that, unlike the developing literacy environment in L1, foreign language students are learning the spoken language at the same time they are learning to read. That is, these students have extremely limited spoken language resources to bolster their burgeoning reading ability. Secondly, understanding the reading process among these students is difficult because, as in other foreign languages across the American landscape, attrition is extremely high after two years, or whenever the language requirement is satisfied. Consequently, a relatively small percentage of students enter the 3rd and 4th year, years where they are finally beginning to acquire more sophisticated reading skills. This means that much of our research data come from first and second year learners of these languages, and very little from large samples of advanced learners.

READING RESEARCH IN CHINESE AS A FOREIGN LANGUAGE (CFL)

Given this background, it should not be surprising that a great deal of CFL research is devoted to understanding and articulating the process of how learners adapt to the learning of characters, with the hope that pedagogical innovation can be derived from the research. As previously mentioned, Chinese orthography is generally classified as logographic, where each character represents a word or morpheme, and is sometimes portrayed as a meaning-based system. This notion has gained more prominence when the opaque and unsystematic sound-to-symbol correspondence is taken into account, leading to a host of oversimplified descriptions in the professional literature of how Chinese orthography actually operates.

In fact, recent interest in the L1 Chinese reading process has led to far more in-depth descriptions of the orthography (Chen & Tzeng, 1992; Wang, Inhoff, & Chen, 1999) that are more informative. Some believe, for instance, that the classification of Chinese as a "logography" is misleading and recommend that it be classified as "logographic-phonetic" (DeFrancis, 1989) or that a character be termed a "morpheme-syllable" (Hoosain, 1991). Additionally, an estimated 90% of Chinese characters are classified as "compound" characters, with these characters each containing what is termed a radical (or semantic) element that gives a clue as to its meaning, and a phonetic element that hints at its pronunciation. It should be noted that these clues are also not consistent, with experts believing that in modern usage, only about 26% of compound characters are pronounced just like their phonetic elements, with this percentage decreasing as character frequency increases (Zhu, 1987). Yet this enhanced understanding of how Chinese characters are constructed does not tell us how learners perceive them, or go about the task of learning and memorizing them.

THE STUDY OF CFL LEARNER STRATEGIES

Given some of the factors listed above that are compounded by the rudimentary language ability students have when they learn to read Chinese, it is no wonder that the time commitment necessary to learn characters is often cited by learners as one of the primary barriers to learning these languages. Consequently, it should come as no surprise that much of the CFL research base is dedicated to how learners devise ways to remember, store, and learn Chinese characters. One of the common assumptions is that students purposefully exploit the phonetic and semantic makeup of Chinese characters as learning aids. In fact, such a strategy is considered to be so obvious that instructors routinely teach it, assuming that it will be a trusty and dependable strategy that students will use easily. Yet some research seems to indicate that this is not the case.

In one study, McGinnis (1999) collected survey data from students who had completed four and a half weeks of an intensive nine-week, first-year course to determine the strategies they employed to learn Chinese characters. His data indicated that students employed a variety of approaches, including rote repetition, character-specific mnemonic aids in the form of devising personal "stories" as to how specific characters look or sound, or the use of semantic and phonetic components. He discovered that students did not clearly favor any one approach for character learning, and that the use of radical and phonetic components was not a method most favored by students.

In a similar study conducted among first-year students who had spent more time in learning Chinese, Ke (1998) found that students believed that memorizing a character holistically was more effective. They also felt that continually practicing the writing of characters was more important than breaking down the individual character components into their semantic and phonetic parts. An interesting finding, however, was that students who perceived the learning and use of character components as more important strategies performed better in tasks of character recognition and production. Additionally, these learners felt that practicing characters in the context of vocabulary items (such as two-character compounds) was more effective than learning characters individually.

From a theoretical perspective, it may be that at the initial stage of character acquisition when learners are developing an understanding of the rules by which the Chinese orthographic system operates (sometimes termed "orthographic awareness"), they understand that they need to study recurring components such as radicals and phonetics. However, due to the sheer number of recurring components in the system, learners need to have learned enough characters to generate rules that would help them learn and memorize characters effectively. Although at the initial stage the learners may be taught to use and value these strategies, they are not able to take advantage of them to decompose characters. Instead, they must resort to other strategies having nothing to do with the semantic and phonetic makeup of the characters. As their orthographic awareness increases, however, so does their reliance on the knowledge of character components for character learning. This seems to be supported by the finding in the McGinnis (1999) study where students halfway through their study of a nine-week beginning Chinese course favored rote repetition and the creation of mnemonics not related to the radical or phonetic components for learning characters. In contrast, a sizable number of Ke's (1998) group who had achieved a higher level of orthographic awareness through their one-year study of Chinese felt that learning character components as an aid to character learning was more effective than writing characters repetitively.

A study conducted by Everson (1998) confirmed the importance for CFL learners of achieving a sound-symbol match for learning characters. In this study, learners who had completed one year of Chinese were given a naming task whereby they would pronounce in Chinese a series of two-character words displayed to them that were part of their first-year curriculum. Later, they were required to give the meaning for these and other characters so that the relationship between the naming and meaning task could be correlated. The results indicated that the ability to pronounce character combinations was closely related to being able to identify their meaning in English; that is, when a student could identify the meaning of a Chinese character combination, there was about a 90% likelihood that he or she also could pronounce it. The processing strategy that did not seem to occur was that learners could identify the meaning of character combinations they could not pronounce. This finding suggests that learners use their spoken language resources to anchor the meaning of the characters, which to the learner at this stage may still be perceived as so many arbitrary shapes. Interestingly enough, Yang (2000) replicated this study among heritage learners of Chinese and obtained the same results. Although bolstered by more developed spoken language resources, these learners also showed the same reliance upon these resources for learning characters.

Whether CFL learners are able to acquire a comprehensive enough understanding of the orthography over one year of Chinese study to infer the pronunciation and meaning of unfamiliar characters is still open to question. In one such study, Everson, Ke, and Jackson (2000) evaluated this ability among learners about to complete their first year of university level Chinese. To do this, they showed unfamiliar characters to the students which contained semantic elements (radicals) that the students had demonstrated they already knew. Additionally, they selected additional unfamiliar characters that contained characters as their phonetic element that the students had also demonstrated that they knew. The researchers were interested in learning whether the students would make the proper phonetic or semantic association, and thus be able to guess the meaning or pronunciation of the unknown characters. Although the students performed better on the semantic task than they did the phonetic task, the findings indicated that being able to perform these associations was difficult, and quite variable among learners. It may be that learners at this stage were still not sensitive to the component parts of characters, and therefore not able to use this knowledge to a high degree of reliability. In addition, because the number of phonetics is so large, learners probably do not master them to the same degree as the more finite set of radicals.

Given the data generated from these studies, Ke (1996a) has proposed a model of orthographic awareness, which states that learners of Chinese develop this awareness in three developmental states. In the first, or accumulation stage, learners are primarily adding whole characters to their lexicon without a great deal of component processing. At this stage, learners may certainly value the learning and use of radicals and phonetic components. However, due to the sheer number of these components, learners cannot break down the characters into their meaningful components because they have not yet accumulated enough characters in their mental lexicons to generate the recurring components. In addition, the learner's orthographic awareness for those recurring components that do not belong to either radical or phonetic components is basically nonexistent. Although they may be accumulating knowledge of various graphic features and character components, they have to rely on creating idiosyncratic mnemonics based on how a character appears to look or sound or must memorize it as a whole and practice it repetitively. At the high end of the accumulation stage, learners may be able to make good guesses about the semantic categories of novel characters in which the most perceptually and/or semantically salient and most frequently occurring radicals are embedded. As regards the phonetic components, their number greatly exceeds the number of radicals, while illustrative characters for the phonetic components are not as easy to come by as those for the radicals. Therefore, even at the high end of the accumulation stage, learners are unlikely to be able to make good guesses about the pronunciation of most novel characters.

The second stage, referred to as the transitional stage, is where learners habitually apply their knowledge of the structure of the orthographic system for deriving the sound and meaning of characters. Learners at this stage already have accumulated a significant number of characters and have begun to generate the frequently used radicals and phonetic components from their relatively large lexicon to aid in the recognition of novel characters. At the higher end of this stage, learners display consistent strategies for guessing the meaning and pronunciation of novel semantic-phonetic compound characters. At this stage, the pattern of character acquisition also should show a hierarchy in terms of recurring components; that is, certain recurring component and graphic features will appear harder for learners to acquire than will others. Factors contributing to this acquisition hierarchy may include the frequency with which a component occurs in characters, the graphic saliency of components, and the number of strokes that make up a component.

There is some evidence of this ability occurring in advanced CFL students. In one study, Everson and Ke (1997) used think-aloud protocols to investigate the strategies employed by two groups of CFL learners. The first group called "intermediate learners," had completed two years of university level Chinese, while the readers in the "advanced group" had about five years of Chinese, and were advanced graduate students studying Chinese religion and philosophy. Their task was to read a newspaper article that they had never seen before. The researchers attributed much of the reading comprehension breakdown that occurred among the intermediate students to inadequate word recognition ability. The intermediate learners had trouble processing the characters in an accurate and rapid manner and experienced difficulty isolating meaningful word units in the text. The advanced learners, because of their extensive knowledge of Chinese orthography, morphology, and language in general, could more easily isolate what they did not know, and made intelligent, purposeful, and less random decisions about how to remedy problematic situations. The advanced learners also indicated in their think-aloud protocols a tendency to pronounce the characters in Chinese, especially using the sound cues within the characters to attempt pronunciation of characters they did not recognize. When coupled with their impressive use of context and analysis of the visual features, their ability to successfully work through unfamiliar vocabulary was striking.

The final stage in Ke's (1996a) orthographic awareness model is referred to as the component-processing stage. At this stage, learners can recognize and produce characters from the perspective of recurring components, including those components that are not sound- or meaning-based. In addition to making informed guesses as to the meaning and pronunciation of most unfamiliar characters, they can also determine quite successfully whether a novel character has a possible or impossible combination of character components. The errors that CFL learners make at this stage should be those that native speakers make. Very often, the errors they make will be phonological in nature. Like all good theories and models, more research must be conducted to determine whether they will stand up to additional scrutiny. Nonetheless, this model can provide guidance for researchers wishing to understand the development of word recognition processes among CFL learners.

READING IN JAPANESE AS A FOREIGN LANGUAGE (JFL)

As with CFL research, there has been great interest in how JFL learners come to deal with the demands of new orthographies. In fact, research conducted early in the 1990s provided evidence that among beginning L2 learners of Japanese, symbol identification speed was a factor distinguishing good from poor readers (Koda, 1990) and general efficiency in lower-level processing skills significantly contributed to successful text comprehension (Koda, 1992). To expand the construct of cross-orthographic lower-level processing, research has been conducted to establish the theoretical importance of the learner's first language as a determinant in how one approaches the L2 reading process, a factor receiving renewed interest in L2 models of reading (Bernhardt, 2000). In her article detailing the role of word recognition in L2 reading, Koda (1996) discusses frameworks that need to be considered when investigating this facet of the reading process. One framework, the notion of orthographic distance, predicts that L2 word recognition will be facilitated to the extent that the reader's L1 shares similar structural properties with the L2. An additional consideration is "orthographic depth" (Katz & Frost, 1992) or how consistently and transparently the sounds in the language map onto the language's written system. When the learner's L1 differs from the L2 in orthographic type and to the degree that the sound-symbol correspondence is systematic, this framework predicts that the learner will be at a disadvantage when compared to learners whose L1 orthography more closely resembles that of the L2 orthography. A related question is whether learners seem to transfer their L1 word recognition strategies when reading in the L2.

To investigate these effects, a common research strategy has been to compare the performance on different reading tasks among learners of Japanese who come from different L1 reading backgrounds. Koda (1989), for example, conducted a study among beginning learners of Japanese to determine if students whose L1 orthographies shared certain characteristics with Japanese (i.e., the use of Chinese characters in Korean and Chinese) would perform over a variety of tasks differently than American students. The results indicated that the Korean and Chinese students held a large advantage due to their knowledge of *kanji*, and that their knowledge of *kanji* translated into vocabulary knowledge that separated the groups even more as the complexity of the task increased. This finding should not be surprising given the nature of *kanji* as a meaning-based script that facilitates reading in Japanese to a large extent for Chinese and Korean learners, yet is a writing system that must be learned from the very beginning by American students.

Another strand of inquiry that researchers have pursued is determining the extent to which learners employ the availability of phonological information in word recognition. Again, harkening back to the theory that one's L1 orthography will be an important determinant in how the L2 orthography is processed, theorists believe that learners whose L1 employs an alphabet will be at a disadvantage when learning to read in a script where phonological information is not readily accessible. That is, the primary processing experience with spelling, letter cluster analysis, and other forms of phonological processing employed by L1 alphabetic users will not be as effective for reading scripts that are non-alphabetic in nature. In fact, research results from experiments with American learners of Japanese contrasted with Chinese learners seems to bear this out.

For example, in a study involving first year, second semester learners of Japanese, Chikamatsu (1996) employed a lexical decision task among American and Chinese JFL learners. In this study, subjects were shown a series of words from their vocabulary experience written in varying forms of *kana*, the Japanese syllabary scripts, and asked to indicate whether or not these were legal words. Based on their reaction time in making these decisions, the results indicated that the American subjects utilized phonological information more than Chinese subjects, while the Chinese subjects seemed to rely more on visual strategies in making their decisions. Similarly, a study by Mori (1998) investigated whether American learners would differ in a short-term memory task from Chinese and Korean learners when presented with pseudo-*kanji* characters that differed in the degree to which phonological elements were presented as pronunciation aids in the characters. Her results indicated that the American learners were less flexible in strategy use for remembering novel *kanji* than the Chinese and Korean learners whose L1 employs characters either exclusively or partially. The data indicated that the American learners were disrupted when the makeup of the pseudo-characters prevented them from using a phonological analysis to remember the characters.

TEXT LEVEL PROCESSING

In addition to research focusing on how JFL learners deal with words or characters, there has also been a strand of research focusing on whether JFL learners derive an appreciation for text structure, and whether or not textual coherence is an aspect of reading that affects JFL readers. In a study involving native readers of Japanese as well as L2 learners, Horiba (1993) had subjects read texts that reflected varying degrees of coherence. Her results indicated that L1 readers' recall of high coherence text was better than that of a low coherence text, with advanced L2 readers achieving the same results, but after a second reading. The study indicated that L2 readers have difficulty detecting higher order causal structure in text, but that this ability appears to increase with proficiency, though repeated readings seem to be necessary. In a similar study, L2 readers showed no difference in reading texts that were either high or low coherence; what seemed to separate proficient from less proficient L2 readers was their ability to draw inferences from the text (Horiba, 1996). Recent research (Kitajima, 1997) seems to indicate that at certain proficiency levels of JFL, instruction in aspects of text structure such as co-referential ties can help to enhance reading comprehension, thus highlighting the potential for more research involving classroom instructional intervention.

EXPANDING THE CFL/JFL RESEARCH HORIZON

This chapter has described some of the research that has been carried out to investigate the reading processes of CFL and JFL learners, and highlights some of the areas of inquiry that have attracted research activity. To conclude by pointing out implications for further research, it might be useful to speculate how CFL/JFL research ties in with research and theory building in L2 reading in general.

First, understanding the labor-intensive nature of reading in Chinese and Japanese for L2 learners has focused on investigating the nature of processing words and text in orthographies qualitatively different from alphabetic systems. Even though L2 reading models such as Bernhardt's (1991, 2000) have recognized the critical role of word recognition and phono-graphemic features in L2 reading, much of the data bolstering her model have involved learners of French, German, and Spanish, languages more closely related to the L1 of the research subjects. With regard to these two aspects of lower-level processing, her synthesis of the research predicts "rapidly declining error rates in word recognition and phono-graphemic confusions over time" as one conclusion (Bernhardt, 2000, p. 797). Given the data summarized in the CFL/JFL studies, one wonders if a decreasing phono-graphemic feature and word recognition error rate would occur at such a rapid pace, indicating that these errors may persist for longer periods of time among these learners. More research needs to be conducted to test these hypotheses further.

Second, Bernhardt (2000) identifies *vocabulary* as an area of study throughout the late 1990s that has received increased scrutiny. The whole notion of vocabulary development as it applies to CFL readers, however, is still largely underconceptualized due to the nature of Chinese orthography and how it is learned. For instance, students of French, German, and Spanish from the very first day of class learn vocabulary words in these languages using the same orthography as do native speakers. Even in Japanese language classes, the syllabary systems used by native speakers are quickly taught so that students can begin to learn vocabulary using authentic orthographic systems. In Chinese, however, in order to develop spoken language skills at a rapid rate, students learn oral Chinese via romanization, which we have noted represents Chinese sounds using the Roman alphabet, with diacritical marks to represent the tones. Most Chinese curricula then introduce Chinese characters during the first two years at a very controlled rate, trying (often unsuccessfully) to introduce the characters for vocabulary the students have already learned through romanization. What becomes noteworthy is when students progress into their 3rd and 4th year of Chinese and encounter a flurry of authentic texts with less control and systematicity given to how vocabulary is introduced. This results in their spoken and reading vocabulary often being very different. Unlike the results quoted in the Everson (1998) study, one might wonder whether experienced advanced students develop strategies for coping with the high volume of characters needed to confront authentic materials, so that they no longer need to know how to pronounce each and every character they encounter in order to read effectively. Therefore, investigating and accounting for the different vocabulary resources of advanced learners and how they are used, learned, and how they develop will remain a fascinating research challenge for the future.

An interesting strand of research in this area has been begun by Lin (2000) who charted the development of different levels of CFL learners to ascertain the strengths of receptive/passive and active vocabulary. Her data indicate a relationship between language proficiency and a learner's active vocabulary developing over time, which encompasses the ability to write and produce Chinese characters. Language practitioners have always suspected that there was a relationship between reading and writing among CFL learners, with initial correlational research pointing in this direction. Ke (1996b), for instance, found that among first year learners of Chinese, a somewhat straightforward relationship between character recognition and production existed. That is, although students were able to recognize characters better than they were able to produce them, those who were poor at recognizing characters were poor at producing them, and those who were good at production were also good at recognition. Some, however, who performed well in recognition were poor producers. Other research (Shen, 2000) has also demonstrated a relationship between reading comprehension and extended writing in Chinese among second year students. Both Lin and Shen have called for a greater integration of writing into the curriculum as a healthy initiative with which to develop balanced vocabulary and literacy skills. More research, however, will need to be conducted if we are to explain the nature of these relationships.

An additional topic in the area of vocabulary development that is receiving increased attention is the attempt to determine what strategies learners use to figure out the meaning of unknown *kanji*, and to document how these strategies are derived. An example of this type of research was conducted by Mori and Nagy (1999) who supplied students with different contextual conditions with which to guess the meaning of unknown *kanji* compounds (words consisting of two or more Chinese characters). The researchers determined that the subjects used an integrated strategy of inferring meaning from both the *kanji* combinations themselves and the surrounding context; yet, when only one source was available to the subjects, their ability to guess the meanings decreased significantly. Moreover, they determined that the ability to use *kanji* clues to guess the meanings of unknown combinations and the ability to use context was not correlated.

Lastly, research should be conducted that explores the effects of learner belief systems as they pertain to the study of these languages. Recent studies in both CFL and JFL indicate that this is an area of interest to a number of researchers. In one study conducted among beginning and intermediate learners of JFL, Everson and Kuriya (1998) found that in reading a portion of an authentic newspaper article, student think-aloud protocols revealed their reading to be a highly laborious task. More surprisingly, however, were the strong and vocal learner opinions about the difficulty of learning *kanji.* These opinions were so prominent in the think-aloud protocols that the researchers put forward the theory that many learners had developed an adversarial relationship with *kanji,* so relied upon the *kana* systems which they could phonologically decode to get meaning out of the passage. Given that this passage contained a very high percentage of *kanji,* this strategy did not yield particularly positive results.

Some researchers have taken this strand of research a step further to try and establish a relationship between learner belief systems and their choice of learning strategy. Mori (1999), for instance, began an interesting line of inquiry by trying to determine if there was a relationship between the strategies employed by learners to figure out the meaning of unknown words in Japanese and their beliefs about language learning and knowledge in general. Her results indicated a modest relationship between these factors, indicating that the strategies learners employed to deal with unknown words at least partially reflected the learners' belief systems. Other research investigating learner beliefs seems to indicate that the writing system itself may be a source of anxiety for students learning to read in languages such as Japanese (Saito, Horowitz, & Garza, 1999). This study suggests that again, as in much of the research investigating anxiety, there seems to be a relationship between student anxiety level and performance as measured by their final grades. Such research highlights the elusive and multifaceted nature of acquiring reading skills for these students, as well as the various factors that need to be investigated if we are to understand this process in a meaningful way.

REFERENCES

Bernhardt, E.B. (1991). *Reading development in a second language: Theoretical, empirical, & classroom perspectives.* Norwood, NJ: Ablex.

Bernhardt, E.B. (2000). Second-language reading as a case study of reading scholarship in the 20th century. In M.L. Kamil, P. Mosenthal, P.D. Pearson, & R. Barr (Eds.), *Handbook of reading research* (Vol. III, pp. 793–811). Mahwah, NJ: Erlbaum.

Brecht, R.D., & Rivers, W.P. (2000). *Language and national security in the 21st century.* Dubuque, IA: Kendall/Hunt Publishing.

Brod, R., & Welles, E. B. (2000). Foreign language enrollments in United States institutions of higher education, fall 1998. *ADFL Bulletin, 31*(2), 22–29.

Chen, C.H., & Tzeng, O.J.L. (Eds.). (1992). *Language processing in Chinese.* Amsterdam: Elsevier Science Publishers B.V.

Chikamatsu, N. (1996). The effects of L1 orthography on L2 word recognition: A study of American and Chinese learners of Japanese. *Studies in Second Language Acquisition, 18,* 403–432.

DeFrancis, J. (1989). *Visible speech: The diverse oneness of writing systems.* Honolulu: University of Hawaii Press.

Everson, M.E. (1998). Word recognition among learners of Chinese as a foreign language: Investigating the relationship between naming and knowing. *The Modern Language Journal, 82,* 194–204.

Everson, M.E., & Ke, C. (1997). An inquiry into the reading strategies of intermediate and advanced learners of Chinese as a foreign language. *Journal of the Chinese Language Teachers Association, 32*(1), 1–20.

Everson, M.E., Ke, C., & Jackson, N.E. (2000). *The development of orthographic awareness among beginning learners of Chinese as a foreign language.* Unpublished manuscript.

Everson, M.E., & Kuriya, Y. (1998). An exploratory study into the reading strategies of learners of Japanese as a foreign language. *Journal of the Association of Teachers of Japanese, 32*(1), 1–21.

Hoosain, R. (1991). *Psycholinguistic implications for linguistic relativity: A case study of Chinese.* Hillsdale, NJ: Erlbaum.

Horiba, Y. (1993). The role of causal reasoning and language competence in narrative comprehension. *Studies in Second Language Acquisition, 15,* 49–81.

Horiba, Y. (1996). Comprehension processes in L2 reading: Language competence, textual coherence, and inference. *Studies in Second Language Acquisition, 18,* 433–474.

Katz, R., & Frost, L. (1992). The reading process is different for different orthographies: The orthographic depth hypothesis. In R. Katz & L. Frost (Eds.), *Orthography, phonology, morphology, and meaning* (pp. 67–84). North Holland: The Netherlands. Elsevier Science Publishers B.V.

Ke, C. (1996a). *A model for Chinese orthographic awareness.* Unpublished manuscript.

Ke, C. (1996b). An empirical study on the relationship between Chinese character recognition and production. *The Modern Language Journal, 80,* 340–349.

Ke, C. (1998). Effects of strategies on the learning of Chinese characters among foreign language students. *Journal of the Chinese Language Teachers Association, 33*(2), 93–112.

Kitajima, R. (1997). Referential strategy training for second language reading comprehension of Japanese texts. *Foreign Language Annals, 30,* 84–97.

Koda, K. (1989). The effects of transferred vocabulary knowledge on the development of L2 reading proficiency. *Foreign Language Annals, 22,* 529–542.

Koda, K. (1990). Factors affecting second language text comprehension. *Literacy theory and research: Analyses from multiple paradigms.* Thirty-Ninth Yearbook of the National Reading Conference. Chicago: The National Reading Conference.

Koda, K. (1992). The effects of lower-level processing skills on foreign language reading performance: Implications for instruction. *The Modern Language Journal, 76,* 502–512.

Koda, K. (1996). L2 word recognition research: A critical review. *The Modern Language Journal, 80,* 451–460.

Lin, Y. (2000). Vocabulary acquisition and learning Chinese as a Foreign Language (CFL). *Journal of the Chinese Language Teachers Association, 35*(1), 85–108.

McGinnis, S. (1999). Student goals and approaches. In M. Chu (Ed.), *Mapping the Course of the Chinese Language Field,* (pp. 150–188). Kalamazoo, MI: Chinese Language Teachers' Association.

Mori, Y. (1998). Effects of first language and phonological accessibility on kanji recognition. *The Modern Language Journal, 82,* 69–82.

Mori, Y. (1999). Beliefs about language learning and their relationship to the ability to integrate information from word parts and context in interpreting novel kanji words. *The Modern Language Journal, 83,* 534–545.

Mori, Y., & Nagy, W. (1999). Integration of information from context and word elements in interpreting novel kanji compounds. *Reading Research Quarterly, 34*(1), 80–97.

Saito, Y., Horwitz, E.K., & Garza, T.J. (1999). Foreign language reading anxiety. *The Modern Language Journal, 83,* 202–218.

Shen, H. (2000). The interconnections of reading text based writing and reading comprehension among college intermediate learners of Chinese as a foreign language. *Journal of the Chinese Language Teachers Association, 35*(3), 29–47.

Walton, A.R. (1992). *Expanding the vision of foreign language education: Enter the less commonly taught languages.* NFLC Occasional Papers. Washington, DC: National Foreign Language Center.

Wang, J., Inhoff, A.W., & Chen, H.C. (Eds). (1999). *Reading Chinese script: A cognitive analysis.* Mahwah, NJ: Erlbaum.

Yang, J. (2000). Orthographic effect on word recognition by learners of Chinese as a foreign language. *Journal of the Chinese Language Teachers Association, 35*(2), 1–17.

Zhu, Y.P. (1987). *Analysis of cueing functions of the phonetic in modern Chinese.* Unpublished manuscript.

CHAPTER 2

TECHNOLOGICAL LITERACY AND FOREIGN LANGUAGE LITERACY IN A TECHNOLOGICAL ERA:

CONSIDERATIONS OF TWO INTERACTING CONSTRUCTS FOR FOREIGN LANGUAGE EDUCATION

Michael Fast

ABSTRACT

This paper discusses two types of literacy—alphabetic and technological—their characterization, their relationship, and their relevance to the field of foreign language education. In keeping with current interpretations within many disciplines, alphabetic literacy is viewed not merely as competencies in reading and writing, and based on texts of an academic nature, but as a set of competencies of many interrelated communication skills, and based on discourse generated in a range of computer and non-computer media. Of crucial concern for foreign language education are the social and cultural contexts in which such skills are practiced. Technological literacy concerns the set of competencies required to integrate a range of technologies, and especially communication technologies, into a domain of behavior. Both types of literacies are viewed as key to currently defined discourse-based methodologies for foreign language instruction.

INTRODUCTION

This chapter examines the notion of literacy as viewed from the field of computer-supported foreign language instruction. It focuses on two constructs related to literacy, or perhaps two interacting perspectives on a single broad construct, and in terms not of stable psychological phenomena, but as dynamic sociocultural and educational trends with significant political overtones. One construct, technological literacy, concerns a divergent use of the term "literacy" (viz. alphabetic literacy). Like numerate, geographic, visual, scientific, aesthetic, and assessment (among others), all of which have been used to extend the meaning of the term "literacy," digital, electronic, technological, network, and computer are also used to describe what some consider to be a specialized set of socially important skills (e.g., Selfe, 1999; Tuman, 1992; Tyner, 1998). Technological literacy has been deemed crucial for effective functioning in contemporary society and therefore a matter of urgent curricular attention within the school system. As the U.S. Department of Education report "Getting America's Students Ready for the 21st Century: Meeting the Technology Literacy Challenge" (1996) pointed out:

> [C]omputers and information technologies are transforming nearly every aspect of American life. They are changing the way Americans work and play, increasing productivity, and creating entirely new ways of doing things. Every major U.S. industry has begun to rely heavily on computers and telecommunications to do its work.

> But so far, America's schools have been an exception to this information revolution. Computers and information technologies are not part of the way American students learn. (p. 1)

Technological literacy, then, for the purposes of the present context of interest, is used in the sense cited above to refer to a broad set of competencies required for the successful integration of computer and information-based technologies into the field of foreign language education. It embraces competencies implied by related terms such as electronic, digital, computer, and networking literacies (see Tyner, 1998, p. 94, for specific definitions of these literacies). Successful integration would be measured in terms of whether or not technological use led to the development of foreign language communication skills.

The second construct, literacy in a foreign language, is used for the purposes of this chapter to refer to an equally non-traditional interpretation of the term "literacy." It retains standard references to the skills of reading and writing. But, as we shall see later in the chapter, the tendency in recent years has been to broaden the meaning of the term "literacy" within foreign language pedagogy, as in other fields, to embrace skills beyond reading and writing, and beyond the printed medium. This has occurred to accommodate a shifting focus from skills as separate sets of behavior, to viewing their relatedness, interdependence, balanced importance, and relevance to the cultural and social context of use of those skills. It also reflects an increasing influence of technology to mediate oral and written interaction. Literacy in a foreign language now embraces a range of socially important skills to include, in Kern's (1995a) words: "particular ways of thinking, valuing, and behaving that are essential to becoming communicatively competent in both the spoken and written modes" (p. 62). Literacy studies have come to favor the term "multiple literacies" (e.g., the New London Group, 1996) to describe the range of oral, written, and media-related skills that are important for successful participation in society, the workforce, and the global economy of the 21st century. In a similar vein, Graff (1995) has pointed out in defining alphabetic literacy that "[it is] one exceptionally valuable set of competencies among others with which it interacts" (p. xix).

It is argued in this chapter, then, that technological literacy and literacy in a foreign language, rather than being independent sets of functional skills, are part of a broader set of socially and culturally important competencies. Literate people are able to interact through a range of skills with a range of discourses, including those that are facilitated or mediated by computer-driven technologies (or any other technology). Of particular importance to the foreign language education field is the fact that modern computer-driven technologies facilitate immediate access to the creation of and interaction with a range of culturally rich and communicatively authentic written and spoken discourses in the target language. All of the ingredients of such discourses, including their authenticity, their cultural content, their media content, their relatedness to a social reality, help to facilitate the educational purpose of their use, the development of foreign language skills. In Kramsch's (1995) terms, they facilitate the teaching of language as "an explicit cultural practice" (p. xxiv). Technology sustains the vision of a pluralistic interpretation of the term "literacy," of literacies. Without such technological resources, foreign language learners are limited to exposure either through travel to the country of the target language and culture (the optimum but most impractical solution for many language learners, especially in a sustained way), or through an impoverished set of typically pedagogical discourses in the classroom setting.

TECHNOLOGICAL LITERACY

Technological literacy has significant implications for foreign language education. Its potential impact targets issues such as teacher and student training in the development of appropriate skills, the design and attainment of curricular goals and objectives, teaching and testing, equity of access to resources, and the politics of foreign language department governance. Although not universally held to be the case (see, for example, Hirvela, 1988), computer-related technologies are seen as offering radically different ways of supporting many foreign language pedagogical needs, especially in the communicative, discourse-based paradigm that currently characterizes the field. The technologies themselves range from different types of synchronous and asynchronous communications resources, and computer-driven distance learning environments, to Web-based hypermedia text resources, interactive and learner-adaptive multimedia software, and emerging voice-driven technologies. The state of technological literacy of those involved in the foreign language education process is crucial, at all levels, and with a complex range of technologies. There are recommendations expressed in the K-12 "Standards for foreign language learning in the 21st century" (American Council on the Teaching of Foreign Languages, 1999) that support the idea that:

> ...students should be given the opportunity during their school careers to take increasing advantage of new technological advances ... [that will] help students strengthen linguistic skills, establish interactions with peers, and learn about contemporary culture and everyday life in the target country. (p. 35)

The incentive to integrate a broad range of computer-based technologies at the college level, especially from administrative quarters looking for ways to make foreign language instruction more efficient, is equally pervasive, although not without substantial criticism by some from a more traditional humanities perspective.

The most recent technological impact on foreign language education has been the Internet, viewed by Warschauer (1999) as important for two related dimensions: interpersonal communications, and Web-based hypermedia. Kern (1998) concurs with this perspective:

> The most profound effects of computer technology on literacy and language learning will likely arise not from language pedagogy software but from the new forms of information dissemination and social interaction made possible by local and global computer networks. The implications of networked communication for language learning are important not only because computer networks potentially expand the number and diversity of people one can

communicate with, but also because they influence the ways in which people use language to interact with one another. (p. 58)

These two areas of recent technological development are interesting especially because they clearly demonstrate how communication through integrated skills, through the use of multiple literacies, has become of vital interest for the foreign language learning community.

The availability of target language texts on the Internet, certainly if English is the target language but also in rapidly increasing amounts for other languages, makes the Internet an important provider of authentic materials for language learning. Such texts are to be found in diverse sources, diversely presented, frequently with multimedia support, and instantaneously available. They constitute a corpus of materials for language learning that is dynamic in nature, never constant, always reflecting immediate and personal needs, unlike the texts of textbooks that are so generic, so divorced from the students' ongoing needs. They represent what is most current in the language (in local news sources), they are the texts of day-to-day behavior (bus-timetables, street maps, personal ads, articles for sale, etc.), they are the texts of the cultural vigor of a language (video files of films, sound files of songs, images of local celebrations, interviews with well-known personalities). They are typically distributed in Hypermedia format, that is, they facilitate nonlinear interaction. Texts can be read in a depth-wise fashion by following links at key locations throughout a text that take the reader to other supporting texts. When the Hypermedia format is custom-applied to target foreign language texts, access can be made available to sources of information that can play a significant role in aiding in the process of language development—access to dictionary databases for instantaneous definitions or translations, to grammar explanations that help to clarify a complex construction in context, to audio overlays, to additional multimedia texts that enhance learning by providing further contextualization. This type of reading, although different from reading from printed media, significantly improves upon the latter for language learners because of its immediate accessibility, its nonlinear characteristics, its multimedia contextualization, and built-in redundancy.

The changes that such Internet-based textual environments can make to foreign language education cannot be underestimated. They are changes that can invest much greater responsibility on learners for their selection, for the ways in which they are interacted with, for the time and space of interaction with them. And what is more important, their availability finally or rather potentially decentralizes the foreign language textbook and the teacher in the learning process, a situation that has long been the desire of motivated, energetic, and pedagogically-current language instructors. Teachers and textbooks, as central personalities in the language learning process, are counterproductive to the development of skills that demonstrate an ability to produce culturally and socially relevant discourse.

Without technological literacy, foreign language teachers are unable to resolve many of the language learning objectives that have become important in a contemporary pedagogy. Such objectives pertain to an expanded interpretation of literacy outlined above, and efficiently realizable within expanded learning environments, almost exclusively through the use of computer-driven technologies. Students without appropriate technological literacy who wish to be able to exploit technologies in language learning also need to be trained in the technical as well as the philosophical content of this type of literacy. This is as true for the technologies that provide Internet-based text resources as it is for the types of technologies described in the next section.

Even more important for foreign language education has been the second dimension highlighted by Warschauer (1999)—Internet-facilitated interpersonal communication. Such communication is of two varieties, synchronous and asynchronous, that is communication conducted in real-time with immediate audio or written response, and communication conducted with delayed response. A range of technologies are currently available that allow for synchronous and asynchronous communication in a foreign language, including electronic mail, bulletin boards, listServes, various conferencing resources, and MOOs or MUDs (multiple-user domains object-oriented). Kern (1998) defines the value of these technologies in the following way:

> The implications of networked communication for language learning are important not only because computer networks potentially expand the number and diversity of people one can communicate with, but also because they influence the ways in which people use language to interact with one another ... [They] present new opportunities for reorganizing classroom interaction, for extending person-to-person communication to worlds beyond the classroom, and for developing literacy and cultural literacy among foreign language learners. (p. 58)

Research in this dimension of technology applied to foreign language acquisition has been substantial in recent years, reflecting the realization within the profession that this type of technology has a significant role to play. Conclusions are somewhat typical across studies and tend to suggest that students say more in electronically mediated interaction, are more accurate, more motivated, interact on a greater variety of topics, exhibit a greater range of language functions, initiate more often, and develop more discourse management strategies than is found in face-to-face interaction (see, e.g., González-Bueno, 1998; Kern, 1995b; Ortega, 1997; St. John & Cash, 1995; Warschauer, 1996).

Like the Hypermedia texts of the Internet, communication resources also exhibit important qualities that are difficult to obtain in formal classroom environments for language learning. Classrooms facilitate face-to-face interaction, between students, between teachers and students. Such interaction suffers from a number of problems if the goal of language learning is to facilitate the development of communicative skills that allow one to function in the real world, the world of diverse discourses, diverse participants, of culturally replete and socially relevant interaction. Classroom interaction is, inevitably, pedagogical in nature, and even when it attempts not to be, in role-plays and dialogue construction activities and scenarios for discussion, the capacity to mirror reality and social and cultural authenticity is severely diminished. In affective terms also, face-to-face interaction, while certainly a feature of communication in the real world, becomes a barrier for sustained interaction. In asynchronous environments especially, time for reflection and absence of pressure, are important ingredients for beginning language learners.

Non-computer mediated interaction in the classroom limits students' involvement in communication, in terms of quantity and quality. It is bound by a pedagogical task, it is influenced by a pedagogical environment, and it is irrelevant to students' ongoing needs, except in very generic terms. Computer-mediated communication vastly expands students' opportunities for interaction, improving its quantity and quality, and making it highly relevant to students' needs because it is shaped by them, even desired by them. It also expands the learning environment of the student to extra-classroom space and time. In addition, interaction can be facilitated with native speakers who are not part of the learning environment, creating socially relevant and culturally rich conditions for interaction.

Again, technologically naïve teachers and students have problems in technology-mediated learning environments. The problem is not merely technical but philosophical too, making it difficult for both teachers and students to understand the relevance of such technologies to the language learning process.

LITERACY IN A FOREIGN LANGUAGE

The second construct, foreign language literacy in a technology-dominated social and educational environment, has implications of a different but clearly related kind for foreign language education. At stake here is what has been an object for international preoccupation for a number of years. Gee (1990) states the problem in the following way, suggesting a broader social crisis than that of illiteracy:

In the U.S. and Great Britain today, we are once again in the midst of a widely proclaimed "literacy crisis', with virtual calls to arms in a war against illiteracy nationally and internationally. In the U.S., these calls to arms reached their peak in the Reagan administration, … The proclaiming (and subsequent waning) of "literacy crises" is a recurrent feature of the histories of Western "developed" capitalist societies, the "crisis" often masking deeper and more complex social problems, and reflecting less socially acceptable fears. (p. 27)

Such literacy crises typically receive considerable national and international attention, in the form of high profile sociocultural and political commentary (e.g., like that of William Bennett, 2001), or in the form of international studies and meetings (for example, "Literacy in the information age: Final report of the international adult literacy study," by the Organization for Economic Co-operation and Development, 2000; or the Commission of the European Communities' report: "Meeting: Literacy in the European Community," 1991).

While it is outside the purview of this chapter to discuss the reasons why illiteracy is a prevalent feature of Western "developed" societies, statistical evidence is certainly available (e.g., the OECD's 2000 report comparing many European countries and the United States along a number of literacy indices) to suggest that illiteracy exists to varying degrees and especially when higher-order writing and reading tasks, deemed necessary for day-to-day functioning in the workforce and social environments (OECD, 2000), are required. Technology looms large among social critics like Postman (1992) and Roszak (1986) as a prime contributor to the phenomenon of illiteracy.

Two issues bear discussion at this point, in light of the ways in which literacy has been characterized above for the field of foreign language education. First, claims of illiteracy typically refer to standard definitions of literacy, i.e., based on competencies relating to reading and writing, and as Kern (1995a) states, often "associated with learnedness and literary appreciation" (p. 61). Such a definition falls considerably short of a currently accepted understanding of literacy that embraces oral skills and written skills within a single construct. Importantly, all language skills are considered intimately linked and equally important for many communication tasks. As Kern (1995a) states:

Scholars in disciplines such as rhetoric, composition, educational psychology, sociology, and cultural theory have recently critiqued mainstream notions of literacy (e.g., Baker & Luke, 1991; Brandt, 1990; Flower, 1994; Gee, 1990; Heath, 1991; Lunsford, Moglen, & Slevin, 1990; Street, 1984). These educators challenge skill-based definitions of literacy focused on the ability to read and write in ways commensurate with a prescriptive, normative standard.

They question the notion of a monolithic, generalizable concept of literacy, and favor the idea of multiple literacies—roughly defined as dynamic, socially and historically embedded practices of producing, using, and interpreting texts for variable purposes. (p. 61)

The traditional definition of literacy would seem to suggest that claims of illiteracy, if not somewhat unrealistic in the light of their disregard for other types of skills that are equally important for social communication, are certainly likely to generate inadequate solutions that focus on erroneous goals.

The second issue is technology, which we have demonstrated is fundamental in a contemporary social and educational environment to any definition of literacy. Its importance derives from the fact that many texts, many discourses, many environments for linguistic interaction are technology mediated and to the point where technology imposes its own characteristics on the nature of the discourse. This does not produce impoverished discourse; it generates different types of discourse with as much social and cultural validity as discourses that are not technology mediated. And yet, technology is claimed as an influence on the incidence of illiteracy. This again suggests an unrealistic assessment of the situation and certainly if measures are adopted in light of this frequently held claim, would produce incongruous results.

The implications for foreign language education are significant above all because traditional perspectives on literacy and consequent claims for illiteracy suggest a fundamental questioning of current methodological approaches to foreign language instruction, which have given considerable emphasis to the development of oral-based skills since the 1960s, although more recently have adopted a more balanced treatment of all skills. Oral-based competencies became the center of interest in foreign language education over the last 3–4 decades partly as a reaction against earlier methodologies that focused on culturally elitist literacy content, partly because of theoretical study in language and language acquisition that has been characterized by an interest in oral language, and partly as a result of a move toward student-centered approaches to curriculum design and pedagogical methodology which have highlighted the development of pragmatic oral skills. The literacy-orality debate has been most strident at the college level where expectations, if not real practice, for appropriate tertiary level foreign language study (which does not necessarily concern advanced level study) are typically literacy oriented in the traditional sense of the term.

In summary, a dilemma is apparent between the claims of widespread illiteracy which are typically attributed to the broad technological environment in which we live (Bennett, 2001, cavalierly states that "Parents need to turn off the television, computer and video games"), and the value that technology is seen to offer education, specifically for the purposes of this chapter to foreign language education. A conflict exists between the restricted reading-writing sense in which literacy is normally defined for the purposes of sociopolitical claims of illiteracy, the overtly oral characteristic of foreign language curricula of the last 30 years or so, and the more recent move to define foreign language curricula and foreign language literacy, as with other fields, in much broader discourse-based terms to embrace communication skills of a greater range and delivered by a range of media. Tyner (1998), reflecting upon Levine's (1986) remarks on linguistic and social practices of literacy over time, captures the dilemma in the following way:

> Levine contained his remarks to address the difficulty in unifying oral and written forms of communication. When digital and other electronic forms of communication are added to the mix, the task of finding "conceptual order and integration" between the various strands of literacy is exacerbated. (p. 44)

CONCLUSIONS

This chapter has attempted to demonstrate the inextricable relationship between linguistic communication skills and the media through which they are practiced. In the technology-rich environment in which we live, especially of Internet and communication-based computer technologies, technological literacy cannot be separated from alphabetic literacy. Similarly, alphabetic literacy has to be shaped, not exclusively, but certainly in part, by the types of linguistic and communicative skills utilized in a technological environment. Such skills, as has been claimed, are not uniquely written text-related, nor are they predominantly literary in nature. Such a claim does not infra-value literacy discourse. It places it in a broader context and relates it to different needs.

For foreign language education, such expanded interpretations of literacy are claimed to be crucial to the understanding of a new pedagogy. Foreign language education has for many years had an unfortunate relationship with technology. It has recognized the value of tape-recorders to providing models of linguistic behavior beyond that of the teacher, and to providing review of audio material through replay techniques. It has seen video technology as an important visual and cultural contextualizer of language. But both technologies clashed with pedagogical methodologies that were eminently form-focused, message-free, unrelated to discourse, and socially unrealistic.

An essentially Vygotskyan-shaped methodology of recent years in foreign language education has placed the emphasis on socially and culturally relevant conditions for communication in the target language. And for such conditions to prevail in the learning environment, technology is key.

REFERENCES

American Council on the Teaching of Foreign Languages. (1999). *Standards for foreign language learning in the 21st century.* National Standards in Foreign Language Education Project.

Baker, C.D., & Luke, A. (Eds.). (1991). *Towards a critical sociology of reading pedagogy: Papers of the XIIth World Congress on reading. Pragmatics and beyond.* Amsterdam: John Benjamins.

Bennett, W.J. (2001, April 24). A cure for the illiteracy epidemic. *The Wall Street Journal.* Available: *http://interactive.wsj.com/archive/retrieve.cgi?id=SB988068125345265925.djm* [subscribers only].

Brandt, D. (1990). *Literacy as involvement: The acts of writers, readers, and texts.* Carbondale: Southern Illinois University Press.

Commission of the European Communities. (1991). *Meeting: Literacy in the European Community.* Commission of the European Communities. Luxembourg: Office for Official Publications of the European Community.

Flower, L. (1994). *The construction of negotiated meaning: A social cognitive theory of writing.* Carbondale: Southern Illinois University Press.

Gee, J.P. (1990). *Social linguistics and literacies: Ideology in discourses.* New York: Falmer Press.

González-Bueno, M. (1998). The effects of electronic mail on Spanish L2 discourse. *Language Learning & Technology, 1*(2), 55–70.

Graff, H.J. (1995). *The labyrinths of literacy: Reflections on literacy past and present.* Pittsburgh, PA: University of Pittsburgh Press.

Heath, S.B. (1991). The sense of being literate: Historical and cross-cultural features. In R. Barr, M.K. Kamil, P.B. Mosenthal, & P.D. Pearson (Eds.), *Handbook of reading research* (Vol. 2, pp. 3–25). New York: Longman.

Hirvela, A. (1988). Marshall McLuhan and the case against CAI. *System, 16*(3), 299–311.

Kern, R. (1995a). Redefining the boundaries of foreign language literacy. In C. Kramsch (Ed.), *Redefining the boundaries of language study* (pp. 61–98). Boston: Heinle and Heinle.

Kern, R. (1995b). Restructuring classroom interaction with networked computers: Effects on quantity and characteristics of language production. *Modern Language Journal, 79,* 457–476.

Kern, R. (1998). Technology, social interaction, and FL literacy. In J. Muyskens (Ed.). *New ways of learning and teaching: Focus on technology and foreign language education.* American Association of University Supervisors, Coordinators, and Directors of Foreign Language Programs annual volume. Boston: Heinle and Heinle.

Kramsch, C. (1995). Introduction: Making the invisible visible. In C. Kramsch (Ed.), *Redefining the boundaries of language study* (ix–xxx). Boston: Heinle and Heinle.

Levine, K. (1986). *The social context of literacy.* London: Routledge and Kegan Paul.

Lunsford, A.A., Moglen, H., & Slevin, J. (Eds.). (1990). *The right to literacy.* New York: Modern Language Association.

The New London Group. (1996). A pedagogy of multiliteracies: Designing social futures. *Harvard Educational Review, 66*(1), 60–92.

Organization for Economic Co-operation and Development. (2000). *Literacy in the information age: Final report of the international adult literacy survey.* Paris: Organization for Economic Co-operation and Development/Minister of Industry, Canada.

Ortega, L. (1997). Processes and outcomes in networked classroom interaction: Defining the research agenda for L2 computer-assisted classroom discussion. *Language Learning & Technology, 1*(1), 82–93.

Postman, N. (1992). *Technopoly: The surrender of culture to technology.* New York: Vintage Books.

Roszak, T. (1986). *The cult of information: The folklore of computers and the true art of thinking.* London: Paladin.

Selfe, C.L. (1999). *Technology and literacy in the twenty-first century: The importance of paying attention.* Carbondale: Southern Illinois University Press.

Street, B.V. (1984). *Literacy in theory and practice.* Cambridge: Cambridge University Press.

St. John, E., & Cash, D. (1995). Language learning via e-mail: Demonstrable success with German. In M. Warschauer (Ed.), *Telecollaboration in foreign language learning: Proceedings of the Hawai'i Symposium.* Honolulu: University of Hawai'i, Second Language Teaching and Curriculum Center.

Tuman, M.C. (Ed.). (1992). *Literacy online: The promise (and peril) of reading and writing with computers.* Pittsburgh, PA: University of Pittsburgh Press.

Tyner, K. (1998). *Literacy in a digital world: Teaching and learning in the age of information.* Mahwah, NJ: Erlbaum.

U.S. Department of Education. (1996). *Getting America's students ready for the 21st century: Meeting the technology literacy challenge. A report to the nation on technology and education.* Washington, DC: Office of Educational Technology. Available: http://www.ed.gov/Technology/Plan/

Warschauer, M. (1996). Motivational aspects of using computers for writing and communication. In M. Warschauer (Ed.), *Telecollaboration in foreign language learning: Proceedings of the Hawai'i Symposium.* Honolulu: University of Hawai'i, Second Language Teaching and Curriculum Center.

Warschauer, M. (1999). *Electronic literacies: Language, culture, and power in online education.* Mahwah, NJ: Erlbaum.

CHAPTER 3

WHAT SHOULD TEACHERS KNOW ABOUT BILINGUAL LEARNERS AND THE READING PROCESS?[1]

Andrew D. Cohen and Rosalind Horowitz

ABSTRACT

This chapter targets what it is that teachers who teach bilinguals should know about the reading process for the new century. First, we describe teachers in the United States who work with bilingual learners. Second, we examine research on bilinguals and reading programs. A series of questions are posed that are germane to the design of reading programs in L1, L2, or both languages. Third, we describe bilinguals and the reading process. Fourth, the chapter identifies theory and research that teachers will find useful to consider before and during instruction. We ask: *What is it that teachers need to know and do who serve bilingual students? What theory and research-based knowledge must teachers use in decision-making, if they are to apply new standards of excellence in instruction?* Fifth, assessment of bilingual students' reading is briefly discussed. We highlight that the bilingual learner will demonstrate individual differences in the acquisition and development of language and reading. If bilingual students are to excel in a variety of communication contexts, teachers must consider those contexts and the range of reading acts vital for school, work, and daily life.

INTRODUCTION

The President of The Carnegie Corporation of New York and former President of Brown University, Vartan Gregorian (2001), has argued that higher education's greatest challenge is to develop a new model for teacher education for the new century.

He indicates that "Many colleges and universities marginalized their schools of education, treating them as revenue generators ... increasing enrollments and reducing educational quality." A new model of teacher education must place teacher education at the center of the university and apply research from across the disciplines and entire university (de León, 2001). The development of teachers is a formidable, daunting task, constantly changing. We believe teacher education in the new century will be influenced by an emerging knowledge base on bilingual learners acquiring second-language English literacy (August & Hakuta, 1987, pp. 266–270) and biliteracy uses in oral and literate contexts (Hornberger, 1989). Biliteracy refers to the ability to read and write in two languages and the ability to talk about what has been read and written; unfortunately, bilingual programs that encourage biliteracy are rare.

This chapter is written for teachers or paraprofessionals who will teach reading to students who are bilingual, from preschool to adulthood, and who may collaborate with university researchers. We include recent research findings, from 1997–2001, but also report from the literature classic studies on bilinguals who are beginning to read—in a first or second language, or both. Bernhardt (2000) so aptly refers to second language reading as a "complicated case study of reading scholarship" that will enlarge our theories of reading and human development.

The "bilingual" has fulfilled, in some measure, a unique role within each generation and community. This individual speaks two languages, has had exposure, at least through these languages, to two cultures that influence ways of knowing the world. There are different degrees of bilingualism. Bilinguals are **not** a homogeneous group. It is difficult to generalize about them, given they may differ in a myriad of ways: their degree of bilingualism, the sequence in which they acquired the two languages, the uses that they have for their first language (L1) and their second language (L2), and the relative dominance of one or the other, the degree to which they code-switch between the two languages, the extent to which they think in their L1 and L2, and their language preferences for reading. Bilinguals could be in any program, studying reading in their L1, their L2 (here referring to both second and foreign language), or in both languages at the same time.

By virtue of including *should* in the title, "*What should teachers know about bilingual learners and the reading process?*" there is an implied moral imperative that somehow teachers need to know something they do not. The reality is that many teachers today in states such as Texas and California may be bilingual or multilingual. Half of all Hispanics residing in the United States live in just these two states (*U.S. Census Report,* 2000). These and other teachers who interact on a daily basis with bilinguals acquire insights about their Hispanic students' language abilities and needs. They may be able to design classroom research about bilinguals in ways that would benefit other teachers. The information flow between teachers and university professors needs to be two-way and interactive.

This chapter summarizes select research about the bilingual's entry into the reading process. Although the rich body of theories and knowledge of reading by monolinguals is applicable to second-language readers, it is apparent that a specialized body of knowledge, based on research on bilinguals entering literacy is essential for optimal achievement of bilingual children or adults. Below are some caveats relating to the interpretation of the research findings that follow.

TEACHERS OF BILINGUAL LEARNERS

Our teacher education classes in Minnesota and Texas include students quite different from twenty or thirty years ago. Prospective teachers have had careers in other fields or other capacities in schools. In a survey of 99 paraprofessionals in elementary schools in a low-income urban district in San Antonio, Texas, Horowitz (1997) found that 21% of bilingual paraprofessionals, largely Hispanics, had spent as many as 25 years in the school district. Sixty-six percent indicated that their own reading habits had changed as a result of tutoring bilingual children. Similarly, bilingual students in teacher education classes reported they were improving their own reading and writing, concurrently.

Teachers and paraprofessionals, today, place reading improvement as a high priority objective for bilinguals. Despite this priority, students in teacher training may not receive exposure to the research on bilinguals, their reading processes, or biliteracy. Those in schools of education would be enriched by relevant courses, for example, on sociolinguistics, second language reading, language and culture, the social psychology of literacy or the rhetorical foundations of early language and literacy acquisition (Calfee & Scott, 2001).

It is estimated that 2.5 million new teachers are needed for the next decade. In addition to the teacher shortage, retention is also a serious problem, as 50% of beginning teachers in city schools leave within three to five years (see Gregorian, 2001). Reform in teacher training has targeted early literacy of bilinguals to establish a foundation for a child's success in later school years. Links among theory, research, and on-site practice are needed so teachers of bilinguals can create exemplary classrooms in the communities they serve. This chapter focuses on Hispanic populations and particularly the Mexican-American, bilingual learner. However, where appropriate for understanding these and other bilingual learners, studies from additional cultures are referenced.

The U.S. Census, 2000, reported that the Hispanic population increased by 57%, from 22.4 million in 1990 to 35.3 million in 2000, compared with a 13.2% increase for the total U.S. population. Mexican-Americans represented 58.5% of all Hispanics. The relative youthfulness of the Hispanic population was evident with 35% of Hispanics under age 18, whereas 25% of the U.S. population was under 18. Approximately 9.8 million children between ages five and seventeen speak a language other than English, with about two-thirds, 6.7 million, speaking Spanish (U.S. Census, American Fact, 2000).

In 1990, in approximately 900,000 homes in the United States, English was reported as "not spoken well" or "not spoken at all." By the year 2000, this number increased resulting in approximately 1.2 million, a 7.82% increase, over the ten years, with English reported as "not spoken well" or "at all."

Given these demographics, teachers will need to prepare a substantial number of students to make the transition to English and second language literacies. As communication changes, bilinguals will be required to use new technology, for example, e-mail, the Internet, fax, online resources, and mass media. Bilingual learners will need to develop oral flexibility and savvy in uses of literacy, moving beyond the personal, contextualized discourse of an immediate family-neighborhood to English used in formal, public, institutional settings. For many, oral-based traditions have been the primary vehicle for learning and expression. Thus, bilinguals will require guidance in order to construct information from complex, written sources used in the institution of schools and work contexts (Hoggart, 1957/1992; Horowitz & Samuels, 1987).

RESEARCH ON BILINGUALS AND READING PROGRAMS

Little research has been conducted about bilingual instruction in reading programs. This is the case for first or second language literacies or biliteracy, albeit it by linguists, second language researchers, or reading researchers. Those who speak native Spanish and learn to read in English as a second language have been portrayed in the research as at risk of not becoming a reader or subject to school failure. There are single, isolated studies but few syntheses that place this research within a broader context of the developmental psychology or sociology of learning and teaching. Whereas Hakuta (1986) made the prediction that bilingualism in education promised to be a rich arena for research that would draw talented scholars and generate fascinating studies, such research has been slow in the coming and scattered in perspective.

Recently, the teaching of beginning reading in a first language to bilinguals has been viewed favorably, with books produced in Spanish and English, on bilingualism and literacy, targeted specifically for teachers (Brisk & Harrington, 2000; Carrasquillo & Segan 1998). Moreover, children's books for literacy learning have also been created in two languages to contrast language systems and reading processes.

In *Preventing Reading Difficulties in Young Children*, Snow, Burns, and Griffin (1998) convey evidence that the development of literacy in a first language in the early grades is necessary for the development of metalinguistic awareness and vital to alphabetic reading in a second language. This publication underscores that those children whose first language is Spanish may benefit in their ability to read English—through developing reading in Spanish, their L1.

Cohen and Laosa (1975) identified factors that influenced decision making about whether to introduce reading in L1, L2, or both languages based on research. Decision-making about which language to use in introducing reading depended upon multiple factors—the **specific reading program and text types, the sociolinguistic contexts of the program, and student characteristics, including age, motivation, learning or language preferences, proficiency in each language, and experiences with the languages.** Thirty years later, these are some of the same factors that influence decision making about which language to use to introduce reading. For example, they asked, if bilingual instruction takes place, in what way is literacy introduced in the two languages? The simultaneous introduction of L1 and L2 literacy may benefit some bilingual children but overwhelm others. Further, what is the level of the motivation of the bilingual child to be in the particular program of instruction they are assigned to (e.g., sheltered instruction, newcomer program, transitional bilingual education, developmental bilingual education, foreign/second language immersion, or two-way immersion; see Genesee, 1999)? To what degree does the text bilinguals are assigned fit reading ability and interests, so that they are motivated to read? Are bilinguals learning the L2 in a discourse environment where both L1 and L2 are being used interchangeably (sometimes referred to as a *coordinate bilingualism* situation) or in an environment that is removed from contact with the native language (referred to as a *compound bilingualism* situation)? Some learners may prefer to keep their languages separate (see the discussion of mental translation in reading which appears below).[2]

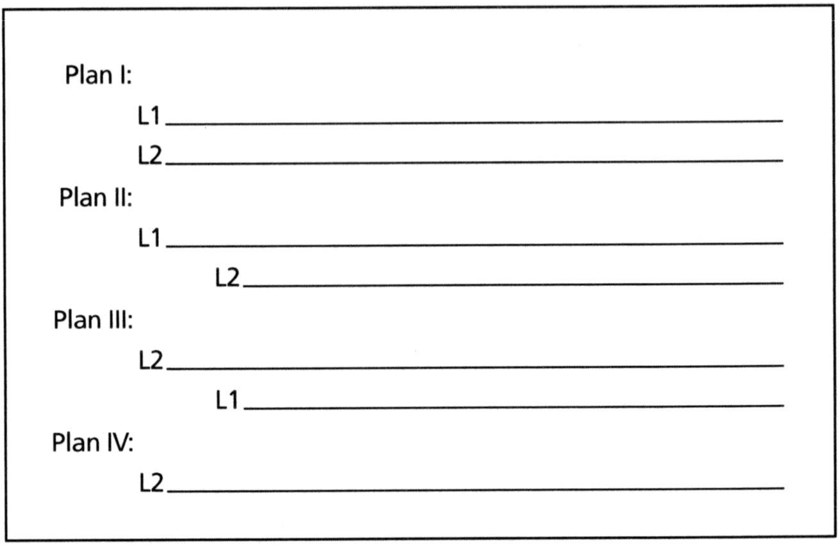

Plan I:

L1 _____

L2 _____

Plan II:

L1 _____

L2 _____

Plan III:

L2 _____

L1 _____

Plan IV:

L2 _____

Figure 1.   Reading programs for bilinguals.

Given the above discussion, the following are alternative ways of foster-ing beginning reading-research and positioning L1 and L2 instruction (see Figure 1).

Plan 1 introduces literacy instruction in L1 and L2 simultaneously. Plan 2 introduces beginning reading in L1 and after its development introduces reading in L2. Plan 3 suggests developing reading in the L2 (e.g., English) and after its development working on reading in L1 (e.g., Spanish). Plan 4 focuses on reading in L2 and excludes L1 reading. For a more detailed list of different types of bilingual programs see Garcia (1996, 1999).

BILINGUALS AND THE READING PROCESS

There is agreement that what distinguishes bilinguals the most is how dif-ferent they may be from one another, whether the factors are internal to the learners or conditioned by the external context in which they have learned languages (Grosjean, 1982; Hakuta, 1986). There are urban, rural, migrant, and immigrant bilinguals who come to schools with different kinds of daily experiences with language. In addition, there are distinct groups nested within a cultural group or minority. For instance, research on the literacy and school needs of Mexican American gang affiliates in Texas suggests they may differ from other groups of adolescents and Mexi-can American adolescents in educational needs and preferences in ways that teachers may or may not perceive (Horowitz, in progress; Orange & Horowitz, 1999).

Because of vast student differences, teachers should explore a variety of programs. Bilinguals should be assessed using multiple methods and as a group and individually, as they read in L1 and L2. Findings, to date, on second-language reading have been largely based on assessments of adult learners who are fluent in a first language—not children or adolescents (Weber, 1991). Quantitative studies have been the common form of research and have produced findings about beginning reading, basic reading skills, and comprehension of monolinguals (see *Report of The National Reading Panel* 2000 and *The Nation's Report Card. Fourth*-Grade *Reading 2000*). However, there is clearly a need for in-depth case studies, developmental and longitudinal studies of reading processes, and learning outcomes when reading in L1 and/or L2.

Case studies of monolinguals' reading processes were first conducted at the turn of the century, incorporating foreign terms (Huey, 1908; Judd & Buswell, 1922). Since some bilingual learners also may have special difficulties when reading in the L2 given the nature of their schooling (Miramontes, 1990), it can be most informative for teachers to systematically document student reading experiences. Fortunately, case reports of bilinguals in classroom contexts have emerged recently that give teachers detailed profiles of individuals developing as readers (Jiménez, 1997; Jiménez, Garcia, & Pearson, 1995, 1996; Moll, Saez, & Dworin, 2001; Moll & Gonzalez, 1994).

We will now examine a series of statements about bilinguals and the reading process, based on recent findings in the research literature, bearing in mind the above caveats. Although there are overlaps across categories, the statements have been categorized under the following nine headings: (1) A Comparison of Young Bilinguals vs. Monolingual Readers, (2) Model of Language Transfer in Bilingual Reading Development—The Best Language for Starting Literacy, (3) The Process of Reading in a Second Language, (4) Transfer of Reading Skills and Strategies Across Languages, (5) The Fit Between the L1 and L2 Writing Systems, (6) The Texts Used with Bilingual Learners, (7) The Grouping of Students in the Classroom, (8) The Bilingual's Training in Reading Strategies, and (9) The Home Environment as a Context for Literacy. The chapter will conclude with a few suggestions about assessment and about future research to conduct.

THEORY AND RESEARCH FINDINGS

1. A Comparison of Young Bilinguals versus Monolinguals and Reading

Practice with oral language before, during, and outside schooling can be beneficial for all learners. Horowitz (1984) and Horowitz and Samuels (1987) reviewed theories and research contrasting oral-literate language and comprehension by bilinguals and monolinguals, respectively. Some theorists point to the similarities in acquiring oral and written language, whereas others view oral and written communication as serving different functions, resulting in different language and cognitive processes. Researchers may view beginning reading as uncovering the oral language, matching print to speech, but later in development readers will go directly to meaning, bypassing speech. Oral and literate experiences (e.g., talk at home and reading in school) of monolinguals and bilinguals are never purely separate and will interact (Horowitz, 1995b). Edelsky (1989) cautioned that oral language development is not necessarily a prerequisite to written language development. For example, it is possible that written language will influence oral language and how children perceive speech (Olson, 1994). Also, it is possible to become a high level reader in a language one does not speak, but this is usually after the establishment of oral and written skills in the L1. Jiménez (2001) discussed how bilinguals assume unique roles as "oral language brokers" and "interpreters" for parents, teach siblings, and perform oral and written language acts not recognized in the institution of school, yet valuable for high literacy and thinking.

Opportunities to practice oral language are needed for academic success. Spanish-speaking students in Los Angeles learning to read have acquired academic oral language through teacher-led Instructional Conversations (IC's) (Goldenberg, 1994). Patthey-Chavez and Lindsay (1996) found IC's were beneficial for transitional bilingual fourth-grade Hispanic students. These conversations resulted in fluency with writing, reduced anxiety, and sustained attention to and comprehension of written sources. Saunders and Goldenberg (1999) found when teachers used both literature logs and Instructional Conversations with limited-English fourth and fifth graders, the students understood the literature better than when only one of these techniques was used. Instructional Conversations activate schemata, promote complex language, create a nonthreatening environment, involve direct teaching, and include teacher responsiveness to student ideas. These and other speech structures can be practiced to develop vocabulary and syntax, to activate different content area genres that will ultimately be processed as text content.

The Nation's Report Card: Fourth-Grade Reading, 2000, also conveyed that conversations outside of school with family and friends about reading had a positive relationship to student reading performance. Overall, students at this grade who talked about their reading weekly had a higher average reading score than students who reported such talk daily, monthly, or never (U.S. Department of Education, 2001, p. 56).

Bilingual children may be better able to recognize symbolic relations between letters or characters and sounds than monolinguals. Bialystok (1997) examined the understanding of general correspondences between print and language and specific correspondences in alphabetic and non-alphabetic languages on the part of 137 monolingual (English) and bilingual (French-English, Chinese-English) four and five year olds. Bilingual children understood the general symbolic representation of print better than monolingual children. Older Chinese-English bilingual children showed advanced understanding of specific correspondences in English print. A follow-up study by Bialystok, Shenfield, and Codd (2000) examined understanding of print concepts in preschool children bilingual in English and Hebrew. They found that bilingual children were more advanced than monolinguals, regardless of task or whether English or Hebrew was the community language.

Geva and colleagues (1993) demonstrated that learning an L2 concurrently with L1 did not confuse Canadian children. Geva and Siegel (1998) demonstrated that the orthographic features of a language could influence the development of basic reading skills in two languages and that when the script was less complex, young children appeared to develop their word recognition with relative ease. Geva's research has discounted prevailing myths about the abilities of bilinguals.

2. Model of Language Transfer in the Bilingual's Reading Development

Figure 2 illustrates the different ways L1 and L2 may function in a bilingual's oral and written language development and provides a model of language transfer from one language to another. The transfer of literate language skills is influenced by the student's age-experiences, contextual uses of language, the student's familiarity with the writing systems, the texts in given contexts and exposure to and motivation toward oral and written language and literacy in L1 and L2.

First, some children's beginning literacy may be developed through the oral and written L1 (e.g., Spanish). The child produces and processes speech (e.g., at home and school) and may read and write—in L1 (Spanish), (Box A). With experience, exposure, and opportunity, the skills and knowledge acquired in beginning (oral or written) Spanish are transferred to

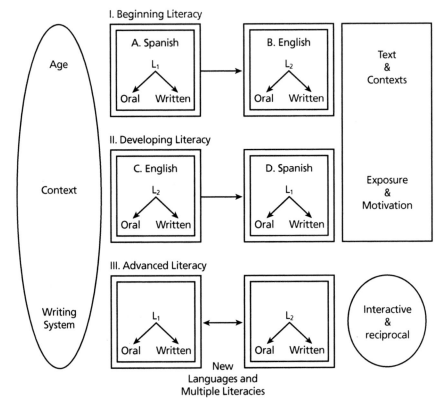

Figure 2.   Boxology. Model of language transfer in the bilingual's reading development.

beginning L2 (English), oral and written language (a second language), (Box B). Recently, state and federal projects have been designed to teach students to read and write in their first language (e.g., Spanish).

At a later stage, a student's L2 (English) may be further developed in oral and written language (Box C) and influences L1 (Spanish) oral and written language (Box D). With continued practice, advanced schooling and reading development, new contexts for learning and language requirements, there is an interdependency, a flow from L1 to L2 and L2 to L1—bidirectionality—with hybrid discourses (sometimes a mixture of English and Spanish and code-switching). The teaching of reading in L1, before L2, or alongside L2 is further explored and clarified through the research cited below.

The Best Language for Starting Literacy

Reading skills transfer from L1 to L2. A recent study of Spanish-English bilinguals examined whether performance on indicators of Spanish reading ability at the end of second grade could predict English reading performance at the end of third grade (August, Calderón, & Carlo, 2000). The researchers examined differences in transfer across phonological, orthographic, and comprehension processes, and evaluated whether transfer effects would vary for Spanish-instructed and English-instructed students. They used a combination of standardized measures and researcher-developed measures to assess phonological awareness, phonemic segmentation (ability to divide words into their component sounds), orthographic skills (letter recognition, word recognition, and ability to read non-words), and comprehension skills in both Spanish and English.

The results indicated that Spanish phonemic awareness, Spanish letter identification, Spanish word recognition, and fluency in letter and word identification in Spanish were reliable predictors of English performance on parallel tasks in English at the end of third grade. The effect of Spanish phonemic awareness on English phonemic awareness emerged for all students. However, the effect of Spanish word decoding on English word decoding emerged **only** for students who had received formal instruction in Spanish reading. These results are consistent with the hypothesis that reading skills acquired in school contexts can be transferred across languages (cf. Cummins, 1994; Gottadro, Harmon, Acevedo, Stanish, & Wolfe, 2001). These preliminary findings were interpreted as support for literacy instruction in Spanish—to Spanish-speaking, English-language learners, thus, helping them acquire literacy skills in English and enhancing their bilingual capability.

It can be beneficial to establish a strong underpinning in L1 literacy at the same time as one develops L2 literacy. Research has demonstrated that for Spanish-English bilinguals in U.S. schools, a focus on the home language is an effective way to stimulate literacy (Brown-Rodríguez & Mulhern, 1993). When instruction has been provided in English only, the children seem to improve their oral English but not their emergent literacy development (Thornburg, 1993).

Research has also shown that late-exit transitional bilingual education programs can benefit bilingual readers (Ramírez, Yuen, Ramey, & Pasta, 1991). In other words, the longer that Spanish-English bilinguals receive reinforcement in the L1 (e.g., Spanish) the better. Consistent with this finding, research has shown that two-way developmental (or maintenance-oriented) bilingual education at the elementary school level is the most promising program model for the long-term academic success of language minority students in comparison to one-way developmental, transitional bilingual education, in-class or pullout ESL instruction (Collier, 1995; Thomas & Collier, 1997). As a group, students in the maintenance-oriented bilingual program maintained grade-level skills in L1 at least through sixth grade and reached the 50th percentile in their L2, generally after four-five years of schooling in both languages. Gains were sustained through secondary education.

Initial literacy in the L2 before L1 literacy, if developed, can be a viable possibility—depending on the learners involved and the instructional program. Studies with language-minority, Spanish-English bilinguals have demonstrated the value of initial literacy in the L1. However, full language immersion programs that begin with reading readiness and reading in the L2 also have been shown to produce good literacy skills in both the L1 and L2. Research in Canada has documented successful results of French immersion education for English Canadians, where initial literacy takes place in the L2 (see, e.g., Genesee, 1987). Similar results were found for one of the first full immersion programs in the United States, the Culver City Spanish Full Immersion Program (Cohen, 1974, 1975; Snow, Galván, & Campbell, 1983). In the Culver City model, the pupils were required to participate in a program that was exclusively in Spanish during the early years, and the research reports were generally positive with regard to success at reading in both Spanish (L2) and English (L1), with the introduction of the latter delayed until grade two.

L1 and L2 may both contribute to reading in English. Reese, Garnier, Gallimore, and Goldenberg (2000) demonstrated that students entering kindergarten with greater Spanish (L1) literacy development **and** oral English proficiency (a) maintained grade level Spanish reading and (b) transitioned to L2 reading, attaining higher verbal English reading in middle school. This study found intergenerational literacy and cultural factors were predictors of early literacy in Spanish and that early literacy experiences influenced later literacy, regardless of the language.

3. The Process of Reading in a Second Language may be Different than Reading in a First Language and may Vary by Individual Reader

Readers may potentially use similar strategies across languages. However, their actual strategy use for a given text in a given language will depend on the genre and difficulty level of the text, their individual language proficiency and reading ability. A qualitative think-aloud study of fourth-grade bilingual Latino students found that those who were strong readers had reading profiles that were similar across languages. Their actual strategy use varied according to text genre (which made a difference), text difficulty, their relative proficiency in the two languages, and their reading ability (Garcia, 1998).

The choice of reading strategies may be influenced by the topic and student interest. Horowitz (1991), for example, found that Mexican-American, Spanish-speaking adolescents had specific expectations about reading certain topics. Text types, such as a more oral-like or more written-like text, could influence comprehension and recall. A more oral-like text was comprehended best when it was listened to and a more written-like text was comprehended best when it was read by high school students (Horowitz & Rubin, 1999).

Bilinguals may use fewer L2 reading strategies and less effectively than strategies in L1.   Strategy research with young learners found that third- and fifth-grade bilingual Latinos used fewer and less sophisticated cognitive and metacognitive strategies in English than monolingual Anglo students (Padrón, Knight, & Waxman, 1986). However, in a qualitative think-aloud study focusing on documenting the reading strategies of sixth- and seventh-grade bilingual Latino readers, Jiménez et al. (1996) reported that there was no substantial difference in the comprehension monitoring and meaning-making strategies by three monolingual Anglo readers and eight bilingual Latino readers. The three bilingual students who were not successful English readers used the fewest and least sophisticated strategies.

Few studies have been conducted wherein bilinguals use L2 strategies for reading very specific kinds of content area texts. Cohen (1984), for one, studied how bilinguals deal with the texts that appear in reading comprehension tasks on tests. Bilinguals may use fewer strategies when reading a content area text on a test than monolinguals because they are struggling with decoding and lack automaticity.

Mental translation in L2 reading requires extra time and may be influenced by individual strategy preferences for particular reading tasks.   A study conducted with intermediate learners of French at the University of California, Berkeley (Kern, 1994) and a replication with beginning, intermediate, and advanced learners of Spanish at the University of Minnesota (Cohen, 1998; Hawras, 1996) helped identify at least five strategic purposes that nonnative readers reported for using mental translation while reading. Mental translation of language was used as a strategy for remembering points in the text (for chunking material into semantic clusters, for keeping the train of thought), for creating a network of associations, for enhancing the familiarity of the text, for clarifying grammatical roles, and for checking on comprehension. These mental translations require extra time and control in attention.

4. Transfer of Reading Skills and Strategies across Languages

Children with higher L1 phonological awareness and word recognition may be more successful at L2 word recognition too. It would appear that if young bilinguals are good readers in their L1, they are likely to be good readers in an L2 as well. A study of Spanish-speaking first graders in the United States showed that the children's Spanish phonological awareness and word recognition significantly predicted their English word recognition and pseudo-English word recognition, indicating cross-linguistic transfer (Durgunoglu, Nagy, & Hancin-Bhatt, 1993). Children who had phonological awareness and Spanish word recognition skills performed better on the transfer tasks than those children who could read some Spanish words but who demonstrated low Spanish phonological awareness.

Not all bilingual readers have an intuitive sense of transfer or make use of cross-linguistic strategies. Research with successful and less successful sixth- and seventh-grade bilingual English readers revealed that the successful ones saw reading in two languages as essentially comprising the same skills across the two languages. Consequently, they were able to transfer knowledge and strategies across languages (Jiménez et al., 1995, 1996). They could also make use of bilingual reading strategies such as using cognates (words of a similar origin), code-switching, and translating in order to enhance their reading comprehension. The weaker readers felt they had to keep their two languages separate or they would become confused.

5. The Fit between the L1 and L2 Writing Systems

The degree of similarity between L1 and L2 writing systems may or may not have an impact on reading across languages. The Japanese syllabary system is different from the English alphabet. But ease of transition from one system to another is not predictably difficult. It depends on the individuals' style preferences, language proficiency in the two languages, perceptions of these differences, and so forth. As Fillmore and Snow (2000, p. 26) point out, syllabic systems actually have the advantage of being rather easy for young children, since syllables are psychologically more accessible units than phonemes,[3] which are simply sounds and often are difficult to segment.

In alphabetic writing systems, letters typically represent phonemes. Representing sounds alphabetically can be a challenge in languages like English that often ignore phoneme identity to preserve the spelling identity of morphemes.[4] For example, in English the spelling S is used for plural morphemes whether they are pronounced /s/ or /z/—even though in other contexts, such as at the beginning of words, the /s/ and /z/ sounds are spelled distinctively (compare the spelling and pronunciation of *dogs* and *cats* to that of *zoo* and *Sue*). Perhaps of more significance than the similarity of the writing systems is the manner in which initial literacy is approached in an L1 (Valdés, 1996).

6. The Texts Used with Bilingual Learners

The cultural familiarity of texts plus linguistic modification or simplification may facilitate reading by bilinguals.   A study with Turkish students learning Dutch in the Netherlands found that if third graders read *culturally appropriate material* with *linguistic simplification*, they did better than monolingual children (Droop & Verhoeven, 1998). However, when they read *culturally appropriate texts* that were *linguistically complex*, there was no significant difference in performance between the Turkish and Dutch students. In other words, linguistic complexity can wash out the effects of cultural familiarity.

There are not many basal reading series in Spanish (see, e.g., Escamilla, Andrade, Basurto, & Ruiz, 1990, 1991) nor many that incorporate English and Spanish; few tradebooks exist in Spanish, and neighborhood libraries have been slow to purchase Spanish or bilingual books for children. However, new software may include books with translations, vocabulary, or pronunciations that will assist bilinguals learning L2.

7. The Grouping of Bilingual Students in the Classroom

Assignment of bilinguals to reading groups needs to be flexible and according to specified criteria.   Fillmore and Snow consider it acceptable to group students by reading level so that they can discuss their books with one another. However, they point out that it is imperative that the teacher make sure such grouping is "*targeted*" (i.e., used for a particular instructional purpose), *flexible* (i.e., as soon as individual children have acquired the targeted skill they leave that group), and *objective* (i.e., based on well-specified criteria directly related to the instructional target, not on global measures of readiness) (Fillmore & Snow, 2000, p. 8). For example, some children may need more time with particular instructional foci (e.g., digraphs or vocabulary enrichment or long vowel spellings). Otherwise, tracking can have a profound negative effect on the child.

8. Spanish-English Bilinguals and Training in Reading Strategies

There is empirical evidence that Spanish-English bilinguals can be trained to be more strategic readers. Research results have been positive in studies aimed at improving bilingual readers' use of metacognitive and cognitive reading strategies—namely, reciprocal teaching, question-answer relationships (QARs), and self-generated questions while reading (Muñiz-Swicegood, 1994; Padrón, 1992). Likewise, in a qualitative study with five low-literacy seventh grade Latino students, Jiménez (1997) reported that the students benefited from cognitive strategy lessons that: (1) used culturally familiar texts, (2) emphasized reading fluency, and word recognition skills, and (3) taught the students how to resolve unknown vocabulary, ask questions, and make inferences. In addition, effective cognitive strategies lessons taught students how to use bilingual strategies such as searching for cognates, translating, and transferring knowledge from one language to the other.

9. The Home Environment as a Context for Literacy

The home reading environment will influence how biliteracy develops at school. For most of the century, Spanish-speaking children in Texas have not been permitted to speak Spanish while acquiring English in schools. There is some evidence that today's bilingual second- and third-generation parents wish to preserve the first language in order to increase cross-generational communication and loyalty (Snow et al., 1998). It has also been noted there may be special forms of literacies in biliteracy not found in English or monolingual classrooms. Some of these first language literacies may stem from family literacy or historical-cultural practices (Moll et al., 2001). Programs target parents to read Spanish in order to build intergenerational literacy and reading routines and contexts for literacy in a household (Goldenberg, 1994).

Limited-English-proficient children in bilingual programs may have little access to books. Pucci (1994) estimated an average of one book in Spanish per Spanish-speaking child in some school libraries. Building on ecological research, Neuman and Celano (2001) studied the extent to which printed sources were available in low income vs. middle income schools and neighborhoods. There were significantly fewer written sources available in low-income preschool, libraries, and neighborhoods, a finding that has been substantiated in similar research in San Antonio, Texas.

ISSUES OF ASSESSMENT

The instruments and tasks used in evaluating bilingual reading processes, comprehension, and recall must be appropriate for this population. Research by Cohen (1984, 1993, 1994a, 1994b, 1994c) has included assessment of the bilinguals' testing strategies, their cognitive operations during math tasks, and their approaches to reading and text summaries. Beginning readers who are learning to read in L1 have recently been assessed for phonemic awareness, word recognition skills, and reading and listening comprehension, using *The Spanish Tejas Lee*. This is a Spanish modification of the *Texas Primary Reading Inventory* (TPRI)—adopted by 800 school districts throughout Texas. *The Spanish Tejas Lee* has recently been evaluated in a number of locations in Texas, including through a San Antonio Implementation Study, coordinated by the second author. It is designed to be used with Spanish-speaking, bilingual K-2 students to assess their English and Spanish reading readiness and to determine that the child will be reading on grade-level (in both languages) by third grade.

Looking beyond early reading, the multiple meanings of a given word may create difficulties for bilinguals as they enter specialized content area reading. Recent research suggests that teachers are capable of determining the difficulties that Hispanic students have with reading and study and that standardized tests are not the only vehicle for reliable assessment (Frontera & Horowitz, 1995; Meisels, Bickel, Prima, Nicholson, Yange, Atkins-Burnett, 2001). Ralph Tyler astutely warned about the dangers of comparing performance of students across schools in different districts (Horowitz, 1995a). He suggested that performance on standardized reading tests may be influenced by the neighborhood and that comparisons across neighborhoods or school districts may not be valid (cf. Neuman & Celano, 2001).

ISSUES FOR FURTHER RESEARCH

While we have considered many issues of concern about bilinguals and the reading process that were not as well conceptualized or even raised some 35 years ago, at the start of US federally-funded bilingual education programs, there are still pressing questions to resolve:

a. *The best language for starting literacy and the processing of literate discourse needs further teacher and university research.* The research is currently examining beginning literacy in L1 for particular individuals and contexts. In this case, the transfer assumption that underlies bilingual education needs further explication: What gets transferred?

When and how does transfer occur between L1 and L2, given oral language or reading?

b. *The process of reading in a second language and the difficulties encountered by a range of children (by age, social group, first language, developmentally) need to be researched.*   Research results are not widely evaluated or published on the type of L1 reading instruction offered to young Spanish-English bilingual readers (García, 1998) or its benefits. Durgunoglu et al. (1993) questioned whether young bilingual children who do not have phonological awareness in their first language should be taught these skills in L1 or L2. Two topics for further investigation would be the extent to which bilingual children need to be taught phonological or orthographic elements that are characteristic of their second language but not of their native language, and whether this type of instruction can accelerate the students' second language literacy development.

c. *Knowledge is needed about the types of texts that can be most effective in facilitating content reading in L1 and L2.*   Researchers in collaboration with classroom teachers should consider text structures, the role of illustrations, culturally-based content, the use of L1 and L2 readings in a single text, and the nature of the topics and content being taught in content areas to bilingual, ethnic minority and majority populations.

d. *The home and school connection is receiving greater attention in studies of literacy development.*   What should parents do to foster bilingualism and biliteracy? How do neighborhood and community resources, and opportunities to practice speaking and reading in English, influence reading development? In what ways can parents become more active in their child's reading activities? In what ways can schools stay connected to families?

e. *Teacher training and knowledge of family and intergenerational literacy practices or non-literacy can be instrumental in the teaching of reading.*   As Auerbach (1991) purports, teachers and researchers can benefit from building a new model of the family as a positive source of literacy learning. In the past, low-income, minority families may have been viewed as an impediment rather than an asset to literacy. With children reading to parents who are non-readers, adults and children experience bi-directionality in literacy development.

g. *Finally, writers who describe immigration patterns of Latinos point to the cognitive correlates of acquiring a second language—characterizing the gains but also the psychological and emotional challenges.*   For example, Stavans (1995), a native of Mexico City, portrays the transition from one language and culture to another as "living on the edge" and Rose (1989), who describes growing up Italian in a Los Angeles ghetto writes about "living on the boundary." More needs to be known about the acquisition and outcomes of biliteracy—cognitive-affective experiences, the intellectual joys and trepidations, the change in consciousness of second language learners as they reframe use of their first language and acquire a new language and literacy.

An important body of research on children's theories of mind can be expanded to include children's views of themselves as L2 and biliteracy learners (Olson, 1994). We wonder what theories today's children hold in their minds about second language learning. How do children perceive the roles of English and other languages, e.g., Spanish in their lives or schooling (Jiménez, 2001)? What might teachers do to foster positive self-perceptions of bilingualism and biliteracy? These questions remain untouched in the research.

As a result of the increase in English as a second language learners and population shifts, the International Reading Association hosted a North American Consultation on Second Language Literacy Research in Washington, DC on July 17, 2001. The goal was to review the research knowledge base with teacher and university experts from across North America and the world. A conclusion was that we have limited research about how to introduce reading to bilinguals. There was a realization that teachers need to know about the research that has been conducted and how to add to it. Further, the conference stressed that it is not clear how the studies in Canada and other nations differ from or resemble United States studies. Moreover, how transportable current knowledge is from one community, region, or people, to another remains an issue of concern.

The teacher of bilinguals in the new century is, without doubt, a critical figure. This teacher should foster new speech genres and literacies that will advance the lives of bilingual learners—far beyond what we could have imagined in the past century. Bilingual and biliterate learners will have access to a myriad of resources in the new century, but will also have the potential to analyze and influence the way we think and act on these resources in our communities and society.

AUTHOR NOTE

Appreciation is extended to Marty Chamness, Ruby Kainth and Wendy Angleman, students at The University of Texas-San Antonio, for their assistance with the manuscript.

NOTES

1. An earlier, more limited version of this chapter was presented at the Sympo-sium, *Defining and Developing New Standards of Excellence for Professional Development of Literacy Teachers* held at the American Educational Research Association (AERA) Conference, Seattle, Washington, on April 13, 2001. This Symposium was orga-nized by Rosalind Horowitz on behalf of the Special Interest Group on Basic Research in Reading and Literacy at AERA. A debt of gratitude goes to Georgia Earnest García (e.g., García, 2000) for her fine work in reviewing research on bilin-gual children's reading from 1989 to 1997. Her work inspired and informed this work. This chapter expands upon her review by adding research studies from 1997 through July 2001.

2. Although Baetens Beardsmore (1982) and others might contend that there is little empirical support for the *coordinate-compound* distinction, there is probably some truth to the notion that language contexts can vary in the extent of overlap or separation of the languages in the learning process.

3. *Phonemes* are the smallest meaning-distinguishing structure of the sound sys-tem, e.g., for English, [s] [š], *see, she*).

4. *Morphemes* are the smallest meaning-bearing language structure, e.g., *dog, -ly*.

REFERENCES

August, D., Calderón, M., & Carlo, M. (2000). *Transfer of skills from Spanish to English: A study of young learners*. Report for practitioners, parents, and policy makers. ED-98-CO-0071. Washington, DC: Center for Applied Linguistics.

August, D., & Hakuta, K. (1997). *Improving schooling for language-minority children. A research agenda*. Washington, DC: National Academy Press.

Auerbach, E.R. (1991). Toward a social-contextul approach to family literacy. In M. Minami, & B.P. Kennedy (Eds.), *Language issues in literacy and bilingual/multibil-ingcultural education* (pp. 391–408). Cambridge, MA: Harvard Educational Review.

Bernhardt, E.B. (2000). Second-language reading as a case study of reading schol-arship in the 20th century. In M.L. Kamil, P.B. Mosenthal, P.D. Pearson, & R. Barr (Eds.). *Handbook of reading research* (Vol. III, (pp. 791–811)). Mahwah, NJ: Erlbaum.

Baetens Beardsmore, H. (1982). *Bilingualism: Basic principles*. Clevedon, Avon: Mul-tilingual Matters.

Bialystok, E. (1997). Effects of bilingualism and biliteracy on children's emerging concepts of print. *Developmental Psychology, 33* (3), 429–440.

Bialystok, E., Shenfield, T., & Codd, J. (2000). Languages, scripts, and the environ-ment: Factors in developing concepts of print. *Developmental Psychology, 36*, 66–76.

Brisk, M.E., & Harrington, M.M. (2000). *Literacy and bilingualism. A handbook for all teachers*. Mahwah, NJ: Erlbaum.

Brown-Rodríguez, F.V., & Mulhern, M.M. (1993). Fostering critical literacy through family literacy: A study of families in a Mexican-immigrant community. *Bilin-gual Research Journal, 17*, 1–16.

Calfee, R., & Scott, L. (2001, April 13). What should the 21st century literacy teacher know and be able to do? In *Defining and developing new standards of excellence for professional development of literacy teachers*. Symposium conducted at The American Educational Research Association Conference, Seattle.

Carrasquillo, A., & Segan, P. (Eds.). (1998). *The teaching of reading in Spanish to the bilingual student* (2nd ed.). Mahwah, NJ: Erlbaum.

Cohen, A.D. (1974). The Culver City Spanish Immersion Program: The first two years. *The Modern Language Journal, 58*, 95–103.

Cohen, A.D. (1975). Progress report on the Culver City Spanish Immersion Program: The third and fourth years. *Workpapers in Teaching English as a Second Language, 9*, University of California, Los Angeles, 47–65. Educational Resources Information Center, 121 093.

Cohen, A. (1984). On taking language tests: What the students report. *Language Testing, 1*(1), 70–81.

Cohen, A. (1993). The role of instructions in testing summarizing ability. In D. Douglas & C. Chapelle (Eds.), *A new decade of language testing: Collaboration and cooperation* (pp. 132–160). Alexandria, VA: TESOL, 132–160.

Cohen, A. (1994a). *Assessing language ability in the classroom* (2nd ed., Ch. 5, pp. 115–159). Boston: Newbury House/Heinle & Heinle.

Cohen, A. (1994b). The language used to perform cognitive operations during full-immersion math tasks. *Language Testing, 11*(2), 171–195.

Cohen, A. (1994c). English for academic purposes in Brazil: The use of summary tasks. In C. Hill & K. Parry (Eds.). *From testing to assessment: English as an international language* (pp. 174–204). London: Longman.

Cohen, A.D. (1998a). *Strategies in learning and using a second language*. Harlow: Longman.

Cohen, A. (1998b). Strategies and processes in test taking and SLA. In L.F. Bachman & A.D. Cohen (Eds.), *Interfaces between second language acquisition and language testing research* (pp. 90–111). Cambridge: Cambridge University Press.

Cohen, A.D., & Laosa, L.M. (1976). Second language instruction: Some research considerations. *Curriculum Studies, 8*(2), 149–165.

Collier, V.P. (1995). Acquiring a second language for school. *Directions in Language & Education, 1*(4), (ERIC ED394 301).

Cummins, J. (1994). Interdependence of first and second language proficiency in bilingual children. In E. Bialystok (Ed.), *Language processes in bilingual children* (pp. 70–89). Cambridge: Cambridge University Press.

de León, A.G. (2001). Carnegie Challenge. 2001. *Higher education's challenge: New teacher education models for a new century*. New York: Carnegie Corporation.

Droop, M., & Verhoeven, L. (1998). Background knowledge, linguistic complexity, and second-language reading comprehension. *Journal of Literacy Research, 30*, 253–271.

Durgunoglu, A., Nagy, W.E., & Hancin-Bhatt, B.J. (1993). Cross-language transfer of phonological awareness. *Journal of Educational Psychology, 85*, 453–465.

Edelsky, C. (1989). Bilingual children's writing: Fact and fiction. In D.M. Johnson & D.H. Roen (Eds.), *Richness in writing: Empowering ESL students* (pp. 165–76). New York: Longman.

Elley, W.B. (1991). Acquiring literacy in a second language: The effect of book-based programs. *Language Learning, 41,* 375–411.

Escamilla, K., Andrade, A., Basurto, A., & Ruiz, O. (1990, 1991). *Descubriendo la lectura: An early intervention Spanish literacy project.* Annual Conference Journal. Washington, DC: National Association for Bilingual Education.

Fillmore, L.W., & Snow, C.E. (2000). *What teachers need to know about language.* Paper prepared for the ERIC CAL Clearinghouse on Language and Linguistics. Available at http://www.cal.org/ericcll

Frontera, L., & Horowitz, R. (1995). Reading and study behaviors of fourth grade Hispanics: Can teachers assess risk? *Hispanic Journal of Behavioral Sciences, 17*(1), 100–120.

García, G.E. (2000). Bilingual children's reading. In M. Kamil, P. Mosenthal, P.D. Pearson, & R. Barr (Eds.), *Handbook of reading research* (Vol. III, pp. 813–834). Mahwah, NJ: Erlbaum.

Garcia, O. (1999, July 12–16). *Bilingualism and biliteracy through schooling. An international Symposium.* Brooklyn, NY: Brooklyn College, Long Island University.

Garcia, O. (1996). Bilingual education. In F. Coulmas (Ed.), *The handbook of sociolinguistics* (pp. 405–420). Oxford: Blackwell.

Genesee, F. (1987). *Learning through two languages: Studies of immersion and bilingual education.* Cambridge, MA: Newbury House.

Genesee, F. (Ed.). (1999). *Program alternatives for linguistically diverse students.* Santa Cruz, CA: Center for Research on Education, Diversity & Excellence, University of California, Santa Cruz.

Geva, E., & Siegel, L. S. (1998). Orthographic and cognitive factors in the concurrent development of basic reading skills in two languages. *Reading and Writing: An Interdisciplinary Journal, 12*(1–2) 1–31.

Geva, E., Wade-Wooley, L., & Shany, M. (1993). The concurrent development of spelling and decoding in two different orthographies. *Journal of Reading Behavior, 25,* 383–406.

Goldenberg, C. (1994). Promoting early literacy development among Spanish speaking children: Lessons from two studies. In E.H. Heibert & B.M. Taylor (Eds.), *Getting reading right from the start: Effective early literacy interventions* (pp. 171–199). Boston: Allyn and Bacon.

Gottardo, A., Harmon, M., Acevedo, D., Stanish, H., & Wolfe, M. (2001). *The development of English reading in Spanish-speaking children.* Paper presented at the Society for Scientific Study of Reading Conference, Boulder, CO.

Gregorian, V. (2001, July 6). How to train—and retain—teachers. *The New York Times,* p. A17.

Grosjean, F. (1982). *Life with two languages.* Cambridge, MA: Harvard University.

Hakuta, K. (1986). *Mirror of language. The debate on bilingualism.* New York: Basic Books.

Hawras, S. (1996). *Towards describing bilingual and multilingual behavior: Implications for ESL instruction.* Double Plan B Paper, English as a Second Language Department, University of Minnesota, Minneapolis.

Hoggart, R. (1957/1992). *The uses of literacy.* New Brunswick & London: Transaction.

Hornberger, N. H. (1989). Continua of biliteracy. *Review of Educational Research,* *59*(3), 271–296.

Horowitz, R. (1984). Orality and literacy in bilingual-bicultural contexts. *NABE Journal, 8*(3), 11–26.

Horowitz, R. (1991). A reexamination of oral versus silent reading. *Text, 11*(1), 133–166.

Horowitz, R. (1995a). A 75-year legacy on assessment: Reflections from an interview with Ralph W. Tyler. *Journal of Educational Research, 89*(2), 68–75.

Horowitz, R. (1995b). Orality in literacy: The uses of speech in written language by bilingual and bicultural writers. In D.L. Rubin (Ed.), *Composing social identity in written language* (pp. 47–74). Hillsdale, NJ: Erlbaum.

Horowitz, R. (1997). *The unique contributions of Latina paraprofessionals to the teaching of reading.* Invited colloquium, Department of Human Development and Applied Psychology, The Ontario Institute for Studies in Education (OISE) of The University of Toronto, Ontario, Canada.

Horowitz, R. (in progress). *Educational and literacy enhancement for gang affiliated Hispanic adolescents.* The University of Texas—San Antonio.

Horowitz, R., & Rubin, D. (1999). *Oral-based versus literate-based discourse. Effects on reading and listening comprehension.* Paper presented at the Society for Scientific Study of Reading (SSSR). Montreal, Quebec, Canada.

Horowitz, R., & Samuels, S. J. (Eds.). (1987). *Comprehending oral and written language.* London and San Diego: Academic Press.

Huey, E.B. (1908). *The psychology and pedagogy of reading.* Cambridge, MA: MIT Press.

Jiménez, R.T. (2001). "It's a difference that changes us": An alternative view of the language and literacy needs of Latina/o students. *The Reading Teacher, 54,* 736–741.

Jiménez, R.T. (2000). Literacy and the identity development of Latina/o students. *American Educational Research Association Journal, 37,* 971–1000.

Jiménez, R.T. (1997). The strategic reading abilities and potential of five low-literacy Latina/o readers in the middle school. *Reading Research Quarterly, 32,* 224–243.

Jiménez, R.T., García, G.E., & Pearson, P.D. (1995). Three children, two languages, and strategic reading: Case studies in bilingual/monolingual reading. *American Educational Research Journal, 32,* 31–61.

Jiménez, R.T., García, G.E., & Pearson, P.D. (1996). The reading strategies of bilingual Latino/a students who are successful English readers: Opportunities and obstacles. *Reading Research Journal, 27,* 427–471.

Judd, C.H., & Buswell, G.T. (1922). *Silent reading: A study of the various types.* Chicago: The University of Chicago.

Kern, R. G. (1994). The role of mental translation in second language reading. *Studies in Second Language Acquisition, 16,* 441–461.

Meisels, S.J., DiPrima Bickel, D., Nicholson, J., Xue, Y., & Atkins-Burnett, S. (2001). Trusting teachers' judgements: A validity study of curriculum-embedded performance assessment in kindergarten to grade 3. *American Educational Research Journal, 38,* 73–95.

Miramontes, O. (1990). A comparative study of English oral reading skills in differently schooled groups of Hispanic students. *Journal of Reading Behavior, 22,* 373–394.

Moll, L.C., Saez, R., & Dworin, J. (2001). Exploring biliteracy: Two student case examples of writing as a social practice. *The Elementary School Journal, 101*(4), 435–449.

Moll, L.C., & González, N. (1994). Critical issues: Lessons from research with language-minority children. *Journal of Reading Behavior: A Journal of Literacy, 26,* 439–56.

Muñiz-Swicegood, M. (1994). The effects of metacognitive reading strategy training on the reading performance and fluent reading analysis strategies of third grade bilingual students. *Bilingual Research Journal, 18,* 83–97.

National Reading Panel (U.S.) (2000). *Teaching children to read: An evidence-based assessment of scientific research literature on reading and its implications for reading instruction. Reports of the subgroups.* Washington, DC: National Institute of Child and Human Development, National Institutes of Health.

Neuman, S., & Celano, D. (2001, Jan/Feb). Access to print in low-income and middle-income communities: An ecological study of four neighborhoods. *Reading Research Quarterly, 36,* 8–26.

Olson, D. (1994). *The world on paper.* Cambridge: Cambridge University Press.

Orange, C., & Horowitz, R. (1999). An academic standoff: Literacy task preferences of African American and Mexican-American male adolescents versus teacher expected preferences. *The Journal of Adolescent and Adult Literacy, 43*(1), 28–39.

Oxford, R.L. (1990). *Language learning strategies: What every teacher should know.* New York: Newbury House/Harper & Row.

Padrón, Y. (1992) The effect of strategy instruction on bilingual students' cognitive strategy use in reading. *Bilingual Research Journal, 16,* 35–52.

Padrón, Y., Knight, S. L., & Waxman, H. C. (1986). Analyzing bilingual and monolingual students' perceptions of their reading strategies. *The Reading Teacher, 39,* 430–33.

Patthey-Chavez, G.G., & Lindsay, C. (1996). Task, talk, and text: The influence of instructional conversation on transitional bilingual writers. *Written Communication, 13*(4), 515–563.

Pucci, S.L. (1994). Supporting Spanish language literacy: *Latino* children and free reading resources in schools. *Bilingual Research Journal, 18*(1–2), 67–82.

Ramirez, J.D., Yuen S.D., Ramey, D.R., & Pasta, D. (1991). *Longitudinal study of structured English immersion strategy, early-exit, and late-exit transitional bilingual education programs for language minority children. (Final Report, Vols. 1 &2).* Santa Mateo, CA: Aguirre International (ERIC ED 330 216).

Reese, L., Garnier, H., Gallimore, R., & Goldenberg, C. (2000). Longitudinal analysis of antecedents of emergent Spanish literacy and middle-school English reading achievement of Spanish-speaking students. *American Educational Research Journal, 37,* 633–662.

Rose, M. (1989). *Lives on the Boundary.* New York: Penguin Books.

Saunders, W.M., & Goldenberg, C. (1999). *The effects of instructional conversations and literature logs on the story comprehension and thematic understanding of English proficient and limited English proficient students.* Technical Report. Center for

Research on Education, Diversity & Excellence. University of California, Santa Cruz.

Snow, C., Burns, S.M., & Griffin, P. (Eds.). (1998). *Preventing reading difficulties in young children.* Washington, DC: National Research Council, National Academy Press.

Snow, M.A., Galván, J.L., & Campbell, R.N. (1983). The pilot class of the Culver City Spanish Immersion Program: A follow-up report, or whatever happened to the immersion class of '78? In K.M. Bailey, M.H. Long, & S. Peck (Eds.), *Second language acquisition studies* (pp. 115–125). Rowley, MA: Newbury House.

Stavans, I. (1995). *The Hispanic condition: Reflections in culture and identity in America.* New York: Harper Collins.

Thomas, W.P., & Collier, V. (1997). *School effectiveness for language minority students.* NCBE Resource Collection Series #9. Washington D. C.: National Clearinghouse for Bilingual Education, George Washington University.

Thornburg, D. (1993). Intergenerational literacy learning with bilingual families: A context for the analysis of social mediation of thought. *Journal of Reading Behavior, 25,* 321–352.

U.S. Department of Education. Office of Educational Research and Improvement. National Center for Education Statistics. The nation's report card: Fourth-grade reading 2000. NCES 2001-499, by P.L. Donahue, R.J. Finnegan, A.D. Lutkus, N.L. Allen and J.R. Campbell. Washington, D.C. 2001. (government required format)

Valdés, G. (1996). *Con respeto: Bridging the distances between culturally diverse families and schools: An ethnographic portrait.* New York: Teachers College Press.

Weber, R.M. (1991). Linguistic diversity and reading in American society. In R. Barr, M.L. Kamil, P. Mosenthal, & P.D. Pearson (Eds.), *The handbook of reading research* (Vol. II, pp. 97–119). New York: Longman.

CHAPTER 4

TEACHING FOREIGN (SECOND) LANGUAGES TO AT-RISK LEARNERS:

RESEARCH AND PRACTICE[1]

Richard L. Sparks, Elke Schneider, and Leonore Ganschow

ABSTRACT

The study of a foreign language (FL) is an expectation for many secondary and postsecondary level students. About 10–15% of them are likely to experience severe difficulties learning a FL in classrooms and/or passing FL courses. Researchers have found that most poor FL learners have underlying native language (NL) learning problems and lack a strong aptitude for learning FLs. Recent research has also indicated that instructional approaches to literacy found successful with at-risk NL learners also benefit at-risk FL learners. In this chapter the authors describe some of these NL and FL learning problems and present research that supports a language basis as the primary source of difficulty. They also describe instructional practices for at-risk FL learners and conclude with suggested directions for future research.

INTRODUCTION

The study of a foreign language (FL) in the United States is an expectation for all primary and/or secondary students in some states, and a majority of universities require a FL either as a prerequisite for entering college or prior to graduation (Brod & Huber, 1996). Students classified as having specific learning disabilities (LD) and others not classified as LD often experience considerable difficulty passing FL courses in traditional classroom settings. (For reviews, see Ganschow & Sparks, 2000; Ganschow, Sparks, & Javorsky, 1998.) Likewise, some individuals from multicultural backgrounds who are required to learn the language of the dominant culture (second language learners) face substantial difficulties (Peer & Reid, 2000). Students who struggle with a second language (SL) sometimes fail to receive the proper instruction early in their schooling and are often misclassified as mentally retarded (Cummins, 1984; Durkin, 2000; Fawcett & Lynch, 2000).

Researchers have demonstrated that these at-risk FL/SL learners often have underlying (sometimes subtle) NL learning problems. (For review of FL learning difficulties, see Sparks & Ganschow, 1991, 1993a; Sparks, 1995; for SL learning difficulties, see, e.g., Dufva & Voeten, 1999; Durkin, 2000; Fawcett & Lynch, 2000.) Recent findings also indicate that an instructional approach to literacy that has been successful with at-risk NL learners (e.g., students classified as LD) provides the foundations necessary for learning a FL among this population. (For review, see Sparks & Miller, 2000.) To date, this finding has not been reported in the SL literature. Likewise, there is increasing evidence that some students who struggle to learn a FL but are not classified as LD have achievement and FL aptitude profiles similar to the classified LD population (Sparks & Javorsky, 1999a; Sparks, Philips, Ganschow, & Javorksy, 1999a,b). For this reason, in this paper the authors have elected to use the term "at-risk" to refer to both students with classified LD and those who have difficulty but are not so classified.

To date, there is a limited body of literature on the FL difficulties of at-risk learners and appropriate instruction. The first and third authors themselves have done the bulk of this research, based on their work with at-risk students, including those classified as LD. There is a need for FL and SL educators to understand the nature of these language problems, and, in particular, why a FL/SL is inordinately difficult for some learners and how teachers might help them. In this chapter the first and third authors discuss research findings about the language difficulties of struggling FL/SL learners; the second author, a SL/FL educator, illustrates their instructional needs and teaching methods/programs; the three authors together then examine directions for further exploration.

RESEARCH ON FL LEARNING PROBLEMS

In the 1980s, FL educators placed heavy emphasis on motivation and anxiety (Gardner, 1985; Horwitz, Horwitz, & Cope, 1986), learning styles and personality (Ehrman, 1990), and learning strategies (Oxford, 1990) as main contributors to FL learning problems. This emphasis, however, was contrary to findings about the learning difficulties of NL learners. In NL research, cognitive variables (e.g., weak phonological processing, inadequate grammatical rule systems) were emphasized as causal factors in poor reading, spelling, and writing. (See Stanovich, 1998, for a review of this research.) Likewise, NL researchers had found that mismatch of teacher-student learning styles was not related to difficulties in learning to read and write, nor had instruction matched with students' learning styles been found to improve reading and language skills (e.g., see Liberman, 1985; Stahl, 1999; Stahl & Kuhn, 1995).

Some FL educators criticized affective explanations for learning problems. For example, Skehan (1991) reported that researchers had not explained how to measure or teach learning strategies or how failure to use a particular learning strategy (e.g., memory) might impact FL learning and yet not affect learning one's NL (Sparks, 1995). In Skehan's words, good language learners "are the ones for whom the use of effective strategies are possible, while for poor learners they are not" (1991, p. 288).

According to NL researchers, problems learning to read, spell, and write one's NL are *language-based* (e.g., see Bradley & Bryant, 1985; Brady & Shankweiler, 1991; Vellutino, 1991). Moreover, Sparks and Ganschow's early research with university students who had FL learning problems suggested that the students also exhibited difficulties in their NL (Ganschow & Sparks, 1986; Sparks, & Ganschow, 1993b; Sparks, Ganschow, & Pohlman, 1989).

FL researchers did not include measures of NL skills or FL proficiency in their studies on affect, learning styles and personality, and learning strategies. In Sparks and Ganschow's view, the failure to control for participants' levels of NL skill and/or FL proficiency in these studies was a methodological weakness: One cannot draw inferences about causal connections between high levels of anxiety about FL learning and poor FL learning without knowing a student's level of language skill (Sparks & Ganschow, 1991, 1993b, 1995a). In a similar criticism of studies involving motivation and FL learning, Au (1988) indicated that these studies have an "obvious confounding variable—subjects' level of L2 achievement . . . The possibility of highly integratively motivated subjects engaging in more active choice behaviors merely or mainly as a result of having better L2 proficiency cannot be ruled out" (p. 86).

Given their interest in possible linkages between NL and FL learning, Sparks and Ganschow undertook a series of research studies to investigate the types of language learning difficulties experienced by at-risk FL learners and the kinds of instruction that would prove beneficial. They selected the following four research questions to highlight in this chapter because of their relevance to FL and SL educators:

1. What language difficulties do poor FL learners exhibit?
2. What are the primary NL and FL aptitude differences between good and poor FL learners?
3. Are there FL proficiency differences among students with differing levels of NL skill and FL aptitude? and
4. What kinds of instruction are most beneficial for at-risk students who have difficulties learning a FL?

The studies that answer these questions are described here. The research questions, their answers, and the studies are also summarized in Table 1.

Table 1.   Summary of research questions, answers, and research studies by Sparks, Ganschow, and colleagues.

Question	*Answer*	*Research Studies*
What language difficulties do poor FL learners exhibit?	Native language learning difficulties, generally	Ganschow & Sparks (1986, 1991); Sparks, Ganschow, & Pohlman (1989); Sparks & Ganschow (1993b). For explanation of LCDH, see Sparks (1995); Sparks & Ganschow (1991, 1993a, 1995a).
What are the primary NL and FL aptitude differences between good and poor FL learners?	Phonological/orthographic skills (word recognition, spelling, pseudoword reading), FL aptitude (on the MLAT), and sometimes grammar.	Ganschow & Sparks (1995); Ganschow, Sparks, Anderson et al. (1994); Ganschow, Sparks, Javorsky, Pohlman et al. (1991); Sparks & Ganschow (1995a); Sparks & Ganschow (1996); Sparks, Ganschow, Fluharty, & Little (1996).
Are there FL proficiency differences among students with differing levels of NL skill and FL aptitude?	Yes, students with stronger NL skills, especially in the phonological/orthographic domain, and FL aptitude (on the MLAT) achieve higher levels of FL proficiency (and FL course grades) than students with weaker NL skills and FL aptitude.	Sparks, Artzer, Patton, Ganschow, Miller, Hordubay, & Walsh (1998); Sparks, Ganschow, Artzer, & Patton (1997); Sparks, Ganschow, Artzer, Siebenhar, Plageman, & Patton (1998).

Table 1.   Summary of research questions, answers, and research studies by Sparks, Ganschow, and colleagues.

Question	Answer	Research Studies
What kinds of instruction are most beneficial for at-risk students with FL learning problems?	Direct multisensory structured language (MSL) instruction in the phonology/ orthography, grammar, and morphology of the FL is beneficial to at-risk FL learners.	Ganschow & Sparks (1995); Sparks, Artzer, Patton, Ganschow, Miller, Hordubay, & Walsh (1998); Sparks & Ganschow (1993c); Sparks, Ganschow, Artzer, & Patton (1997); Sparks, Ganschow, Pohlman, Patton, & Skinner (1992). For a description of MSL approach, see Schneider (1999); Sparks, Ganschow, Kenneweg, & Miller (1991); Sparks & Miller (2000).

1. What Language Difficulties Do Poor FL Learners Exhibit?

In the 1960s, FL educator Paul Pimsleur and his colleagues worked with students labeled FL "underachievers," or students who performed less well in FL courses than in their other courses (Pimsleur, Sundland, & McIntyre, 1964). They hypothesized that "auditory ability" (which they defined as sound and sound/symbol learning) posed difficulties for these students. Harvard counselor Kenneth Dinklage (1971) also reported cases of students who could not fulfill the university's FL requirement and speculated that their problems were similar to dyslexia (difficulties with reading and spelling, discrimination of sounds and syllables, verbal memory).

Ganschow and Sparks (1986) conducted the first reported study with students classified as LD who were studying a FL. They presented the diagnostic histories of four college students with FL learning problems, all of whom were found to have histories of overt or subtle NL learning difficulties. In another study, Gajar (1987) compared university students with and without classified LD on the *Modern Language Aptitude Test* (*MLAT*) (Carroll & Sapon, 1959), a FL aptitude test. This test has five subtests that have been found through factor analysis to be predictive of FL learning: phonetic coding, grammatical sensitivity, inductive language learning ability, and rote memory. The students who were classified as LD did poorly on all five *MLAT* subtests. Their poorest performance was on measures of sensitivity to grammatical structure and memory for language.

In the 1980s, Ganschow and Sparks (1991) developed a FL screening instrument designed to predict a "risk factor" for FL learning. The items on this instrument were based on their knowledge of characteristics of students classified as LD. In a study using this instrument, they found that the students who achieved low FL grades had histories of and/or current difficulties with aspects of NL learning. In another study, Sparks, Ganschow, and Pohlman (1989) reported the results on a battery of NL (reading, spelling, grammar, vocabulary) and FL aptitude (*MLAT*) assessments of a group of 22 students classified as LD who had failed FL courses in high school and college. They again found that the students exhibited overt or subtle problems in one or more aspects of their NL skills as well as low FL aptitude on the *MLAT.*

These studies led them to develop their Linguistic Coding Differences Hypothesis (LCDH) (Sparks, 1995; Sparks & Ganschow, 1991, 1993a; Sparks, Ganschow, & Pohlman, 1989). The major premise underlying the LCDH is that students who have difficulty learning a FL are likely to have (or have had) overt or subtle NL learning problems. This hypothesis is based on NL research by Vellutino and Scanlon (1986), who showed that poor readers and writers have substantial difficulty with the phonological/ orthographic (i.e., sound and sound/symbol) and syntactic (grammar) rule systems of written language, but not the semantic (meaning) system. In the LCDH, the authors proposed that components of the NL—phonological/orthographic, syntactic, semantic—provide the foundation for learning a FL. They also proposed that both NL and FL learning depend on basic language learning mechanisms and that problems with one language component are likely to have a negative effect on both language systems. Furthermore, they speculated that the phonology/orthography of the FL would likely pose the greatest difficulty, a finding reported in the NL reading literature (Brady & Shankweiler, 1991; Gough, Ehri, & Treiman, 1992).

Some FL educators have had similar ideas about the connections between NL and FL learning. For example, Carroll (1973) speculated that FL aptitude is a "residue" of native (first) language ability. Wells (1985) reported that there were wide individual differences in the speed at which individuals acquire their first language. Skehan (1986) found that students' NL ability correlated with their skill in learning a FL. Cummins (1984) suggested a "linguistic interdependence" between languages. Spolsky (1989) included intact NL skills in phonology/orthography and grammar as "necessary" skills for learning a FL.

The aforementioned studies supported Sparks and Ganschow's hypothesis that poor FL learners exhibit weaknesses in some NL skills and in aptitude for learning a FL (as measured by the *MLAT*).

2. What Are the Primary NL and FL Aptitude Differences Between Good and Poor FL Learners?

To answer this question, Sparks and Ganschow conducted a number of studies. Among them were comparisons between good and poor FL learners at the college and high school levels. In a study of college learners, these authors and their colleagues examined profiles of students who were successful (grades of A and B) and unsuccessful (failed and were waived from the college FL requirement) (Ganschow, Sparks, Javorsky, Pohlman, & Bishop-Marbury, 1991). They compared the two groups on measures of IQ, FL aptitude (using the *MLAT*), and native oral and written language. They found no significant differences between the groups on measures of IQ and reading comprehension but noted significant group differences on the *MLAT* and on measures of oral and written phonology/orthography and written syntax. In another study with college FL learners, the authors found that students with relatively low scores on NL phonological/orthographic measures (i.e., word recognition, pseudoword reading, spelling) achieved lower grades in FL courses than students with stronger scores on the phonological/orthographic measures (Ganschow, Sparks, Anderson, Javorsky, Skinner, & Patton, 1994).

In several studies conducted with high school students, findings showed that good and poor FL learners with comparable cognitive ability (IQ) exhibited significant differences on measures of NL skill. In one study with high school students, the researchers compared low risk (A or B in first quarter of FL study) and high risk (D or F in first quarter) FL learners on measures of IQ, FL aptitude (using the *MLAT*), and NL skill (Sparks, Ganschow, Javorsky, Pohlman, & Patton, 1992). Findings showed significant differences on measures of FL aptitude and NL phonology/orthography and syntax but not semantics (i.e., reading comprehension). In another study, a comparison between not-at-risk and at-risk students studying Latin, they obtained similar results (Sparks, Ganschow, Fluharty, & Little, 1996).

Sparks and Ganschow also studied the relationship between FL teachers' and parents' perceptions of students' NL and FL skills and compared these perceptions with students' scores on standardized measures of NL skill and FL aptitude. In two complementary studies with high school students, the authors compared FL learners who were divided into high, average, and low groups according to their scores on NL skill measures (i.e., word recognition, pseudoword reading, spelling, vocabulary, grammar) and the *MLAT* with FL teachers' perceptions (Sparks & Ganschow, 1996) and parents' perceptions (Sparks & Ganschow, 1995b) of the students' language learning skills. Findings of both studies showed that students who scored lower on NL measures of phonology/orthography and the FL aptitude measure (*MLAT*) were perceived by FL teachers and parents as having weaker FL academic skills (i.e., reading, writing, speaking, listening). These students also achieved lower grades in FL courses than students who scored higher on the testing measures.

Other researchers have also found language differences between good and poor FL learners. For example, Humes-Bartlo (1989) reported that fast language learners in fifth grade bilingual classes had more highly developed NL skills than the slow language learners. Olshtain, Shohamy, Kemp, and Chatow (1990) found that proficiency in the NL played the most important role in FL learning among a group of 11–12 year old Hebrew-speaking students learning English. Among Dutch students learning English, Hulstijn and Bossers (1992) found that some individual differences in a SL/FL were explained by individual differences in students' NL. In a group of seven year old Finnish children learning English, Dufva and Voeten (1999) found that proficiency in NL skills was highly significant for learning a FL.

Recent research supports the particular impact of phonological and phonological/ orthographic skills on FL learning. In a study with Finnish children, Service (1992) reported that phonological/orthographic tests (pseudoword repetition and writing) combined with the ability to predict syntactic-semantic structures predicted English learning. Service and Kohonen (1995) found that phonological memory was important for learning FL vocabulary (see also Cheung, 1996; Papagno, Valentine, & Baddeley, 1991).

Related issues in FL/second language research involve first and SL reading. Two questions of interest are whether the processes in reading development differ in the NL and FL and whether a student has difficulty learning to read a FL because his/her oral proficiency in the FL is inadequate. In a summary of recent research on this issue, Geva (2000) reported that English as a second language (ESL) students who experience difficulties comprehending text have weak oral language skills in the SL and poor word recognition, a skill that relies on phonological/orthographic ability. She and her colleagues found that the ability to reflect on and conceptualize the sounds of one's NL appears to be related to the ability to read words and understand oral language in the FL (e.g., Geva & Siegel, 2000; Wade-Woolley & Geva, 2000). Other researchers have supported the notion that phonological processing skills in one language are important predictors of word recognition skills in another language (e.g., Cisco & Royer, 1995; Durgunoglu, Nagy, & Hancin-Bhatt, 1993).

The aforementioned studies support the hypothesis that poor FL learners have particular difficulties with tasks involving phonological/orthographic processing. Likewise, SL researchers have found that individual differences in language skills, especially phonological/orthographic (sound/symbol) processing and verbal memory, predict the development of reading in NL and FL children in various alphabetic and non-alphabetic languages (Geva & Wang, 2001).

3. Are There FL Proficiency Differences among Students with Differing Levels of NL Skill and FL Aptitude?

Sparks and Ganschow were interested in measures of FL learning that extended beyond FL grades and further evaluated students' FL proficiency. This FL proficiency testing used guidelines developed by the American Council on the Teaching of Foreign Languages (ACTFL, 1989) to measure students' skill in reading, writing, speaking, and listening to the FL. In a small pilot study, the oral and written FL proficiency of not-at-risk and at-risk FL learners after two years of FL study was examined (Sparks, Ganschow, Artzer, & Patton, 1997). The at-risk learners were enrolled in a special section of a Spanish course because they had either exhibited a history of language learning problems, failed a previous FL course, or had been classified as LD. The two groups exhibited significant differences on NL and FL aptitude measures, but no differences on the FL proficiency measures. Upon closer investigation, however, findings showed that 100% of the not-at-risk students but only 71% of the at-risk students met or exceeded the expected range of performance (Novice High/Intermediate Low, according to ACTFL Guidelines) in FL Writing after two years of FL study; also, 75% of the not-at-risk students but only 43% of the at-risk students met or exceeded the expected range of performance in FL speaking/listening (based on oral proficiency interviews using ACTFL guidelines). The findings suggested that not-at-risk students might achieve a higher level of FL proficiency than at-risk FL learners, at least on writing and listening/speaking measures of FL proficiency.

To replicate and extend the aforementioned study, Sparks and his colleagues compared the performance of not-at-risk FL learners and three different groups of at-risk FL learners studying Spanish in high school (Sparks, Artzer, Patton, Ganschow, Miller, Hordubay, & Walsh, 1998). The three at-risk groups were receiving different types of FL instruction in different settings. They found significant overall differences between the at-risk and not-at-risk groups on measures of NL skill (i.e., spelling, pseudoword reading, word identification) and FL aptitude. Subsequent testing of the students' FL proficiency revealed significant differences between the not-at-risk group and two (of the three) at-risk groups.

In another study, they divided a group of high school students who had completed the second year of a FL course according to their FL proficiency level (high, average, and low proficiency) and examined the extent to which there would be group differences in NL skills, FL aptitude, and FL grades (Sparks, Ganschow, Artzer, Siebenhar, Plageman, & Patton, 1998). Evaluators trained according to ACTFL Guidelines designed and administered the oral and written FL proficiency measures in Spanish, French, and German. Results showed significant differences among the three proficiency groups on the NL and FL aptitude measures; most group differences were between high and low-risk learners. There were also group differences in final FL grades at the end of both first-year and second-year FL courses.

These findings support Sparks and Ganschow's hypothesis that NL skills impact upon one's oral and written FL proficiency. These studies and others (e.g., Dufva & Voeten, 1999) raise questions about how to improve the FL proficiency of at-risk FL learners.

4. What Kinds of Instruction Are Most Beneficial for At-Risk Students with FL Learning Problems?

In deciding on an instructional model that would likely show the most promise for working with at-risk FL learners, the authors drew on the research in NL learning, especially the literature on learning to read and spell. In NL studies, researchers have clearly shown that learning to read and spell depends to a great extent on the strength of one's skills in phonological/orthographic processing (e.g., Paulesu et al., 2001; Stanovich, 1998). This finding has been supported across a variety of languages including Danish, French, German, Greek, Hebrew, Italian, Portuguese, Spanish, Turkish, and Swedish (see review by Geva, 2000). Even in a nonalphabetic language (e.g., Chinese), research indicates that phonological processing skills play a role in learning to read (Hu & Catts, 1998; Leong, 2000; Suk-Han-Ho & Bryant, 1997). Given these findings, Sparks and Ganschow elected to focus on a model of instruction for at-risk learners that would emphasize direct instruction in the phonology/orthography of a FL. Unlike communicative approaches to FL learning that emphasize implicit acquisition of the sound/symbol and grammatical systems of a FL, a Mustisensory Structured Language (MSL) approach focuses on teaching the FL in a direct fashion and emphasizes skill development (Pritikin, 1999; Schneider, 1999).

A direct instruction model emphasizes the explicit teaching of the structure of a language. Teachers focus on the phonological/orthographic (sound and sound-symbol), syntactic (grammar), and morphological (prefixes, roots, suffixes) systems of that language. In English, MSL approaches have been used successfully to teach students with language learning difficulties and dyslexia to read, spell, and write their NL (e.g., Gillingham & Stillman, 1965/1997). In an MSL approach, students are explicitly taught not only the vocabulary (semantics) of the new language but also its grammar and phonology/orthography. The FL is taught in a "multisensory" format in which students can "hear," "see," and "do" (write) the language simultaneously (see Schneider, 1999; Sparks, Ganschow, Kenneweg, & Miller, 1991; Sparks & Miller, 2000 for a description of MSL approaches).

Sparks, Ganschow and colleagues conducted several studies on an MSL teaching approach for at-risk FL learners. In one study, they examined pre- and posttest scores on NL and FL aptitude measures of three groups of at-risk high school students enrolled in special, self-contained sections of first-year Spanish (Sparks, Ganschow, Pohlman, Artzer, & Skinner, 1992). Two groups received the MSL approach over one year. One of the MSL groups received instruction in both English and Spanish; the other MSL group was taught only in Spanish; and the third group received traditional, textbook-based FL instruction. The MSL group receiving Spanish and English instruction made significant gains on measures of NL phonology/orthography, vocabulary, verbal memory, and FL aptitude (*MLAT*); the MSL group taught only in Spanish showed significant gains on the FL aptitude test; and the traditional instruction group made no significant gains on any of the testing measures.

Sparks and Ganschow (1993c) replicated the aforementioned study with another group of at-risk students in a special, self-contained Spanish classroom who received MSL instruction in both English and Spanish. At the end of a year of instruction, the group had made significant gains on three NL phonological/orthographic measures (phonemic awareness, pseudoword recognition, spelling) and the FL aptitude test (*MLAT*). The authors also followed a group of students from their aforementioned MSL study (Sparks, Ganschow, Pohlman et al., 1992) through a second year of Spanish instruction; in that study, seven students had continued in the self-contained MSL instructional class and three students had transferred to regular Spanish classes. Follow-up testing showed that all MSL students maintained their initial gains on all NL and FL aptitude measures.

The authors then examined the question of whether there would be differences between at-risk FL learners who received MSL instruction and not-at-risk FL learners who received traditional instruction. Sparks and colleagues conducted several studies comparing the two groups on measures of NL skills and FL aptitude. In one study, Ganschow and Sparks (1995) compared the pre- and posttest scores of the female students in the MSL Spanish classes from the two aforementioned studies to not-at-risk female students enrolled in regular Spanish classes. After one year, both groups had improved significantly on the FL aptitude test. The at-risk students who received MSL instruction also showed significant improvement on NL measures of phonology/orthography (spelling, pseudoword recognition, phonemic awareness). Posttest comparisons showed that the not-at-risk students still scored significantly higher than the at-risk students on the FL aptitude test; however, there were no differences on two measures of phonology/orthography (pseudoword recognition, phonemic awareness).

The at-risk group also made significantly greater gains than the not-at-risk group on some of the phonological/ orthographic measures.

To examine the effects of MSL instruction on students' FL proficiency, a follow-up pilot study with eight of the at-risk students from their 1995 study was conducted. They found that the students in the at-risk group who received MSL instruction achieved a Novice-Mid to Novice-High level of oral and written proficiency in the FL on measures designed to evaluate FL proficiency using ACTFL Guidelines after two years of FL study (Sparks, Ganschow, Artzer, & Patton, 1997).

Given these preliminary findings, Sparks and his colleagues conducted a more comprehensive study to compare different methods of instruction (Sparks, Artzer, Patton et al., 1998). They examined the benefits of MSL instruction in Spanish by comparing three different groups of at-risk FL learners and a group of not-at-risk FL students over two years. The at-risk students were either receiving: (a) MSL instruction in a self-contained class; (b) traditional Spanish instruction in a self-contained class; or (c) traditional Spanish instruction in regular classes with supportive tutoring from the school's resource room program. Results showed that all three at-risk groups made significant pre-posttest gains on some NL measures regardless of teaching method. However, the MSL group and the not-at-risk group made greater gains than the other two not-at-risk groups on the FL aptitude test and NL measures of reading comprehension, word recognition, and pseudoword reading. Importantly, on measures of oral and written FL proficiency, the MSL and not-at-risk groups scored significantly higher than the other two at-risk groups, and no differences in FL proficiency were found between the MSL and not-at-risk groups.

The findings of these preliminary studies suggest that direct instruction in the phonological and phonological/orthographic aspects of a FL shows promise as a teaching method for at-risk FL learners. The results also suggest that the more knowledge a student has about the sound and sound/symbol aspects of language, the more skilled she or he is likely to become in a FL (see also Dufva & Voeten, 1999).

INSTRUCTIONAL PRACTICES FOR AT-RISK LEARNERS

What implications do these findings have for FL classroom teachers? In this section the second author begins by introducing the concept of a continuum of FL learning difficulties, a useful concept for FL teachers to consider because learning problems in classes often range from mild to severe. She then describes how the principles of MSL instruction apply to FL instruction and includes strategies for teaching phonology/orthography, syntax, and semantics. Some of the examples in this chapter are in German, but the concepts may easily transfer to other FLs. To date, the authors and other educators have described MSL strategies for teaching *Spanish* (Kenneweg, 1988; Sparks, Ganschow, Kenneweg, & Miller, 1991; Sparks & Miller, 2000), *Latin* (Sparks, Ganschow, Fluharty, & Little, 1996), *French* (Crombie, 2000; Pritikin, 1999), and *German* (Schneider, 1999). In the ESL literature, there are reports of MSL instruction for Hebrew learners of English (Secemski, Deutsch, & Adoram, 2000).

What Is the Continuum of Learning Difficulties?

As FL educators well know, classes often contain students with diverse skills in language. Yet, many FL teachers are not prepared to handle the diverse needs of students in their classrooms. In examining classroom strategies for at-risk FL learners, it may be helpful to begin by suggesting that FL educators place their students on an imagined "continuum" of FL learning strengths and difficulties. It is important to note that placing students on a continuum does not mean that the students are necessarily classified as having a LD. Sparks and Ganschow have found that many students with FL learning problems are not classified as LD because they do not meet the diagnostic criteria for this disability (e.g., see Sparks, & Javorsky, 1999a; Sparks, Philips, & Ganschow, 1996; Sparks, Philips, Ganschow, & Javorsky, 1999a,b).[2] Rather, of primary concern is the extent to which the student has difficulty in one or more of the three linguistic processing skills—phonological/orthographic, syntactic, and semantic—and which skills pose the most difficulty. For example, Sparks, Ganschow, and colleagues found that FL college students with poor phonological/orthographic processing skills are likely to have great difficulty in a beginning level FL course, whereas students with weak syntactic and/or semantic processing skills (and relative strengths in the phonological/orthographic domain) may pass the beginning level course only to fail at the interim or advanced levels, most likely because of increasing syntactic and semantic demands and the course's accelerated learning pace (Sparks & Ganschow, 1993b; Sparks, Ganschow, & Pohlman, 1989).

Table 2 illustrates a sample continuum of FL learners, the types of difficulties they might have, and possible accommodations and instructional needs. Other examples of continua may be found in both the NL and FL literature. (For NL learners, see Ellis, 1985; Kamhi & Catts, 1989; Levine, 1987; for FL learners, see Ganschow & Sparks, 1993; Ganschow, Sparks & Schneider, 1995.) Suffice it to say here that for a given at-risk student, the FL instructor should determine which language skills pose the most difficulty and to what extent. Students who fall at the mild end of the continuum need minimal classroom accommodations; students who fall at the severe end of the continuum may need extensive accommodations as well as individual tutoring; and students who fall somewhere in between and vary in their language strengths may need a combination of tutoring and moderate classroom accommodations.

Table 2.   Continuum of FL Learning Difficulties and Some Accommodations[a,b]

Level of Difficulty	Instructional Accommodations
Mild	• Student may need periodic out-of-class tutoring with peer tutor. • Student should consult as needed with classroom teacher about areas of difficulties and to discuss strategies to help learn a given concept. • Student would benefit from explicit instruction on difficult linguistic concepts (especially those that differ from the NL).
Moderate	• Student is likely to need regular (twice weekly) out-of-class tutoring. • Student is likely to need a FL tutor who is familiar with the needs of at-risk students. • Student, peer tutor, and teacher should communicate regularly to discuss concepts to cover in the tutoring session • Student is likely to find explicit instruction in the linguistic domains necessary in order to pass the FL. • Teacher and student should consider appropriate testing accommodations, such as extended time for tests, providing one-to-one testing on listening/speaking tasks.
Severe	• Student most likely will need a special FL class with modified instruction. MSL instruction is likely to be the most beneficial. • Student may need additional out-of-class tutoring, even in the modified environment. • Student most likely will need a FL teacher who is familiar with the instructional needs of at-risk students. • Student may profit from taking a FL by itself or with a reduced course load. • Student most likely will need some special testing accommodations.

[a]   See also Sparks & Ganschow (1993d); Ganschow, Sparks, & Schneider (1995).

[b]   Availability of instructional accommodations may be contingent on whether the student is classified as LD and has documentation that supports these accommodations. (See Sparks, 2001, and Sparks & Javorsky, 1999b, for a discussion of legal issues involved in FL testing and instructional accommodations.)

What is MSL Instruction?

MSL teaching principles were originally developed to assist students classified as having dyslexia. Dyslexia (from Greek: dys = impaired, lexia = word) is a language disorder that specifically affects an individual's ability to read and spell. Students diagnosed as dyslexic have severe problems with reading and spelling. MSL strategies have been used to remediate NL reading/spelling difficulties in the United States for more than 50 years (Gillingham & Stillman, 1965/1997). (For discussions about MSL instruction in other languages and in English as a second language, see, Peer & Reid, 2000; Schneider, 1999.) In brief, the basic principles of MSL instruction might be summarized using the following adjectives: explicit, multisensory, structured, cumulative, sequential, repetitive, metalinguistic (cognitive), synthetic-analytic, and phonetic-alphabetic (Gillingham & Stillman, 1965/1997). Each principle is described below.

An assumption of MSL instruction is that at-risk students do *not* discover and learn linguistic patterns on their own; instruction must be explicit. The role of the teacher is to teach the linguistic patterns directly. The instruction is multisensory because many at-risk students seem to benefit from seeing, saying, hearing, and writing the language and by actively engaging in language activities. Thus, students receive direct instruction in the sound-symbol relationships of the language (*phonetic-alphabetic*). They learn how words are composed of sounds and syllables, how sounds are blended together to form words, and how words may be taken apart in order to spell them (*synthetic-analytic*). MSL instruction involves the use of all learning channels simultaneously as often as possible (i.e., simultaneous reading, writing and saying/hearing of letters, syllables, or words in sentences) (*multisensory*). The teacher provides highly *structured* lessons that carefully progress in small linguistic units from easy to increasingly more complex (*sequential*); a new concept is taught only after a previous concept has been mastered (*cumulative*). MSL instruction offers consistent opportunities for over-learning so that the skills become automatic (*repetitive*). Finally, the teacher encourages the at-risk student to problem-solve through teacher guided, thought-provoking questions. In response to the instructor's questions, the student verbalizes his/her processing about language (*metalinguistic or cognitive*) (for NL, see Baker & Brown, 1984; Brown & Palincsar, 1982; for FL, see Schneider & Ganschow, 2000). The goal of metalinguistic instruction is to enable the student to think about language so that like a "good" language learner, she or he can determine how language is structured, compare the NL with the FL when necessary, and self-correct errors. Throughout the learning, the MSL instructor serves as facilitator, continuously assesses the students' level of knowledge, and revises the lesson as needed.

How Does MSL Instruction Apply to FL Instruction?

When applying MSL principles to alphabetic FLs, the instructor begins by focusing on the phonology/orthography of the language and uses the aforementioned MSL principles. As soon as a few sounds and symbols have been mastered within the context of simple words, phrases, and sentences (that may include non-phonetic, or "sight" words), the instructor begins to apply the MSL principles to the syntactic and semantic components as well. It should be noted here that the teaching of phonology/orthography, syntax, and semantics will differ depending on the language. French, for instance, may require more focus on pronunciation and spelling than Spanish because of its many silent letters and unfamiliar sounds for native speakers of English (Pritikin, 1999; Simon, 2000). German and Spanish, on the other hand, may require less focus on pronunciation and spelling because these languages are highly grapho-phonetic and have simpler sound-symbol patterns than English (Schneider, 1999). However, German and Spanish may require more attention in the area of grammar, in that they carry more inflectional endings on nouns, verbs, and adjectives than English. (For other comparisons across languages, see Miles, 2000.)

In the next section, the second author identifies selected MSL strategies that can be used to enhance phonological/orthographic, syntactic, and semantic skills and presents ideas for beginning and more advanced levels of instruction. Beginning level at-risk students are defined as those who are just starting the FL or who have not progressed through even the first semester of the language. More advanced level at-risk students are defined as individuals who have passed the first semester of an FL (sometimes with difficulty) but then struggle in subsequent semesters.

How Can We Teach Phonological/Orthographic Skills Using MSL Instruction?

Specific MSL strategies that enhance at-risk FL students' phonological/orthographic skills at the beginning level include making the sound-symbol relationships in the FL explicit by modeling what the mouth muscles do to produce certain sounds, especially those unique to the FL. The teacher provides direct associations between sound and print and asks the student to write and say letters and letter combinations. Here, it may be important to highlight similarities and differences in print and pronunciation between the FL and the NL.

Repeated, structured pronunciation practice can be offered in 3–5 minute visual or auditory reviews of sound/symbol patterns with flash cards. In a visual review, students say the sounds that a particular letter/letter combination can produce (example in German: student sees *a* and says /ä/ as in *Vater*). In an auditory review, students repeat the sound they hear and then write all the spellings that they have learned for this particular sound (example in German: student hears /ä/ and writes *a*, as in Vater— father). Students might collect the more difficult sound-symbol relationships on summary charts kept in a binder with reminders (e.g., a keyword that sounds the same in English: example: in *Vater*, the *a* sounds like the /ä/ in *father*).

Teachers also might assign at-risk students to tape-record short passages at increasing levels of difficulty. The teacher can then provide feedback on pronunciation and prosody after the students have practiced with a tutor and on their own. Some words (depending on the language) do not follow predictable sound/symbol patterns. To learn those non-phonetic words, students might practice simultaneously tracing/writing the letters of the word and saying the letter name rather than its sound.

A word of caution is noted here about the use of audiotapes in language laboratories. At-risk students often have difficulties processing the FL quickly and efficiently as it is spoken and may not find language lab listening/speaking tasks beneficial. It may be necessary to simplify listening tasks or supplement auditory assignments with other media, such as pictures or written texts. NL researchers such as Ehri (1987) have speculated that written language serves as a "visual-spatial model for speech"; thus, seeing the written FL as it is spoken may be more helpful to at-risk students than hearing only the tape.

Specific MSL strategies that enhance at-risk FL learners' phonological/ orthographic skills at a more advanced level might include explicit focus on the syllable patterns of the FL, such as open, closed, or vowel team syllables. It might include learning the syllable division rules in the FL; that is, knowing *where* to break a multisyllabic word for reading and spelling purposes into its individual syllables (examples in German: Mut/ter (mother) = VC/CV; Va/ter (father) = V/CV). Further, teachers might help students identify syllables according to prefix, root-suffix patterns, or their compound elements [example in German: *Unter* + *satz* = *Untersatz* (placemat), or "that which sits under"]. At-risk students might profit from discovering these patterns themselves through "word sorting" tasks. (For NL, see, Templeton, 1980; for FL, see Schneider, 1999.)

Because at-risk FL students can become intimidated by having to speak freely and spontaneously in the FL classroom, it is helpful to provide them with questions ahead of time and occasionally allow them to answer in their NL rather than not at all. Alternatively, at-risk students might use index cards with common FL expressions to assist them in responding in the FL (e.g., an introductory or final greeting phrase, an interruption, agreement, or disagreement phrase). Rather than expecting five-six responses, at-risk students might start with one-two responses and gradually increase their participation as they feel more secure. Instructors might also keep track of the number of times that students participate in conversations by handing out "speaking vouchers" with the student's name. After each conversational contribution, regardless of how small, the at-risk student hands in a voucher and the instructor counts them at the end of each week to provide bonus points.

How Can We Teach Syntactic Skills Using MSL Instruction?

At the syntactic level, there are a number of activities that the teacher can use to structure the language. She or he should establish a common base by explaining linguistic terminology, such as "subject," "predicate," "direct/ indirect object," "preposition," and "pronoun." The teacher can design learning situations in which at-risk students act out FL concepts, such as the difference between direct and indirect objects, passive and active voices or reflexive verbs, what are referred to as "total physical response" activities (Asher, 1969). The teacher can design color-coded packets and shape-coded cards with different parts of speech and grammatical word parts in constructing sentences in the FL (e.g., *round shape* for inflectional endings of verbs, adjectives, and nouns; *rectangular shape* for parts of speech; *different colors* for subjects, predicates, objects, and adverbs). These packets are distributed to groups of three to five students who are instructed to place word parts and words in the correct positions in sentences while verbalizing the thinking process out loud. Laminated cards written on with water-soluble markers make it easy for teachers to reuse the cards to illustrate different concepts. These "card tools" are versatile; they can be applied in one-on-one tutoring, small groups, and large classes. Once the grammatical concept is learned via color, the teacher can switch to white laminated cards as a transition to regular text. Other concepts to color code might include "gender" with noun cards and a separate inflectional ending card (e.g., masculine, feminine, neuter nouns and their endings in German, Spanish, French, or Italian). As languages use different syntactic rules, teachers can create their own color and shape coding system to illustrate specific syntactic rules that may be difficult for their students.

How Can We Teach Semantic Skills Using MSL Instruction?

Specific MSL strategies that enhance at-risk FL students' semantic processing skills in reading and writing at the beginning level first include establishing a base vocabulary. Physical response techniques such as mi-

ming the word or providing an associated picture can help the at-risk learner remember these words. Once the student has learned a base vocabulary of 100–150 words, the teacher could help the student expand his/her vocabulary by forming compound and prefix-root-suffix words. Again, the use of colored cards to categorize words offers students an opportunity to organize their thinking. The teacher tells students to pay explicit attention to the features of certain words, such as connectives or capitalizations (e.g., all nouns in German are capitalized). Once the basic word building concepts are secured, students switch to white cards. As mentioned earlier, teachers can help students build binders that contain lists of word families with specific prefix, root, or suffix patterns, and/or theme charts for a particular topic, such as clothes or foods. It is also beneficial to encourage at-risk students to make up "nonsense" words that follow the FL's word patterns. Nonsense words sometimes help at-risk students remember the concepts. Other activities can include having students collect vocabulary words that contain the same root and/or words that have the same prefix, root, or suffix to illustrate similarities and differences in meaning.

Idiomatic expressions that are unique to each FL can also be taught using MSL strategies. For example, after students are introduced to the concept of idiomatic expressions in English, the instructor can model the use of comparable expressions in the FL. Activities might include asking the students to construct illustrations of English and FL expressions (to enhance memory), or to mime an idiomatic expression and have fellow students guess the expression.

What Other Teaching Strategies Are Appropriate for At-risk FL Learners?

Obviously, MSL instruction is not the only methodology available for achieving success with at-risk FL learners. There are reports in both the FL and dyslexia literature of the instructional needs of at-risk FL learners. Two programs in particular show promise. One program, developed by Demuth and Smith (1987) in the mid 1980s, involved at-risk students at Boston University, who received a year of explicit instruction on the structure of their NL before taking a FL. Demuth and Smith found that after one year, students' pre- to posttest performance on the *MLAT* showed "dramatic" increases. They suggested that the course had a significant positive effect on students' language learning aptitude. Another successful program that has been in operation for ten years at the University of Colorado involves screening and then placing students classified as LD into self-contained, modified language courses in Latin, Spanish, and Italian. Preliminary findings suggest that most students are able to complete the university's FL requirement successfully after several semesters of carefully modified instruction (Downey, Snyder, & Hill, 2000; Hill, Downey, Shepperd, & Williamson, 1995). Mention also should be made of a project at Landmark College, a college specifically for students classified as LD (Landmark College, 2000). The goals of this federally funded project are to examine several instructional formats and to identify teaching practices that are likely to be the most beneficial for at-risk students.

Also in the literature are articles that describe "inclusive" services for at-risk learners within regular FL classes. Readers interested in finding out more about them should refer to Arries (1999), Moore (1995), and Pritikin (1999).

Likewise, there are several models that describe strategies to use in one-to-one or small group tutorial settings with at-risk FL learners. Here, readers are referred to Schneider (1999) and Simon (2000).

Last, students' insights into their own FL instructional needs provide a source of information about instruction. Here, the authors refer readers to Ganschow, Philips, and Schneider (2001), who conducted a survey of 71 college students who had been granted course substitutions for the FL requirement. The students themselves described their difficulties and how some of them might have been successful with accommodations in the FL course. (For other sources on students' insights, see Cabal-Krastel, 1999.)

DIRECTIONS FOR FUTURE RESEARCH

Research evidence suggests strongly that the FL learning problems exhibited by at-risk learners are the result of overt or subtle language learning difficulties and that at-risk learners have particular difficulty with the phonological/orthographic aspects of language. Furthermore, recent research has shown that the development of word decoding and reading comprehension are similar in NL and FL/SL and that word recognition (i.e., word decoding) in an FL plays a significant role in FL reading comprehension. Moreover, preliminary research evidence suggests that a methodology that explicitly teaches the sound/symbol system, grammar, and morphology of the FL enhances the FL learning of at-risk learners. Given these findings, the authors of this paper suggest that the FL learning problems of at-risk learners may be alleviated by focusing on cognitive factors, specifically language variables. In their view, most at-risk learners will need to attend consciously to the structure of language if they are going to become proficient in a FL.

What directions might FL educators take in future studies on the problems of at-risk learners? The authors suggest the following research directions:

- *More research on the efficacy of MSL instruction.*   The only empirical studies using this method have been conducted by Sparks, Ganschow, and their colleagues. (Other studies have been descriptive in nature.) Most of the research has involved at-risk learners studying Spanish. Studies comparing the MSL approach with other methodologies should be conducted by other researchers in a variety of languages.
- *More research on innovative instructional settings.*   There are few research studies involving at-risk learners in different instructional settings. Sometimes innovative programs are described, but the efficacy of the model is not evaluated empirically. Studies comparing at-risk FL learners in innovative instructional settings and in settings with traditional teaching models should be conducted.
- *Research on direct instruction of language other than MSL.*   In past years a number of FL educators taught the structure of language to their students; that is, students were taught directly and explicitly the phonology/orthography (sound/symbol) and grammar system of the FL (Spada, 1997; Stern, 1983). However, in recent years FL educators have moved to teaching methods that emphasize communicative approaches. Comparisons of the results of these methods of instruction should be conducted.
- *Research on application of MSL instruction to ESL.*   Researchers report that decoding skill in one language (e.g., Spanish) is related to decoding skill in another language (e.g., English) and that FL/SL learning is founded on NL phonological/orthographic ability. Because MSL instruction emphasizes direct instruction of the phonological/orthographic system of a new language, this type of instruction may prove beneficial for ESL learners. This type of program for ESL students in Israel has been described (Secemski, Deutsch, & Adoram, 2000); however, to date there have been no empirical studies to determine the efficacy of MSL instruction for teaching ESL.
- *Research on early identification of at-risk FL learners.*   Recent research suggests that strong NL literacy skills have positive effects on FL learning (e.g., see Dufva & Voeten, 1999). There is a need for studies that investigate the efficacy of promoting future FL learning by identifying *early* NL learning deficits and providing specific teaching in NL literacy in the primary grades to determine their effect on subsequent FL learning.
- *Research on the role of other variables that may impede efficient FL learning.*   Little research has been conducted on variables such as short-term verbal memory and verbal naming speed in relation to at-risk FL learners. These variables are important contributors to the

development of NL literacy (Wolf, 2001). Researchers should examine the extent to which these variables also impact FL learning.

- *Research on preferred language of instruction.*   Recent research has shown that students learning to read more transparent orthographies (e.g., Spanish, Turkish, Italian) have less difficulty learning to decode words than students in less transparent, or deep, orthographies (e.g., English) (Spencer, 2000). Studies should be conducted to determine whether some languages might be more easily learned by at-risk learners than others. Also, the value of matching a particular student with a particular FL should be investigated.

CONCLUSION

At-risk students, especially those who experience multiple failures in traditional FL/SL classes, can benefit from the study of a FL/SL if they are provided with appropriate instruction. In this article the authors have explained what research findings suggest about why some students have particular difficulties with languages and methods of instruction that might help these students. However, there is a need for considerably more research on issues such as early identification of those with difficulties, variables that impede FL/SL learning, best instructional practices for at-risk learners, and differences across language of instruction that may help or hinder ease of learning another language.

NOTES

1.   The authors contributed equally in the preparation of this chapter.

2.   General criteria for classification as LD in the United States are established by federal law but the criteria for receiving LD services in school are established by individual states. Most states require the use of a discrepancy between intelligence (IQ), as measured by a standardized intelligence test, and academic achievement, as measured by standardized achievement tests, to determine whether a student meets the required IQ-achievement discrepancy criteria.

REFERENCES

American Council on the Teaching of Foreign Languages (ACTFL) (1989). *American Council on the Teaching of Foreign Languages Proficiency Guidelines.* Hastings-on-Hudson. NY. Author.

Arries, J. (1999). Learning disabilities and foreign languages: A curriculum approach to the design of inclusive courses. *Modern Language Journal, 83,* 98–110.

Asher, J. (1969). The total physical response to second language learning. *Modern Language Journal, 50,* 79–84.

Au, S. (1988). A critical appraisal of Gardner's social-psychological theory of second language (L2) acquisition. *Language Learning, 38,* 75–100.

Baker, L., & Brown, A. (1984). Metacognitive skills of reading. In D.P. Pearson (Ed.), *Handbook of research in reading* (pp. 353–394). New York: Longman.

Bradley, L., & Bryant, P. (1985). *Rhyme and reason in reading and spelling.* Ann Arbor: University of Michigan Press.

Brady, S., & Shankweiler, D. (Eds.). (1991). *Phonological processes in literacy.* Hillsdale, NJ: Erlbaum.

Brod, R., & Huber, G. (1996). The MLA survey of foreign language entrance and degree requirements, 1994–1995. *Association of Departments of Foreign Languages (ADFL) Bulletin, 28,* 35–43.

Brown A., & Palincsar A. (1982). Inducing strategic learning from texts by means of informed, self-control training. *Topics in Learning and Learning Disabilities, 2,* 1–17.

Cabal-Krastel, M. (1999, April). *Listening to the voices of our students: Interpreting qualitative survey data on two types of Spanish classes.* Paper presented at the Symposium on Hispanic Applied Linguistics and Language Teaching Methodology, Kentucky Foreign Language Conference, Lexington, KY.

Carroll, J. (1973). Implications of aptitude test research and psycholinguistic theory for foreign language teaching. *International Journal of Psycholinguistics, 2,* 5–14.

Carroll J., & Sapon, S. (1959). *Modern Language Aptitude Test (MLAT): Manual.* San Antonio, TX: Psychological Corp.

Cheung, H. (1996). Nonword span as a unique predictor of second-language vocabulary learning. *Developmental Psychology, 12,* 867–873.

Cisco, L., & Royer, J. (1995). The development of cross-language transfer of phonological awareness. *Contemporary Educational Psychology, 20,* 275–303.

Crombie, M. (2000). Dyslexia and the learning of a foreign language in school: Where are we going? *Dyslexia, 6,* 112–123.

Cummins, J. (1984). *Bilingualism and special education: Issues in assessment and pedagogy.* San Diego, CA: College-Hill Press.

Demuth, K., & Smith, N. (1987). The foreign language requirement: An alternative program. *Foreign Language Annals, 20,* 66–77.

Dinklage, K. (1971). Inability to learn a foreign language. In G. Blaine & C. McArthur (Eds.), *Emotional problems of the student* (pp. 185–206). New York: Appleton-Century-Crofts.

Downey, D., Snyder, L., & Hill, B. (2000). College students with dyslexia: Persistent linguistic deficits and foreign language learning. *Dyslexia, 6,* 101–111.

Dufva, M., & Voeten, M. (1999). Native language literacy and phonological memory as prerequisites for learning English as a foreign language. *Applied Psycholinguistics, 20,* 329–348.

Durgunoglu, A., Nagy, W., & Hancin-Bhatt, B. (1993). Cross language transfer of phonemic awareness. *Journal of Educational Psychology, 85,* 453–465.

Durkin, C. (2000). Dyslexia in bilingual children—Does recent research assist identification? *Dyslexia, 6,* 248–267.

Ehri, L. (1987). Effects of printed language acquisition on speech. In D. Olson, N. Torrence, & A. Hilyard (Eds.), *Literacy, language, and learning* (pp. 333–367). Cambridge, MA: Cambridge University Press.

Ehrman, M. (1990). The role of personality type in adult language learning: An ongoing investigation. In T. Parry & C. Stansfield (Eds.), *Language aptitude reconsidered* (pp. 126–178). Englewood Cliffs, NJ: Prentice-Hall.

Ellis, A. (1985). The cognitive neuropsychology of developmental and acquired dyslexia: A critical survey. *Cognitive Neuropsychology, 2,* 169–205.

Fawcett, A., & Lynch, L. (2000). Systematic identification and intervention for reading difficulty: Case studies of children with EAL. *Dyslexia, 6,* 57–71.

Gajar, A. (1987). Foreign language learning disabilities: The identification of predictive and diagnostic variables. *Journal of Learning Disabilities, 20,* 327–330.

Ganschow, L., Philips, L., & Schneider, E. (2001). Experiences with the university foreign language requirement: Voices of students with learning disabilities. *Learning Disabilities: A Multidisciplinary Journal, 10,* 111–128.

Ganschow, L., & Sparks, R. (1986). Learning disabilities and foreign language difficulties: Deficit in listening skills? *Journal of Reading, Writing, and Learning Disabilities International, 2,* 306–319.

Ganschow, L., & Sparks, R., (1991). A screening instrument for the identification of foreign language learning problems: Evidence for a relationship between native and second language learning problems. *Foreign Language Annals, 24,* 383–398.

Ganschow, L., & Sparks, R. (1993). Foreign language learning "disabilities": Issues, research and teaching implications. In S. Vogel & P. Adelman (Eds.), *Success for college students with learning disabilities* (pp. 283–320). New York: Springer.

Ganschow, L., & Sparks, R. (1995). Effects of direct instruction in Spanish phonology on the native language skills and foreign language aptitude of at-risk foreign language learners. *Journal of Learning Disabilities, 28,* 107–120.

Ganschow, L., & Sparks, R. (2000). Reflections on foreign language study for students with language learning problems: Research, issues, and challenges. *Dyslexia, 6,* 87–100.

Ganschow, L., Sparks, R., Anderson, R., Javorsky, J., Skinner, S., & Patton, J. (1994). Differences in anxiety and language performance among high- and low-anxious college foreign language learners. *Modern Language Journal, 78,* 41–55.

Ganschow, L., Sparks, R., & Javorsky, J. (1998). Foreign language learning problems: An historical perspective. *Journal of Learning Disabilities, 31,* 248–258.

Ganschow, L., Sparks, R., Javorsky, J., Pohlman, J., & Bishop-Marbury, A. (1991). Identifying native language difficulties among foreign language learners in college: A "foreign" language learning disability? *Journal of Learning Disabilities, 24,* 530–541.

Ganschow, L., Sparks, R., & Schneider, E. (1995). Learning a foreign language: Challenges for students with language learning difficulties. *Dyslexia, 1,* 75–95.

Gardner, R. (1985). *Social psychology and second language learning: The role of attitudes and motivation.* London: Arnold.

Geva, E. (2000). Issues in the assessment of reading disabilities in L2 children—Beliefs and research evidence. *Dyslexia, 6,* 13–28.

Geva, E., & Siegel, L. (2000). Orthographic and cognitive factors in the concurrent development of basic reading skills in two languages. *Reading and Writing: An Interdisciplinary Journal, 12,* 1–30.

Geva, E., & Wang, M. (2001). The development of basic reading skills in children: A cross-language perspective. *Annual Review of Applied Linguistics, 21,* 182–204.

Gillingham, A., & Stillman, B. (1965/1997). *The Gillingham manual: Remedial training for students with specific disability in reading spelling, and penmanship* (8th ed.). Cambridge, MA: Educators Publishing.

Gough, P., Ehri, L., & Treiman, R. (1992). *Reading acquisition.* Hillsdale, NJ: Erlbaum.

Hill, B., Downey, D., Sheppherd, M., & Williamson, V. (1995). Accommodating the needs of students with severe language learning difficulties in modified foreign language classes. In G. Crouse, P. Campana, & M. Rosenbusch (Eds.), *Broadening the frontiers of foreign language education* (pp. 46–56). Lincolnwood, IL: National Textbook.

Horwitz, E., Horwitz, M., & Cope, J. (1986). Foreign language classroom anxiety. *Modern Language Journal, 70,* 125–132.

Hu, C., & Catts, H. (1993). Phonological recoding as a universal process? Evidence from beginning readers of Chinese. *Reading and Writing: An Interdisciplinary Journal, 5,* 325–337.

Hulstijn, J., & Bossers, B. (1992). Individual differences in L2 proficiency as a function of L1 proficiency. *European Journal of Cognitive Psychology, 4,* 341–353.

Humes-Bartlo, M. (1989). Variation in children's ability to learn second languages. In K. Hyltenstam & L. Obler (Eds.), *Bilingualism across the life span* (pp. 41–54). Cambridge, MA: Cambridge University Press.

Kamhi, A., & Catts, H. (1989). *Reading disabilities: A developmental language perspective.* Boston: College Hill Publications.

Kenneweg, S. (1988). Meeting special needs in the Spanish curriculum of a college preparatory school. In B. Snyder (Ed.), *Get ready, get set, go! Action in the foreign language classroom* (pp. 16–18). Columbus, OH: Ohio Foreign Language Association.

Landmark College. (2000). *The Foreign Language Project at Landmark College.* [Brochure]. Putney, VT: Author.

Leong, C. (2000). Exploring reading-spelling connections as locus of dyslexia in Chinese. *Annals of Dyslexia, 50,* 239–259.

Levine, M. (1987). *Developmental variation and learning disorders.* Cambridge, MA: Educators Publishing Service.

Liberman, I. (1985). Should so-called modality preferences determine the nature of instruction for children with reading disabilities? In F. Duffy, & N. Geschwind (Eds.), *Dyslexia* (pp. 93–104). Boston: Little, Brown.

Miles, E. (2000). Dyslexia may show a different face in different languages. *Dyslexia, 6,* 193–201.

Moore, F. (1995). Section 504 and the Americans with Disabilities Act: Accommodating the learning disabled student in the foreign language curriculum. *Association of Departments of Foreign Languages (ADFL) Bulletin, 26,* 59–62.

Olshtain, E., Shohamy, E., Kemp, J., & Chatow, R. (1990). Factors predicting success in EFL among culturally different learners. *Language Learning, 40,* 23–44.

Oxford, R. (1990). Styles, strategies and aptitude: Connections for language learning. In T. Parry & C. Stansfield (Eds.), *Language aptitude reconsidered* (pp. 67–125). Englewood Cliffs, NJ: Prentice-Hill.

Papagno, C., Valentine, T., & Baddeley, A. (1992). Phonological short-term memory and foreign language vocabulary learning. *Journal of Memory and Language, 30*, 331–347.

Paulesu, E., Démonet, J.-F., Fazi, F., McCrory, E., Chanoine, V., Brunswick, N., Cappa, S. F., Cossu, G., Habib, M., Frith, C. D., & Frith, U. (2001). Dyslexia: Cultural diversity and biological unity. *Science, 291*, 2165–2167.

Peer, L., & Reid, G. (Eds.) (2000). *Multilingualism, literacy, and dyslexia: A challenge for educators.* London: David Fulton Publishers.

Pimsleur, P., Sundland, D., & McIntyre, R. (1964). Underachievement in foreign language learning. *International Review of Applied Linguistics, 2*, 113–150.

Pritikin, L. (1999). *A policy of inclusion: Alternative foreign language curriculum for high-risk and learning disabled students.* ERIC Clearinghouse on Language and Linguistics, Center for Applied Linguistics. (ERIC Document Reproduction Service No. ED 428 586)

Schneider, E. (1999). *Multisensory structured metacognitive instruction: An approach to teaching a foreign language to at-risk students.* (Volume 30: Theorie und Vermittlung der Sprache). Frankfurt a. M.: Europäischer Verlag der Wissenschaften: Peter Lang Verlag.

Schneider, E., & Ganschow, L. (2000). Dynamic assessment and instructional strategies for learners who struggle to learn a foreign language. *Dyslexia, 6*, 72–82.

Secemski, S., Deutsch, R., & Adoran, C. (2000). Structured multisensory teaching for second language learning in Israel. In L. Peer & G. Reid (Eds.), *Multilingualism, literacy, and dyslexia: A challenge for educators* (pp. 235–242). London: David Fulton.

Service, E. (1992). Phonology, working memory, and foreign language learning. *Quarterly Journal of Experimental Psychology, 45A*, 21–50.

Service, E., & Kohonen, V. (1995). Is the relation between phonological memory and foreign language learning accounted for by vocabulary acquisition? *Applied Psycholinguistics, 16*, 155–172.

Simon, C. (2000). Dyslexia and learning a foreign language. *Annals of Dyslexia, 50*, 155–188.

Skehan, P. (1986). The role of foreign language aptitude in a model of school learning. *Language Testing, 3*, 188–221.

Skehan, P. (1991). Individual differences in second language learning. *Studies in Second Language Acquisition, 13*, 275–298.

Spada, N. (1997). Form-focussed instruction and second language acquisition: A review of classroom and laboratory research. *Language Teaching, 30*, 73–87.

Sparks, R. (1995). Examining the linguistic coding differences hypothesis to explain individual differences in foreign language learning. *Annals of Dyslexia, 45*, 187–214.

Sparks, R. (2001). Foreign language learning problems of students classified as learning disabled and non-learning disabled: Is there a difference? *Topics in Language Disorders, 21*, 38–54.

Sparks, R., Artzer, M., Patton, J., Ganschow, L., Miller, K., Hordubay, D., & Walsh, G. (1998). Benefits of multisensory language instruction in Spanish for at-risk learners: A comparison study of high school Spanish students. *Annals of Dyslexia, 48,* 239–270.

Sparks, R., & Ganschow, L. (1991). Foreign language learning difficulties: Affective or native language aptitude differences? *Modern Language Journal, 75,* 3–16.

Sparks, R., & Ganschow, L. (1993a). Searching for the cognitive locus of foreign language learning problems: Linking first and second language learning. *Modern Language Journal, 77,* 289–302.

Sparks, R., & Ganschow, L. (1993b). The impact of native language learning problems on foreign language learning: Case study illustrations of the Linguistic Coding Deficit Hypothesis. *Modern Language Journal, 77,* 58–74.

Sparks, R., & Ganschow, L. (1993c). The effects of a multisensory structured language approach on the native language and foreign language aptitude skills of at-risk learners: A follow-up and replication study. *Annals of Dyslexia, 43,* 194–216.

Sparks, R., & Ganschow, L. (1993d). Identifying and instructing at-risk foreign language learners in college. In D. Benseler (Ed.), *The dynamics of language program development* (pp. 173–199). Boston: Heinle & Heinle.

Sparks, R., & Ganschow, L. (1995a). A strong inference approach to causal factors in foreign language learning: A response to MacIntyre. *Modern Language Journal, 79,* 235–244.

Sparks, R., & Ganschow, L. (1995b). Parent perceptions in the screening for performance in foreign language courses. *Foreign Language Annals, 28,* 371–391.

Sparks, R., & Ganschow, L. (1996). Teachers' perceptions of students' foreign language academic skills and affective characteristics. *Journal of Educational Research, 89,* 172–185.

Sparks, R., Ganschow, L., Artzer M., & Patton, J. (1997). Foreign language proficiency of at-risk and not-at-risk learners over two years of foreign language instruction. *Journal of Learning Disabilities, 30,* 92–98.

Sparks, R., Ganschow, L., Artzer, M., Siebenhar, D., & Plageman, M. (1998). Differences in native language skills, foreign language aptitude, and foreign language grades among high, average, and low proficiency learners: Two studies. *Language Testing, 15,* 181–216.

Sparks, R., Ganschow, L., Fluharty, K., & Little, S. (1996). An exploratory study on the effects of Latin on the native language skills and foreign language aptitude of students with and without learning disabilities. *Classical Journal, 91,* 165–184.

Sparks, R., Ganschow, L., Javorsky, J., Pohlman, J., & Patton, J. (1992). Identifying native language deficits in high- and low-risk foreign language learners in high school. *Foreign Language Annals, 25,* 403–418.

Sparks, R., Ganschow, L., Kenneweg, S., & Miller, M. (1991). Using Orton-Gillingham methodologies to teach a foreign language to learning disabled/dyslexic students: Explicit teaching of phonology in a second language. *Annals of Dyslexia, 41,* 96–118.

Sparks, R., Ganschow, L., & Pohlman, J. (1989). Linguistic coding deficits in foreign language learners. *Annals of Dyslexia, 39,* 179–195.

Sparks, R., Ganschow, L., Pohlman, J., Artzer, M., & Skinner, S., (1992). The effects of a multisensory, structured language approach on the native and foreign language skills of high-risk foreign language learners. *Annals of Dyslexia, 42,* 25–53.

Sparks, R., & Javorsky, J. (1999a). Students classified as learning disabled and the college foreign language requirement: Replication and comparison studies. *Journal of Learning Disabilities, 32,* 329–349.

Sparks, R., & Javorsky, J. (1999b). Section 504 and the Americans with Disabilities Act: Accommodating the learning disabled student in the foreign language curriculum: An update. *Association of Departments of Foreign Languages (ADFL) Bulletin, 30,* 36–44.

Sparks, R., & Miller, K. (2000). Teaching a foreign language using multisensory structured language techniques to at-risk learners: A review. *Dyslexia, 6,* 124–132.

Sparks, R., Philips, L., & Ganschow, L. (1996). Students classified as learning disabled and the college foreign language requirement: A case study of one university. In J. Liskin-Gasparro (Ed.), *Patterns and policies: The changing demographics of foreign language education* (pp. 123–159). Boston: Heinle & Heinle.

Sparks, R., Philips, L., Ganschow, L., & Javorsky, J. (1999a). Comparison of students classified as learning disabled who petitioned for or fulfilled the college foreign language requirement. *Journal of Learning Disabilities, 32,* 553–565.

Sparks, R., Philips, L., Ganschow, L., & Javorsky, J. (1999b). Students classified as learning disabled and the college foreign language requirement: A quantitative analysis. *Journal of Learning Disabilities, 32,* 566–580.

Spencer, K. (2000). Is English a dyslexic language? *Dyslexia, 6,* 152–162.

Spolsky, B. (1989). *Conditions for second language learning.* Oxford: Oxford University Press.

Stahl, S. (1999, Fall). Different strokes for different folks? *American Educator, 27–31.*

Stahl, S., & Kuhn, M. (1995). Does whole language or instruction matched to learning styles help children learn to read? *School Psychology Review, 24,* 393–404.

Stanovich, K. (1998). Twenty-five years of research on the reading process: The grand synthesis and what it means for our field. In T. Shanahan & F. Rodriguez-Brown (Eds.), *Forty-seventh yearbook of the National Reading Conference* (pp. 44–58). Chicago: National Reading Conference.

Stern, H. (1983). *Fundamental concepts of language teaching.* Oxford: Oxford University Press.

Suk-Han-Ho, C., & Bryant, P. (1997). Phonological skills are important in learning to read Chinese. *Developmental Psychology, 33,* 946–951.

Templeton, S. (1980). What is a word? In E. Henderson & J. Beers (Eds.), *Developmental and cognitive aspects of learning to spell: A reflection of word knowledge* (pp.15–35). Newark, DE: International Reading Association.

Vellutino, F. (1991). Introduction to three studies on reading acquisition: Convergent findings on theoretical foundations of code-oriented versus whole language approaches to reading instruction. *Journal of Educational Psychology, 83,* 437–443.

Vellutino, P., & Scanlon, D. (1986). Linguistic coding deficits and metalinguistic awareness: Their relationship to verbal and code acquisition in poor and normal readers. In D. Yaden & S. Templeton (Eds.), *Metalinguistic awareness and beginning literacy,* (pp. 115–141). Portsmouth, NH: Heinemann.

Wade-Woolley, L., & Geva, E. (2000). Processing novel phonemic contrasts in the acquisition of L2 word reading. *Scientific Studies of Reading, 4,* 295–312.

Wells, G. (1985). *Language development in the preschool years.* Cambridge: Cambridge University Press.

Wolf, M. (Ed.). (2001). *Time, fluency, and dyslexia.* Baltimore, MD: York Press.

CHAPTER 5

SPANISH LANGUAGE TEACHERS' BELIEFS AND PRACTICES ABOUT READING IN A SECOND LANGUAGE

Terri Ann Gebel and Leslie L. Schrier

ABSTRACT

This study investigated secondary Spanish language teachers' stated beliefs about the construct of reading in a second language, their knowledge about students' roles in the reading process, their preparation to teach reading in a second language and their reported practices of teaching reading in a second language. Because research in teachers' beliefs has established that beliefs may be one of the most effective influences on teachers' practices, this study intended to determine if the stated beliefs were practiced in the secondary Spanish language teachers' classroom.

The results concluded that secondary Spanish language teachers do have strong beliefs about the construct of reading. They believe it to be fundamental to second language acquisition and that it should be taught in the early stages of second language learning.

A conclusion that could be made from the study is that the respondents' stated beliefs and their reported practices evidenced many inconsistencies related to their beliefs about reading and prereading strategies and time allotted for reading in class. The respondents' practices did not always support their stated beliefs.

INTRODUCTION

In the first years of the new century, criticism of the quality of public school education focuses on the individual teacher as a key to educational reform (McNeil, 2000). Within the second language (L2) education field, criticizing the skills and qualifications of the classroom teacher is not a new issue, but one that is rarely substantiated by research that investigates practicing teachers (Schulz, 2000). The foundation of the study that is a focus of this chapter assumes that in order to affect any practice in L2 teaching it is necessary to understand what teachers believe about language learning and how their beliefs transfer to everyday instructional practice. Kagan (1992) found that teachers' prior beliefs were important influences on their practices, both in a direct sense of acting on an innovation, and also in the indirect sense of how receptive the teachers were to the ideas or the findings of the research. Establishing the subjects' beliefs and their correlation to their classroom practices will enable L2 teacher educators to better understand the impact of their methodology courses. To understand the premises of the study presented here a discussion will follow of previous research analyzing teachers' beliefs and practices in the instruction of L1 and L2 reading. Thereafter, a description and discussion of a research study is presented which describes secondary Spanish teachers' beliefs and practices about reading in a L2.[1]

TEACHERS' BELIEFS AND PRACTICES

During the past two decades, teacher education research has made significant strides in studying the complex relationships between teacher beliefs and practices. Influenced by the advances in cognitive psychology, the popularity of ethnographic and qualitative methodology, and the conception of teaching as a thoughtful profession, teacher education researchers have demonstrated an unprecedented interest in and enthusiasm about certain aspects of teacher cognition and their relationship to pedagogical practices in the classroom. These studies signal that research on teaching and learning shifted from unidirectional emphasis on correlates of observable teacher behavior with student achievement to a focus on teachers' thinking, beliefs, planning and decision-making processes.

   The research presented here was strongly influenced by the significant contributions in understanding the relationship between teachers' beliefs and practices that the field of first language (L1) reading achieved. L1 reading research has examined how teacher's personal beliefs about teaching and learning affect their decision-making and behaviors. A substantial number of such studies support the notion that teachers do possess theoretical beliefs about reading and that such beliefs tend to shape the nature of their instructional practices (Blanton & Moorman, 1987; Brophy & Good, 1974; Harste & Burk, 1977; Kamil & Pearson, 1979; Leu & Misulis, 1986; Longberger, 1992; Mangano & Allen, 1986; Rupley & Logan, 1984). For example, Rupley and Logan (1984) reported that elementary teachers' beliefs about reading affected their instructional decision making. Working with teachers from Grades 4, 5, and 6, Richardson, Anders, Tidwell, and Lloyd (1991) found that teachers who believed that sub-skills of reading must be learned before meaning of text can be determined generally used a skills/word approach. On the other hand, those who believed that learning to read is accomplished by reading employed a literary structuralist approach. Those who adopted the whole-language philosophy used authentic literature as a vehicle through which students construct meaning. These findings support Harste and Burke's (1977) claim that "teachers are theoretical in their instructional approach to reading" (p. 32).

Other areas of literacy instruction have also supported the thesis that there is a consistency between teachers' beliefs and practices. For example, Mangano and Allen (1986) found that teachers approach language arts instruction differently depending on their beliefs about writing. Not only were instructional practices found to be consistent with teachers' theoretical beliefs, but also the interactions between teachers and students were found to differ according to teachers' theoretical beliefs about writing instruction. Wing (1989) found that preschool teachers' theoretical beliefs about literacy development not only influenced their instructional practices, but also shaped preschool children's perceptions of the nature and uses of reading and writing.

In L2 reading research there have been few studies investigating the relationship between teachers' beliefs and literacy practices. Johnson's (1992) study indicated that the majority of English as a Second Language (ESL) teachers possess clearly defined theoretical beliefs, which consistently reflect one particular methodological approach. Further, the study showed that ESL teachers who possess clearly defined theoretical beliefs provide literacy instruction that is consistent with their theoretical orientation and that teachers with different dominant theoretical orientations provide strikingly different literacy instruction for nonnative speakers of English.

Taken together, this body of research substantiates Kamil and Pearson's (1979) claim that every teacher operates with at least an implicit model of reading. It also supports the notion that teachers thinking about their roles and the beliefs and values they hold help shape their pedagogy. Specifically, it indicates that teachers teach in accordance with their theoretical beliefs. It further suggests that teacher's theoretical beliefs not only shape the nature of classroom interactions, but have a critical impact on students' perceptions of the literacy processes as well.

The previously mentioned L1 and L2 literacy studies all tend to confirm a constant relationship between teachers' beliefs and practices. However, Fang (1996) elaborated on the inconsistency thesis that reveals that a gap does exist between what research reveals and what may happen in the classroom. There are some research findings that indicate that although teachers may have firm theoretical beliefs that are well established, they might not adhere to these beliefs in actual practice. Inconsistency between teachers' beliefs and their practices is not unexpected. Earlier researchers have noted that the complexities of classroom life can constrain teachers' abilities to attend to their beliefs and provide instruction that aligns with their theoretical beliefs (Duffy, 1982; Duffy & Anderson, 1982; Duffy & Ball, 1986; Paris, Wasik & Turner, 1991; Roehler & Duffy, 1991). Their research suggests that contextual factors can have powerful influences on teachers' beliefs and, in effect, influence their classroom practice.

There is one example in L2 reading research of the inconsistency between foreign language teachers' beliefs and practices in a study reported by Graden (1996). Her study, which compared beliefs about reading and reading instruction of six foreign language teachers, revealed inconsistencies in three tenets on reading about which the teachers felt strongly.[2] The first belief stated by the teachers is that reading proficiency is developed by frequent opportunities for reading practice and that the materials used should represent a variety of authentic texts. However, when observing their instruction, it was noted that the teachers relied extensively on the adopted textbook series that provided little opportunity for reading practice, especially with authentic materials. Additionally, the custodial nature of the classroom level did not allow them to make use of any classroom time to practice reading and none was assigned as homework. The second belief identified as important by the teachers is communication in the target language is preferable for reading instruction, which implies that both the teacher and the students would discuss, converse and interact in the language of instruction. When observed, the teachers used English during the majority of the reading lesson and resorted to use of translation exercises to assess reading comprehension. The third belief that was unanimously agreed upon by the teachers is that oral reading interferes with reading comprehension. Read-aloud activities were used so frequently in the classroom, that the researcher found herself questioning each teacher about the goals and intentions of the reading activity observed. In summary, Graden discovered that the majority of the teachers did not follow through on their beliefs, and, in fact, their actual practice was sometimes in direct opposite of their stated beliefs.

Graden's study did not intend to criticize the practices, but only illustrate that discrepancies do exist. Her research is one example of an inconsistent relationship between the beliefs and practices of second language teachers. These inconsistencies were of no surprise, as earlier researchers have noted that the complexities of the classroom can constrain teachers' abilities to attend to their beliefs, and therefore their instruction is compromised in order to attend to the immediate situation (Duffy & Anderson, 1982; Duffy & Ball, 1986). Duffy (1982) suggested that it is difficult for teachers "to remember that they are supposed to be cognitive information processors who make differential instructional decisions on the basis or rationally developed hypotheses" (p. 361).

It is understood that the complexities of the day-to-day classroom environment influences instruction, however, in other disciplines such as in mathematics and science education, it has been documented that through teacher development opportunities positive changes can and do take place in classroom instruction (e.g., Yager & Penick, 1990; Zbiek, 1998). It seems, however, "foreign language teacher preparation is still long on rhetoric, opinions, and traditional dogma, and short on empirical research that attempts to test those opinions or traditional practices" (Schulz, 2000, p. 518).

One way to begin to document what is emphasized within teacher development is to examine what is valued or emphasized in L2 teacher preparation programs. In 1989, Schrier described what materials were commonly used in many preservice foreign language teacher preparation programs. In updating a portion of the research found in the 1989 study, she reexamined the content of the preservice methodology syllabi (Schrier, 2001). Examining the most current texts in Table 1, Omaggio Hadley's and Shrum's and Glisan's methodology texts, the content for the reading section of the texts varies. Shrum's and Glisan's text integrates the National Standards by referring to interpersonal and interpretive modes of reading. It also addresses reading strategies and what the readers themselves bring to help interpret the text such as topic familiarity, comprehension strategies, and the purpose of the reading task. Omaggio Hadley's approach is more theoretical in nature and refers to tasks that identify the Novice/Intermediate and the Advanced/Superior readers. She relates these reading tasks to student proficiency levels on the ACTFL scale. Both texts examine common reading issues such as top-down, bottom-up approaches and authentic reading materials. Using the texts that Schrier found to be most frequently used as resources in methodology courses, Table 1 illustrates the amount of emphasis given to reading and the teaching of reading in methodology texts used in classes for the preparation of foreign language teachers.

Table 1.   Percentage of Methodology Text Dedicated to Reading Instruction

Author	Percentage of Emphasis on Reading Instruction
Omaggio Hadley (2000)	6%
Rivers (1981)	7%
Allen and Valette (1979)	9%
Chastain (1988)	6%
Schrum and Glisan (2000)	5%

The above texts have been, and many still are, the most frequently used texts; however, Schrier's updated study also found that, as in the1989 study, there was not a majority who selected any one textbook. "Other" material was the most common selection with a listing of a variety of texts and articles being used in the methodology class. In order to compute the percentages given in Table 1, the number of pages dedicated to reading were counted and divided by the total number of pages in the content area of the text. This excluded such sections as the glossary, works cited, and table of contents.

THE STUDY

The instrument used in this study for investigating teachers' beliefs and practices in the teaching of reading in a foreign language is a survey. Fink and Kosecoff (1985) described a survey as constituting an excellent method of collecting information directly from people about their feelings, motivations, plans, beliefs and personal and educational background. The survey method was also determined to be the best way to answer the research questions: (a) what do secondary Spanish language teachers report they believe about the construct of reading, (b) how do secondary Spanish language teachers contend they practice these beliefs in their classrooms, (c) what do secondary Spanish language teachers report that they know about reading, (d) what preparation do secondary Spanish language teachers report to have enabled them to teach reading in a foreign language and, (e) is there a relationship between the secondary Spanish teachers' stated beliefs and their self-reported classroom practices.

The design of the study required a selection of high school Spanish language teachers through a random sample from a list of 8,621 Spanish teachers who were 1998 members of the American Association of Teachers of Spanish and Portuguese (AATSP). This particular population was selected after the results of a pilot study determined that 76% of the pilot study respondents were high school teachers of Spanish. Among high school foreign language teachers, Spanish teachers are the largest single group. The subjects were selected by a random sampling, using the subjects' surnames. The selection process was not apparent to the respondents. The researchers received a response rate from 500 surveys of 58.4% and this is considered adequate by survey design specialists for analysis to begin (Mangione, 1998). Of the total number of respondents, 53.1% had 16 or more years experience teaching a second language and 43.5% hold an MA in Spanish. The data on the returned survey were analyzed in two phases—first an independent analysis using descriptive statistics was done and then an analysis of relationships between variables using non-parametric correlation statistics was done.

Methodology

In the design of the survey, the content of each section was explained at the beginning to clarify any terms that might be ambiguous. In addition, based on the pilot study results, some terms were explicated for added clarification. These terms were: prereading strategies, reading strategies, authentic, and functional literacy. The division of the sections were determined by the research questions being investigated in this study.

Each section provided the investigator with insight about the teachers' own familiarity with the current research on reading and how they apply this knowledge in their classrooms (see Appendix for the complete survey). A closed statement format with a Likert scale was used. A closed format implies that only the choices given may be selected. This format also facilitates subjects' responses (Mangione, 1998). For example, statement one read: *Reading is the most important skill in learning a foreign language.* A category scale of *1 Strongly Agree, 2 Agree, 3 Neutral, 4 Disagree and 5 Strongly Disagree* was elected to elicit responses in the first two sections. The third section used the categories *1 Very Much, 2 Much, 3 Moderate* (Average), *4 Little* and *5 None.* The section providing demographic information utilized simple multiple-choice responses. An attempt was made to keep the survey as simple as possible to answer so as not to be burdensome for the respondents.

FINDINGS

With a return rate of nearly 60% and the descriptive statistics of the data completed,[3] each section of the questionnaire was analyzed in relation to the research questions. What follows is a discussion of the findings from each section. A summary table with the question number and mean, standard deviation and frequency percentage is provided.

What Do Secondary Spanish Language Teachers Believe about the Construct of Reading?

Part I identified the beliefs of the respondents. Secondary Spanish teachers believe reading should be integrated into the beginning levels. They also believe that reading is a building block to L2 acquisition, and that comprehension should be the main objective of a reading activity. Pre-reading and reading strategies can and should be taught are also apparent beliefs of the respondents. Their final belief in this section indicated that technology should be utilized for reading activities.

Just as important as what the respondents believe is what they do not believe. They do not believe that reading is too time-consuming to be incorporated into the classroom activities, nor do they believe that pronunciation and structure should be the main objectives to a reading activity. All of their reported beliefs and non-beliefs concur with research related to the construct of reading in a second language.

The data gathered from Part I of the survey supported the main premises found in L2 reading research: reading is fundamental to L2 acquisition (Bernhardt, 1991). The teachers also agree that extracting meaning from the written text should be the main objective of a reading activity; reading should be given adequate time during a class period as well as beyond the classroom setting; reading skills in a L2 can and should be taught, and reading should begin in the early stages of language study.

The item mean for Part I of the survey is 1.99 with a standard deviation of .866 indicating that the respondents' answers were generally *Strongly Agree* or *Agree*. In fact, the mode for all the items was number one, *Strongly Agree*, or number two, *Agree*. In almost all of items in this section, the respondents were more than 70% in agreement with the statements made about the construct of reading. This reflects a strong belief about the importance of reading in a second language. Table 2 lists a summary of the results from each question.[4]

Table 2.   Teachers' Beliefs about Reading in a Foreign Language

Question Number	Mean	Standard Deviation	Percentage
3	1.5445	.7190	94
5	1.7820	.7977	90
6	2.0171	.9469	80
7	2.8316	.9909	73
8	2.3172	.8975	72
9	2.2138	.9961	70
10	1.4674	.6278	70
11	1.4498	.6278	70
12	2.2500	.9842	70
13	1.8557	.8386	85
14	2.4726	.9823	64
15	1.6829	.7483	90
16	2.1111	.8060	71

$n = 292$

What Do Secondary Spanish Language Teachers Report That They Know about Students' Roles in Reading?

The first aspect of Part II explored what the teachers' beliefs reveal about the overall purpose for reading in a second language. This is not to say the objectives for individual reading activities, but rather, the overall rationale for teaching reading in a second language. For example teachers were asked whether students should attain functional literacy in the target language after a three- to four-year program? This statement received an overwhelming 91.9% yes, the respondents do believe that functional literacy is the ultimate goal of a good reading program (Brooks, 1984; Day & Bamford, 1998; Kellerman, 1981). Do students attain this goal or the individual goals of the respondents' reading activities? Sixty-seven percent of the respondents believe that their students do achieve the goals they set for their reading activities. The question to be asked is why do almost 25% of the students not attain the goals that the teachers set? Are the goals unrealistic or are the reading activities inappropriate? Related to the question of inappropriate reading activities is the response given to the teachers' satisfaction with the reading activities. Only 9% say that they are very satisfied with their reading activities. This is a very confusing response because it was assumed that the respondents were in control of their curriculum;

however, it could be that the questionnaire allowed the teachers to critically reflect on their teaching and hence a self-critical response.

The second area investigated is the students' involvement with the text. Seventy-five percent of the respondents believe the students translate from the target language to their native language. If this is the case, one has to question the objective of the reading activity. Do the teachers want the students to do a literal translation? If so, the translation process is appropriate and is not to be confused with the comprehension process where students will think and recall meaning in the L1 (Bernhardt, 1991). Because respondents report that they believe comprehension should be the main objective and that functional literacy should be the ultimate objective for reading, it is doubtful that a literal translation is the intention of the respondents.

The final aspect of Part II of the survey explored when students should read. The belief that students need to read beyond regular class time is supported by 87% of the respondents; yet only 46.5% felt it was appropriate to allow free reading time in class. This would confirm the personal comments on this section in which some respondents stated that there is not enough regular class time to do guided reading activities, much less, free reading.

The teachers' beliefs expressed in this section are less decisive, yet the underlying tone of the importance of reading to promote L2 acquisition is still evident. The respondents may not be as convinced about their beliefs relating directly to their students which may imply some lack of knowledge for the process of reading or the unwillingness to comment on collective student motivations.

Part II of the survey focused on the research question: What do secondary Spanish language teachers report that they know about students' roles in reading? Although the mode is generally number two, Agree, the responses were not as conclusive as for Part I of the survey, with only items B3 and B4 having different modes. Only one item, B3—*After a three- to four-year program, students should have functional literacy (ability to read and write) in the target language,* with a mode of 1, had more than 90% either Strongly Agreeing or Agreeing to this statement. This corresponds with the respondents' strong belief that reading is a basic skill necessary in a second language. Item B7—*Students need to know the grammatical concepts they will see in the readings before they can read in the foreign language* had a mode of 4—Disagree, which concurs with the reading research that it is not essential to know all of the grammatical structures in order to understand the text.

Possibly, the responses are less decisive for Part II of the survey because it is difficult to know how the student is processing the reading activity and the teachers were reluctant to comment on the students' reading processes. A larger percentage of subjects responded in the neutral category. Generally at least 10% and as many as 35% of the teachers responded with the neutral category in this section. Table 3 provides the summary data.[5]

Table 3.   What Do Spanish Teachers Know about Students' Roles in Reading?

Question Number	Mean	Standard Deviation	Percentage
1	2.2657	.6644	75
2	2.0919	.9294	78
3	1.6316	.7879	91
4	1.7676	.7535	87
5	2.2179	.8545	75
6	2.6538	.9417	46
7	3.2561	1.1138	89
9	2.6386	1.1894	53
10	2.6596	.9077	81

(n = 285)

What Preparation Do Secondary Spanish Teachers Report to Have Enabled Them to Teach Reading in a Second Language?

Some other parts of the questionnaire indirectly provide answers to these questions, however Part III contains the more directed statements by the teachers about their professional preparation. This section of the survey had the greatest reliability with a standardized item alpha of .78. The modes were not as consistent as in the previous parts of the survey. Each category, numbers 1–5 is the mode for at least one item. In other words, there is much variety of opinion among teachers on these issues.

The respondents do not believe that they have received sufficient training to teach reading. Only 5.5% report that they have had "very much" training, while 17% say they have had no training at all to teach reading in a second language, nor do they feel that they are very familiar with reading research. This information is crucial because the respondents adamantly believe in teaching reading and its importance to L2 acquisition and yet they state they have had little to no formal preparation to teach reading.

The response for training received to use technology is also low with more than 50% reporting that they have had little or no training to use technology for reading activities. The personal commentaries indicate that although the respondents report that they believe technology should be used to teach reading activities, almost 72% either strongly agree or agree, the subjects were not always confident of their preparation in this area. This may be due to lack of available time to take courses, lack of course offerings, lack of trained teachers to teach the courses, or lack of the technology itself.

Overall, the respondents do not believe that they have had adequate training. The written comments reinforce what the survey ascertained. The majority of those who wrote comments included a remark relating to the need for methodology coursework in general and more specifically, for courses that would include the teaching of reading. The commentaries also implied that the respondents were willing to take additional coursework, be it in a classroom, distance learning setting or an on-line course. Summary data for this section appears in Table 4.[6]

Table 4.   Teachers' Preparation for Teaching Reading

Question Number	Mean	Standard Deviation	Percentage
1	3.3862	1.1048	92
2	3.2784	1.0930	96
3	3.0825	1.01.3	66
4	3.5663	1.0373	81
5	2.6345	1.0210	91
6	2.0915	1.0255	95
7	2.7289	1.1467	92
9	2.6655	.8970	84
10	2.7345	.8854	81
11	1.7801	.8007	84
12	2.7314	.9179	80
13	2.0828	.9558	92
14	1.0789	2.3552	63
15	3.6862	1.2261	66
16	3.7069	1.0392	75

$n = 292$

How Do Secondary Spanish Language Teachers Contend They Practice Their Beliefs about Reading in Their Classrooms?

Part III of the survey provides most of the responses on how teachers practice their beliefs in their own classrooms. Ten of the items focused on these practices. As stated above, each category, 1–5, Very Much to None, is the mode at least once for the items showing considerable variability. The overall mean for Part III is 2.82. Less than 50% of the respondents are satisfied with their reading activities, and also less than 50% believe they can write clearly defined objectives for reading activities. If they believe that they cannot write appropriate objectives, it is likely that they are unable to design a successful reading activity. On the positive side, 84% of the respondents report that comprehension is their main objective when they do teach a reading activity. This supports the reading research previously discussed, especially that of Swaffar (1988) who has advocated that extracting meaning should be the main objective of a reading activity. However, only 22% of the respondents report that they do teach reading strategies and only 30% do utilize prereading activities very much. These two components are essential in developing successful reading activities. This low percentage may account for the dissatisfaction in their reading activities that the respondents previously indicated.

The last two items relating to the respondents' teaching practices both had low percentages. Item C15—*I use technology in my reading activities* had a mode of five—none. This reply directly relates to the lack of training and was reiterated in the personal comments, which tended to not support technological implementations in reading activities. The final item, C16—*I give my students free reading time during class*, had a mode of four—little. This is parallel to the personal commentaries that the respondents made relating to the time factor for accomplishing preset course expectations. They expressed a great concern for lack of time to teach the other skills, such as speaking and grammar structures, and that it would be extremely difficult to allow free reading time in class.

The results of Part III of the survey link the two research questions addressed above. If the teachers were not adequately trained to teach reading, inadequacy and dissatisfaction would result. The desire for more knowledge exists as indicated by the respondents' personal comments.

Is There a Relationship Between the Secondary Spanish Language Teachers' Stated Beliefs and Their Self-Reported Classroom Practices?

When comparing the findings of the respondents' stated beliefs and their self-reported classroom practices, several inconsistencies are revealed. The first inconsistency was found in the concepts of prereading activities and reading strategies. In Part I of the survey, the respondents stated that they adamantly believed in these concepts, 96.2%, and 95.5% respectively. Yet, in their reported practice, only 70%, and 63% respectively responded that they did use or teach these concepts "much." The question arises as to what do the 25%-30% who stated that they strongly believed in these concepts do in their actual teaching in lieu of prereading activities or lessons on reading strategies?

A second inconsistency is noted between the respondents' belief about utilizing technology in the classroom and their actual use of technology to teach reading activities. Seventy-one percent believe that technology is an important facet of teaching reading, yet only 18.2% utilize it. This is radical discrepancy between teachers' beliefs and practice.

The final major inconsistency is the amount of time to be utilized for reading in the classroom. Here, 85.9% of the respondents report that reading is not too time-consuming in the classroom; while in their reported practice, only 11.7% allow substantial free reading time. In the personal comments, teachers referred to the constraints put on their time by demands such as testing and requirements for the next level. For example, one respondent reported that "...there is so little time to teach reading with all the pressure of year-end testing where grammar and vocabulary are the main focus and must be stressed."

Although inconsistencies were seen between the preceding stated beliefs and the reported practice related to these beliefs, there were also consistencies found between the beliefs and practices. The most important one being that comprehension of the text should be the main objective for a reading activity and the respondents' stated objectives. Eighty percent report that they believe comprehension should be the main objective and 84% say that comprehension is the main objective of their reading activities.

CONCLUSION

When asked to describe their knowledge, beliefs, and practices about teaching reading in the secondary Spanish classroom, Spanish language teachers display consistencies and inconsistencies between beliefs and practice. These variations concur with the results described in Graden's (1996) study, that the subjects studied in her investigation all compromised their beliefs to adapt their activities to the students and the classroom environment (p. 397). The data gathered in this study suggest that the respondents to this survey also compromised their beliefs for one or more reasons to attend to the actual classroom environment. One belief was the value of teaching and employment of prereading strategies. Whereas 96% believe that prereading strategies should be used in reading activities, only 30% responded that they use prereading strategies very much and 22.3% responded that they teach reading strategies. Another discrepancy between belief and practice was time for reading in class. More than 60% allow little or no time for free reading, while 82.2% believe free reading is very important. These are only two examples of the demonstrated discrepancies found in the study.

The powerful reality of the secondary Spanish language classroom can overwhelm the most well prepared and organized classroom teacher. Facing the daunting task of instructing beginning sections that average 32 students or more with sometimes third year courses running to 25 or more students (Semmer, 2000, p.164), the well-meaning Spanish teacher has the odds stacked against her when trying to mesh theory with practice. Nevertheless, some teachers do achieve this matching of both belief and practice.

Ambiguity and inconsistency between teachers' beliefs and practices is not an unusual finding in L1 reading research. It is nevertheless disheartening to discover similar disparities in L2 classrooms in the few studies being done on this topic in L2 reading research. With the advent of more research directed toward describing the teaching and learning process in L2 classrooms, perhaps in the future two problems underscored in the present study may be solved. Perhaps in the future the custodial duties of the classroom teacher will lessen and with that problem solved, the Spanish language teacher will have greater freedom to employ and reflect on theoretically based instruction. Second, hopefully there will be studies that isolate what instructional processes effective teachers use, despite the constraints of the classroom environment, in order to effect meaningful reading instruction with positive outcomes for L2 learners.

APPENDIX:
A SURVEY OF FOREIGN LANGUAGE TEACHERS' BELIEFS AND PRACTICES FOR TEACHING READING IN A FOREIGN LANGUAGE

Please respond to each item by circling only one of the five alternatives. Use the following scale:

1 Strongly Agree
2 Agree
3 Neutral
4 Disagree
5 Strongly Disagree

You could precede the following statements with. In my opinion, or I believe…

1. Reading is the most important skill in learning a foreign language.

1   2   3   4   5

2. Reading is a passive skill.

           1   2   3   4   5

3. Reading should be integrated into the first level of language study.

           1   2   3   4   5

4. Reading is a result of language learning.

           1   2   3   4   5

5. Reading is a building block of language learning.

           1   2   3   4   5

6. Comprehension should be the main objective for a reading activity.

           1   2   3   4   5

7. Vocabulary and structure should be the main objectives for a reading activity.

           1   2   3   4   5

8. Pronunciation should be the main objective for a reading activity.

           1   2   3   4   5

9. Reading skills in one's native language transfer to reading in the foreign language.

           1   2   3   4   5

10. Prereading strategies should be used (background knowledge, schema, vocabulary, etc.) to prepare the students for the reading.

           1   2   3   4   5

11. Reading strategies (techniques to facilitate reading such as finding cognates, context, etc.) can be taught.

           1   2   3   4   5

12. Of speaking, listening, reading and writing, reading is the most difficult skill to teach.

           1   2   3   4   5

13. Reading is too time-consuming to teach in the beginning levels.

           1   2   3   4   5

14. The target language should be used considerably more than the native language when teaching reading.

1   2   3   4   5

15. Reading should be taught in the beginning level of foreign language instruction.

1   2   3   4   5

16. Technology (e.g. computers, Internet, etc.) should be utilized for reading activities.

1   2   3   4   5

II. STUDENTS' ROLES IN READING

Students are the participants in the reading activities. The following section asks for both your beliefs about the students' roles as well as their actual participation in the reading activities.

Please respond to each item by choosing only one of the five alternatives. Use the following scale:

1 Strongly Agree
2 Agree
3 Neutral
4 Disagree
5 Strongly Disagree

1. My students attain the goals I set for the reading activities.

1   2   3   4   5

2. Students need to be able to read for survival in   the   target   language country.

1   2   3   4   5

3. After a three to four year program, students should have functional literacy (ability to read and write) in the target language.

1   2   3   4   5

4. Students need to read in the target language beyond regular class time.

1   2   3   4   5

5. Students generally translate from the L2 to their native language when reading.

1   2   3   4   5

6. Students should be given free reading time in class.

1   2   3   4   5

7. Students need to know the grammatical concepts they will see in the readings before they can read in the foreign language.

1   2   3   4   5

8. Students should be able to read what they can say.

1   2   3   4   5

9. Students should be able to orally use the language that they can read.

1   2   3   4   5

10. Students enjoy reading in the foreign language.

1   2   3   4   5

III. TEACHERS' PREPARATION, TRAINING FOR AND ENGAGEMENT IN THE TEACHING OF READING IN A FOREIGN LANGUAGE (FL)

This section refers to your preparation both as an undergraduate and any ongoing training/courses you have received or are receiving that relates specifically to the skill of reading and teaching reading to your students as well as your actual teaching of reading to your students.

Please respond to each item by choosing only one of the five alternatives. Use the following sale:

1 Very Much
2 Much
3 Moderate (Average)
4 Little
5 None

1. I have been trained to teach reading in a foreign language.

1   2   3   4   5

2. I am familiar with reading research.

1   2   3   4   5

3. I am familiar with terminology used in teaching reading.

1   2   3   4   5

4. I am adequately trained to use technology for reading activities.

1   2   3   4   5

5. I am able to write clearly defined objectives for reading activities.

1   2   3   4   5

6. My experiences with reading in FL as a student were positive.

1   2   3   4   5

7. I teach reading the way I was taught.

1   2   3   4   5

8. I learned to teach reading through experience.

1   2   3   4   5

9. I am satisfied with the reading activities I use in my classes.

1   2   3   4   5

10. Vocabulary and structure are the main objectives of my reading lessons.

1   2   3   4   5

11. Comprehension is the main objective of my reading lessons.

1   2   3   4   5

12. I use more English than the target language when I teach a reading activity.

1   2   3   4   5

13. I use prereading strategies in my reading activities.

1   2   3   4   5

14. I teach reading strategies.

1   2   3   4   5

15. I use technology (e.g., internet, e-mail, etc.) in my reading activities.

1   2   3   4   5

16. I give my students free reading time during class.

1   2   3   4   5

IV. DEMOGRAPHICS

The following section will provide valuable information about the current population of foreign language teachers and the schools in which you teach.

Circle all responses that apply to you.

1. Are you a _____?
    a. male
    b. female

2. Are you a _____?
    a. Native Speaker of Spanish
    b. Nonnative Speaker of Spanish

3. How many years experience do you have teaching a foreign language?
    a. 1–5 years
    b. 6–10 years
    c. 11–15 years
    d. 16 or more years

4. What degree do you hold for the language you are presently teaching?
    a. BA minor
    b. BA major
    c. MA
    d. Other _____

5. What level/s are you presently teaching?
    a. 1st year
    b. 2nd year
    c. 3rd year
    d. 4th year
    e. 5th year or above
    f. Other _____

6. Besides Spanish, how many other languages are taught in grades 9–12 in your district?
   a. 0
   b. one
   c. two or more

7. How many foreign language teachers in grades 9–12 are in your district?
   a. one
   b. two
   c. three to five
   d. more than five

8. Do you remember what text was used in your methods course, was it?
   a. Lee, J. and B. Van Patten. *Making communicative language teaching happen.*
   b. Alice Omaggio Hadley. *Teaching language in context.*
   c. Wilga Rivers. *Teaching foreign language skills.*
   d. Allen, E. D., and R. Vallete. *Modern language classroom techniques.*
   e. Chastain, Kenneth. *Developing second language skills.*
   f. Other

9. How many credits/hours have you taken in foreign language methodology coursework?
   a. 1–3
   b. 4–6
   c. 7–10
   d. more than 10

10. What is the main reason you are teaching a foreign language?
    a. influence from a former foreign language teacher
    b. personal interest in foreign languages
    c. maintain job status at current school
    d. other

NOTES

1. This chapter is a selection from a larger study by Gebel (2000).

2. Graden's results should be viewed with some caution since there were only six participants in the study.

3. For a complete reference to the descriptive data and reliability analysis please refer to Gebel (2000, pp. 176–184).

4. Part I of the survey was intended to establish teachers' reported beliefs about the construct of reading in a second language. In this section of the survey,

four items were reversed or flipped to correlate with the rest of the items in the section. For example, item A7 read *vocabulary and structure should be the main objectives for a reading activity.* Given the reading research, the respondents should disagree or strongly disagree, thus marking numbers 4 or 5 as their response. This would not be consistent with the other items in this section. As a reversed item, A7 would be analyzed as if it read, *vocabulary and structure should NOT be the main objectives for a reading activity.* Now the respondents should have replied strongly agree or agree, numbers 1 and 2. The meaning was not changed, but the response was then consistent with the direction of the rest of the scale.

The items flipped or reversed were A7—*Vocabulary and structure should be the main objectives for a reading activity;* A8—*Pronunciation should be the main objective for a reading activity;* A12—*Of speaking, listening, reading and writing, reading is the most difficult skill to teach;* and A13—*Reading is too time-consuming to teach in the beginning levels.* These items were analyzed and discussed, therefore, as reversed order items.

Also in this section, three items were deleted after the statistical and content analyses were completed. The first item deleted was A1—*Reading is the most important skill in learning a foreign language.* In the initial descriptive analysis, the A1 responses showed a mean of 3.68 with a standard deviation of 2.64. The item was then flipped to correspond with the direction of the scale of the other items in the section. The mean then became 2.32. The standard deviation remained the same as flipping an item will not change the standard deviation. Both the original item and the flipped or reversed item demonstrated that there was no consistent pattern of responses. Also, by deleting item A1, the alpha increased from .28 to .44 providing more reliable data. Upon careful examination of the item and considering the resulting descriptive statistics, the item was determined to be too ambiguous to be of value and did not enhance nor deter from the study if removed.

The second item in this section to be eliminated was A2—*Reading is a passive skill.* The same procedures were followed as for item A1. The mean for this item was 2.32 with a standard deviation of 2.63. As with item A1, the responses showed no consistent pattern with a broad range of responses. The final item in this section to be deleted was A4—*Reading is the result of language learning.* The alpha increased slightly by deleting the item, from .28 to .3. The mean was 2.40 and its standard deviation was 1.15. Also, item A5—*Reading is the building block of language learning* provided the same information and was much more reliable with a mean of 1.76 and standard deviation of .81. The respondents' belief about the impact of reading in a second language could be determined from item A5. The above-mentioned changes were the only ones made to Part I of the survey. The other items were kept and analyzed in their original form.

5.   Unfortunately, there were a number of missing data in this section. Six respondents left this section unanswered. It does not appear to be intentional, but rather the result of the placement of the section in the survey. Part II was on the back side of the three page survey. The missing items affect the total reliability of this section. The initial reliability analysis of this section did not take into account the missing responses and had a standardized alpha of .69. The final analysis factored in the missing responses reducing the standardized alpha to .49. After examining the various analyses and carefully studying the items, it was decided that it was unnecessary to keep both items B8 and B9. Having the two questions might cause confusion to the respondents since they are a reverse sentence order. Upon careful examination of the two items and considering the descriptive statistics, item B8 was deleted. The reliability analysis displayed that there would be less effect on the section reliability of Part II if B8 were deleted. If B9 were deleted the reliability of the

section would reduce to .65, whereas the deletion of B8 would keep alpha, .67, the same as the original alpha. All other items remained the same in this section.

6. This section has the highest reliability of the three parts of the survey. It has a standardized item alpha of .78. Only one item, C8—*I learned to teach reading through experience* was eliminated. After careful content analysis, it was determined that either respondents were confused by the question or they really had no idea whether they learned to teach reading through their own experience as a teacher or during their preparation to teach.

REFERENCES

Aebersold, J., & Field, M. (1997). *From reader to reading teacher.* Cambridge: Cambridge Press.

Allen, E.D., & Valette, R. (1977). *Modern language classroom techniques* (2nd ed.). New York: Harcourt Brace Jovanovich.

Barnett, M.A. (1989). *More than meets the eye: Foreign language reading, theory and practice.* Englewood Cliffs, NJ: Prentice-Hall.

Barr, R., & Duffy, G. (1978, March). *Teacher conceptions of reading: The evolution of a research study.* Paper presented at the meeting of the American Educational Research Association, Toronto. (EDRS: ED 153 200)

Bernhardt, E.B. (1991). *Reading development in a second language: Theoretical, empirical and classroom perspectives.* Norwood, NJ: Ablex.

Blanton, W.E., & Moorman, G.B. (1987). *The effects of knowledge on the instructional behavior of classroom reading teachers.* Research Report No.7. Boone, NC: Appalachian State University, Center on Excellence in Teacher Education.

Brophy, J., & Good, T.L. (1974). *Teacher-student relationships: Causes and consequences.* New York: Holt, Rinehard and Winston.

Chastain, K. (1988). *Developing second language skills: Theory to practice* (3rd ed.). New York: Harcourt Brace Jovanovich.

Day, R., & Bamford, J. (1998). *Extensive reading in the second language classroom.* Cambridge: Cambridge University Press.

Duffy, G. (1982). Fighting off the alligators: What research in real classroom has to say about reading instruction. *Journal of Reading Behavior, 14,* 357–73.

Duffy, G., & Anderson, L. (1982). *Final report: Conceptions of reading project.* East Lansing: Michigan State University Institute for Research on Teaching. (EDRS ED 218 583)

Duffy, G., & Ball, D. (1986). Instructional decision making and reading teacher effectiveness. In J. Hoffman (Ed.), *Effective teaching of reading: Research practice* (pp. 163–70). Newark, DE: IRA.

Fang, Z. (1996). A review of research and teacher beliefs and practices. *Educational Research, 38*(1), 47–65.

Feiman-Nemser, S., & Floden, R.E. (1986). The cultures of teaching. In M. C. Wittrock (Ed.), *Handbook of research on teaching* (3rd ed.) (pp. 37–49). New York: Macmillan.

Fink, A., & Kosecoff, J. (1985). *How to conduct surveys: A step-by-step guide.* Newbury Park, CA: Sage.

Gebel, T.A. (2000). *A survey of Spanish teachers' beliefs and practices for teaching reading in a second language.* Unpublished dissertation, the University of Iowa.

Graden, E.C. (1996). How language teachers' beliefs about reading instruction are mediated by their beliefs about students. *Foreign Language Annals, 29,* 387–398.

Harste, J.C., & Burke, C.L. (1977). A new hypothesis for reading teacher research: Both the teaching and learning of reading is theoretically based. In P.D. Pearson (Ed.), *Reading: Theory, research, and practice* (pp. 32–40). New York: National Research Conference.

Johnson, K.E. (1992). The relationship between teachers' beliefs and practices during literacy instruction for non-native speakers of English. *Journal of Reading Behavior, 24,* 83–108.

Kagan, D.M. (1992). Implications of research on teacher belief. *Educational Psychologist, 27,* 65–90.

Kamil, M., & Pearson, P.D. (1979, Winter). Theory and practice in teaching reading. *New York University Education Quarterly, 10*(2), 10–16.

Kellerman, M. (1981). *The forgotten third skill.* Oxford: Pergamon.

Leu, D., & Misulis, K. (1986, December). *Prior knowledge and the comprehension of basal teacher's guides.* Paper presented at Annual Meeting of National Reading Conference, Austin, TX.

Longberger, R. (1992). The belief systems and instructional choices of preservice teachers. In N. Padak, T. Rasinski, & J. Logan (Eds.), *Literacy research and practice: Foundations for the Year 2000* (pp. 71–8). Pittsburg, PA: College Reading Association.

Mangano, N., & Allen, J. (1986). Teachers beliefs and language arts and their effects on students beliefs and instruction. In J. Niles & R. Lalik, (Eds.), *Solving problems in literacy: Learners, teachers, and researchers* (pp. 136–42). Rochester, NY: National Reading Conference.

Mangione, T. (1998). Mail surveys. In L. Bickman & D. Rog (Eds.), *Handbook of applied social research methods.* Thousand Oaks: Sage.

McNeil, L. M. (2000). *Contradictions of school reform: Educational costs of standardized testing.* New York: Routledge.

Olsen, J., & Singer, M. (1994). Examining teachers' beliefs, reflective change, and the teaching of reading. *Reading Research Instruction, 34*(2), 97–110.

Omaggio Hadley, A. (2000). *Teaching language in context* (3rd ed.). Boston: Heinle & Heinle.

Paris, S.G., Waski, B.A., & Turner, J.C. (1991). The development of strategic readers. In R. Barr (Ed.), *Handbook of reading research* (pp. 609–40). New York: Longman.

Richardson, V., Anders, P., Tidwell, D., & Lloyd, C. (1991). The relationship between teachers' beliefs and practices in reading comprehension instruction. *American Educational Research Journal, 28,* 559–86.

Rivers, W. (1981). *Teaching foreign-language skills* (2nd ed.). Chicago: University of Chicago Press.

Roehler, L., & Duffy, G. (1991). Teachers instructional action. In R. Barr (Ed.), *Handbook of reading research* (pp. 861–84). New York: Longman.

Rupley, W.H., & Logan, J.W. (1984). *Elementary teachers' beliefs about reading and knowledge of reading content: Relationships to decisions about reading outcomes.* ERIC document Reproduction Service No. ED285162.

Semmer, M.S. (2000). Factors that affect the implementation of the Standards. In G. Guntermann (Ed.), *Teaching Spanish with the five C's: A blueprint for success* (pp. 161–181). Orlando, FL: Harcourt.

Schrier, L. (1989). *A survey of foreign language teacher preparation patterns and procedures in small, private colleges and universities in the United States.* Unpublished dissertation, the Ohio State University.

Schrier, L. (2001). Developing precollegiate foreign language teachers: An overlooked mission of foreign language departments. In E.B. Wells & D. Goldberg (Eds.), *Chairing the foreign language and literature department* (Part 2, pp. 71–78). New York: Modern Language Association.

Schulz, R.A. (2000). Foreign language teacher development: MLJ perspectives— 1916–1999. *Modern Language Journal, 84,* 496–523.

Schrum, J., & Glisan, E. (1994). *Teachers' handbook: Contextualized language instruction.* Boston: Heinle & Heinle.

Swaffar, J.K. (1988). Readers, texts, and second languages: The interactive process. *Modern Language Journal, 72,* 123–149.

Swaffar, J., Arens, K., & Byrnes, H. (1991). *Reading for meaning: An integrated approach to language learning.* Englewood Cliffs, NJ: Prentice-Hall.

Wallace, C. (1988). *Learning to read in a multicultural society.* Englewood Cliffs, NJ: Prentice-Hall.

Wing, L. (1989). The influence of preschool teachers' beliefs on young children's conceptions of reading and writing. *Early Childhood Research Quarterly, 4,* 61–74.

Yager, R.E., & Penick, J. (1990). Science teacher education. In W.R. Houston (Ed.), *Handbook of research on teacher education* (pp. 657–73). New York: Macmillan.

Zbiek, R.M. (1998). Prospective teachers' use of computing tools to develop and validate functions as mathematical models. *Journal for Research in Mathematics Education, 29*(2), 184–201.

CHAPTER 6

THE FORM-MEANING INTERFACE:

A STUDY OF JAPANESE-AS-A-FOREIGN-LANGUAGE WRITING

Sufumi So

ABSTRACT

Two studies are reported here to examine the issue of form-meaning relationships in the context of foreign language writing from an educational perspective. One of them, a case study of an intermediate Japanese proficient learner, describes how he approaches composition writing in the target language and, in particular, how much attention he is willing or able to pay to ideational thinking. The other study shifts the focus to composition readers evaluating two versions of the same Japanese compositions, one version exactly as written by Japanese learners and the other with grammatical errors corrected. These two studies led to the propositions that foreign language writers are capable of focusing on the more abstract levels of meaning or semantic integrity of text despite their language deficiencies and that the two general subscales of *content* and *language use* of foreign language texts can be discriminated without being unduly affected by surface-level, morphosyntactic errors.

INTRODUCTION

In this chapter I shall discuss how the traits underlying the writing skill are enacted in the context of foreign language (FL)[1] education. These traits are thinking (adapting the subject matter to be worded in a text), formulating (converting contents of thought into language), and encoding (putting formulations in writing) (Blok & de Glopper, 1992, p. 105). The issue, in a nutshell, concerns what Bereiter and Scardamalia (1987, pp. 299–317) call a "dual-problem space" comprising the content space (or idea production) and the rhetorical space (or text production). In systemic functional linguistic terms it is about the content plane concerned with the construal of meaning through the workings of lexicogrammar and discourse semantics and the expression plane concerned with realizations of meaning in written language (e.g., Martin, 1997).

The present inquiry, which I approach from a strictly educational perspective, is at once reflective and empirical. It includes two separate but related studies, both on writing in Japanese as a foreign language (JFL) in college-level Japanese courses for nonnative speakers in North America. The first study describes a case where a JFL learner in a Japanese reading and writing class was interviewed about his experience of writing in Japanese, his processes of writing in Japanese was documented, and his texts written in Japanese were assessed for various textual aspects. This particular case was studied as part of a large research project (So, 1997) that addressed a number of questions including the one relevant to the theme of this chapter: How do JFL learners deal with semantic and structural constraints in writing a composition in Japanese?

The second study shifts the focus to composition readers who evaluated two versions of the same Japanese compositions, one version exactly as written by JFL learners and the other with grammatical errors corrected. This study asked whether surface errors would impede the reader's evaluation of meaning-related global features of text. The two studies offer the data base, hitherto almost nonexistent, upon which our systematic understanding of form-meaning relationships in FL writing can be built and further developed. Admittedly the data base is small and may be fragmentary; the studies do, however, make the beginnings of the effort in theorizing and model building in the study of FL writing. If such was a far-fetched goal, they still help us formulate our present concerns about writing in FL classrooms. Before presenting the two studies, I shall discuss the broader context of FL education where the two studies can be best situated.

FOREIGN LANGUAGE WRITING AND EDUCATION

Consider purposes of writing in FL classrooms. They may include (a) supporting the acquisition of oral language, which has typically been the case with the now outdated audio-lingual approach to FL instruction, (b) reinforcing the learning of grammar and spelling rules, (c) helping learners integrate all learning in the FL, and (d) strengthening general writing skills by elevating the level of learners' understanding of the dynamics of good writing (Gaudiani, 1981). All of these purposes suggest that writing is simply a technology to transcribe already-known content or ideas. In some way writing in FL classrooms is so ritualized that it requires little thought. In many cases FL courses, especially lower-division courses, have been regarded as "bland and contentless" (Littlejohn & Windeatt, 1989, p. 159). They tend to emphasize the acquisition of surface features of language without providing intellectually stimulating "content." This situation, however, is changing, albeit modestly and probably sporadically. At this junction it may be useful to review the emerging voices of FL professionals who have been concerned about articulating a rationale for FL instruction in curricula at schools, colleges, and universities.

As FL education has become "a secure part" of school and university curricula due to recent institutionalized enforcement of FL requirements in the United States (Lange, 1992, p. 528; see also Davis, 1997) and elsewhere (Dickson & Cumming, 1996), an urgent need has appeared to carefully consider the relationship between FL curricula and the goals of educational programs overall. Historically, language teaching has been influenced primarily by theories and principles of linguistics, psycholinguistics, sociolinguistics, and second language acquisition research (Nunan, 1988; Richards & Nunan, 1992). Only recently have FL professionals begun to see themselves as educators as well as applied linguists. This renewed conception of FL teaching as an educational matter invites us to consider what needs to be learned beyond the linguistic aspects of a target language. Littlejohn and Windeatt (1989) called such learning "additional, non-language, learning" (p. 158) as emphasized by, for instance, Lange (1992). For Lange, however, such learning is a priority rather than "additional" component. He has strongly advocated that FL curricula move toward a view that prizes "its contribution to human development rather than the development of language features" (p. 528).

To understand Lange's proposal, one needs to consider existing FL curricular orientations, particularly their sense of what the curriculum is for. Lange (1990) insightfully analyzed FL curricular orientations using Schubert's (1986) threefold classification of curriculum inquiry: the scientific-technical, also known as empirical-analytical; the practical or hermeneutic; and the critical or emancipatory. Recent trends in FL curriculum have

linked the empirical-analytical orientation and the interpretive or hermeneutic orientation. The former is represented by audio-lingual and gram-
mar-translation teaching while the latter emphasizes the development of
language proficiency as a means of expressing individual meaning and discovering meaning in the world of the individual. Lange suggests that one
such example is Stern's multidimensional curriculum, consisting of linguistic, cultural, communicative, and general language education syllabi (Stern,
1983a, 1983b, 1992). Although curricula of this combined orientation (or
what Lange calls the *connective*) focus on uses of language for communication, the understanding of *the self* and *the surrounding other* as well as any use
of language to act upon human conditions are fundamentally byproducts of
learning linguistic components (i.e., phonology, morphology, syntax, lexicon) and basic communicative functions of language (Lange, 1990). For
this reason Lange suggested that curricular efforts should go beyond the
analytic and scientific to help learners find personal meaning in their learning processes (through a hermeneutic orientation) or to allow them to contemplate and act upon the society in which they live (through an
emancipatory orientation). This suggestion aims toward the development
of the enlightened self or the betterment of human conditions.

Such orientations and purposes are difficult to find in the curricular
writings on FL education (Lange, 1990). There are, however, some excep-
tions. Moskowitz (1978) and Stevick (1990) have presented instructional
techniques for the cause of humanism based on a hermeneutic philosophy
of language learning and teaching. And Crawford-Lange and Lange
(1987) and Kubota (1996) have applied the work of Freire (1973) to reori-
ent language learning from the scientific-analytic acquisition of facts and
information toward emancipatory reflection and action on such facts and
information.

These voices speak for language learning as a total "educative experience" (Dewey, 1938/1963). They overlap with those advocating content-
centered language instruction[2] as a means to counter traditions of language instruction through "bland and contentless" textbooks (Littlejohn &
Windeatt, 1989, p. 159). The intent of content-based instruction is twofold
(Crandall & Tucker, 1990). One is to help learners attain language proficiency beyond the level of basic communicative skills, that is, expanded
foci of instruction for the development of "basic interpersonal communicative skills (BICS)" *and* "cognitive/academic language proficiency (CALP)"
(Cummins, 1980; Cummins & Swain, 1986, ch. 8). The other intent is to
meet the specific needs of language students who come to language classrooms for a variety of reasons. Although integrated language and content
instruction is often associated with *second* language learning where special
language skills are required to carry out cognitively demanding academic
tasks (e.g., learning English as a second language for academic purposes),

it is also gaining acceptance among *FL* professionals who recognize the increasing importance of students developing FL proficiency that goes beyond the BICS level (Crandall, 1993; Crandall & Tucker, 1990; Leaver & Stryker, 1989; Snow, Met, & Genesee, 1989; Sudermann & Cisar, 1992).

This current movement of FL curricular reform is supported by a general understanding of L2 acquisition that suggests an L2 is learned most effectively in contexts that are personally meaningful and socially purposeful, that is, when meaning rather than form is a focus of instruction. But there is a danger in this line of thinking, as Sudermann and Cisar (1992) have cautioned in their critical appraisal of *foreign language across the curriculum* programs. Complex form-meaning relations may be reduced to dualistic or simplistic pedagogical formulas. The reduction has appeared, for example, in the long-standing debate over the value of phonics or whole language in reading instruction or more recently the product-process debate in writing instruction. When two seemingly oppositional views are put forth, there appear voices to admonish extremism, calling for a more balanced, integrated stance as seen in the interactive model of reading instruction (Carrell, Devine, & Eskey, 1988), the "balanced and flexible literacy diet" (Willows, 1996), and the "middle ground" approach to writing instruction advocated by, for example, Arndt (1987), Connor (1987), or Raimes (1985). For the development of balanced FL curricula that place importance on form *and* meaning and language learning *and* non-language learning objectives, I (So, 1994) have suggested that integration of language and non-language goals might be realized successfully through Miller's (Miller, 1988, 1993; Miller, Cassie, & Drake, 1990) holistic curriculum model consisting of three overlapping components of transmission (corresponding to the scientific-technical orientation to curriculum), transaction (the hermeneutic), and transformation (the emancipatory).

Ideologies in FL education are changing progressively and expanding. The purpose, content, and rationale of the FL curriculum are in transition accordingly—from foci on the mechanical learning of linguistic forms isolated from context, to emphases on the meaningful, communicative use of language, and to aims of broadening learners' visions and perspectives. Alongside these curricular shifts is the restructuring of the conception of different modes of language skills such as speaking, listening, reading, and writing. Instead of looking at them as separable skills, their integrality is highlighted. The recent increased and renewed attention to the integrated approach to FL instruction, which of course includes the writing component, is unprecedented. Composition writing is now seen as "a major component of foreign language (FL) instruction, whatever the pedagogical orientation" (Koda, 1993, p. 332). In view of these recent trends in FL curricular orientations, my present inquiry, firmly situated in the educational context, examines form-meaning relations as experienced by one FL learner engaged in the production of compositions in his target language and as perceived by readers evaluating FL texts.

COLIN AS A JFL WRITER

Colin Chan belongs to one typical group of students found in many of North American college classrooms of the Japanese language. He is a Chinese immigrant living in Canada with some education in his native Hong Kong. He is fluent in spoken and written Chinese and English. At the time of this study he was pursuing a bachelor's degree in Japanese Studies from a major Anglophone university in Canada. I have chosen Colin's *tale* (Van Maanen, 1988) to include here, but not the tales of the other twelve participants in the original study (So, 1997), because of his unique approach to teacher-assigned writing tasks. My tale about Colin's JFL writing is divided according to Biggs's presage-process-product model of classroom learning (Biggs, 1991; Biggs & Moore, 1993).

Presage

Colin was rated *intermediate-mid* on the Japanese Speaking Test (Center for Applied Linguistics, 1992) and considered his Japanese in all skills to be poorer than that of his classmates. Colin, however, had a unique view of writing. Writing was an essential means for him to make his thinking clear. He compared the process of composing a piece of writing to that of "playing a jigsaw puzzle"[3] as both seek for a coherent whole. This process, according to Colin, is valid in any kind of writing including course assignments of JFL writing.

Concerning specific problems of writing in Japanese, he spoke of the importance of "getting into the logic of the Japanese mind and seeing things from the Japanese point of view" by "getting exposed to and absorbing the way Japanese people deal with a particular topic and present it in writing." This is, as Colin said, "like falling into the sea of Japanese culture." He continued, "There you can pick up words and expressions in the way Japanese people use naturally."

Being an intermediate-level learner of Japanese, Colin saw language use as "a major barrier" in his production of Japanese essays. But he took this fact calmly and confidently, saying, "Right now I am not at the stage where one can use language like a native but this situation cannot last forever . . . When I read, I try to assimilate the Japanese language, give myself to it, and be friendly to it instead of struggling with it." Such remarks by Colin about

Japanese language learning are suggestive of his unique approach to language and language learning.

To Colin, an experienced—but not professional—writer in his L1 (Chinese), writing in any languages is a culture-bound, meaning-making activity. He wanted to write something in Japanese that "could move the Japanese reader." Creating a piece of writing that "is coherent and well thought-out," as his Japanese instructor spoke of his Japanese writing, was probably an integral part of Colin's conscious and subconscious knowledge. The JFL writing assignments provided Colin with opportunities to "think how to match the content with linguistic expressions" of Japanese.

Process

Concurrent think-aloud protocol data were collected from Colin working on two separate Japanese writing assignments given by his teacher on two different occasions during the year-long Japanese reading and writing course (see So, 1997 for the procedures of collecting and analyzing these data). Table 1 shows how much of his attention Colin focused on each of the four mutually exclusive aspects of writing—gist, discourse organization, language use, and writing procedures—while composing.

Table 1.   A Summary of Colin's Think-Aloud Protocol Data

JFL writing task	Gist (%)	Discourse organization (%)	Language use (%)	Writing procedures (%)
I	76	14	4	10
II	66	5	17	14

Colin, an experienced writer with the intermediate level of proficiency in Japanese, attended much more frequently to gist as he wrote. Much less attention was devoted to the other aspects. Colin's comments given right after the completion of one of the writing tasks help to enhance our understanding of his writing process. He said, "Although it took only a short period of time to finish writing the assignment, important ideas were generated during a long period of time. Extensive preparation before the writing process was required." Obviously he expended quite a bit of mental energy on shaping ideas for the teacher-assigned JFL compositions.

On the other hand, this intermediate-proficient student's very few verbalizations about language issues are curious. It is probable that although he was referring to the processes of idea generation at a pre-writing stage (which were not tape-recorded) in the aforementioned comments and the idea generation might have been done in his L1, he could have been thinking, consciously or subconsciously, about Japanese expressions that would fit the generated ideas—as Cumming's (1989) Francophone expert writers with varying degrees of English proficiency did while writing essays in English—during the "long period of extensive preparation." Because of such preparation, language issues may not have come to the fore of his consciousness for verbalizations during the actual taping.

Product

How would Colin's intensive engagement in content generation and refinement during the production of his Japanese compositions manifest itself in written texts? His texts were assessed by two independent readers for the three major components of content, organization, and language use according to the scoring criteria adapted from Hamp-Lyons's 9-point scale (Hamp-Lyons, 1991a; see So, 1997 for a more detailed description of text assessment). Table 2 provides a summary of assessment results including the comments the readers jotted down voluntarily while doing the assessment.

Table 2.   A Summary of Colin's Essay Scores and Comments

JFL Writing Task	Rater	Content	Organization	Language Use	Comments
I	A	5	4	4.5	The points are not clearly explained. Cryptic.
	B	3	2	2	Grammar is alright up to the clause level. But beyond that level there are too many mistakes that obscure the writer's intended meaning.
II	A	5	6	5	The essay could have been a lot better if the last paragraph were further developed.
	B	9	9	7.5	Very powerful, persuasive.

Note. The maximum score for each dimension is 9 points.

The same reader tended to rate the essay's three aspects similarly. Where there was a difference between the three component scores, it was only between 0.5 and 1.5 points. According to Jacobs, Zinkgraf, Wormuth, Harfiel, and Hughey (1981), this implies that the writer has acquired, in the reader's judgment, "approximately the same mastery level in all aspects of the composition" and that "each cog [aspect] in the machinery of discourse is interacting appropriately with other elements" (p. 32). This result, along with both readers' comments on the Task I essay, certainly speaks to the delicate interplay of form and meaning manifested in the text and in the mind of a reader evaluating that text. As Hamp-Lyons (1991b) states, different facets of writing "are not independent but are interwoven throughout the text, so that readers' judgments of one facet are influenced by the quality of others" (p. 247).

The vast differences in Reader B's scores for the Task I and the Task II essay, which were written at two different times but at an interval of only a couple of weeks, are rather unusual; yet they are revealing. Because the reader was not aware that the two essays were written by the same writer, Reader B was most likely focusing simply on the text, not on who might have written it. The occurrence of halo effect is highly probable with Rater B's rating of the Task II essay; the much higher score given to the essay's language use could be due to its "very powerful, persuasive" (in Reader B's words) content. On the other hand, "too many [grammatical] mistakes" (also in Reader B's words) in the Task I essay must have made Reader B give a very low score to the essay's language use component, which might have interfered with her evaluating the quality of its content properly and led her to rate it very low.

Colin's two essays were later evaluated exclusively from an ideational perspective, applying the SOLO (Structure of the Observed Language Outcome) taxonomy (Biggs & Collis, 1982; Biggs & Moore, 1993; see also So, 1997 for a detailed explanation) designed to assess the cognitive structural complexity of students' written texts. Two other readers were asked to read the text as a semantic representation, thus focusing on meaning and ignoring grammatical or lexical errors inasmuch as they would not bring the resulting text to the point of unintelligibility. This meaning-focused assessment attested to the superior quality of Colin's ideational thinking during the production of JFL written discourse.

Summary

The form-meaning interplay is inexplicably complex and subtle. Meaning can be conveyed only through the "*surface structure* [italics in the original] of language" (Smith, 1994, p. 49) or its physical, observable properties. Deficiency in the language (Japanese in this case) skill is sure to affect the meaning conveyed, and thus its readability. The reverse is true, too. The accurate and fluent use of language can boost the readability of an essay, making its content look more sophisticated or complex than it actually is.

The issue can no longer be left to philosophical arguments alone. In reality, new traditions of FL curricula are demanding that classroom teachers, at all levels of proficiency, focus on the development of not just all modes of language use but thinking skills. Research programs that produce educationally relevant results and that meet these practitioners' current needs are much needed. Considering that there has simply not been enough theoretically motivated research going on involving any aspects of FL education or FL writing in particular (Reichelt, 1999), I chose to pursue a promising idea across a range of topics about and types of inquiry into FL writing, following "inductive research" orientations (Nunan, 1992, p. 13). The study described below addresses the question of how the form-meaning interplay takes place in the mind of the FL composition reader.

EVALUATION OF JFL COMPOSITIONS

The above exploratory case study of Colin's JFL writing suggests that when the multiple-trait scoring procedure is used, it is difficult, or even inappropriate (Jacobs et al., 1981), for the reader to evaluate the content independent of the language use and vice versa. When the single-trait procedure focusing just on the content is employed, however, the same content may be evaluated quite differently. In reality the former is often favored, regardless of assessment purpose, for it "possesses psychometric properties that enhance the reliability of single number scores built from its components" (Hamp-Lyons, 1991b, p. 252) and because it provides diagnostic information highlighting areas of strength and weakness (Hamp-Lyons, 1991b; Jacobs et al., 1981).

Another part of the reality is that composition raters, who are usually FL teachers themselves, have received little or no training in writing instruction and assessment. I would then ask "Can such teacher raters make significant distinctions between content and language of the text so that they may be able to provide specific feedback on different aspects of writing separately?" or more specifically, "Can they base their decisions on global, meaning-related criteria despite the presence of surface errors in lexicogrammar of the text?" The importance of these questions becomes obvious and urgent as the new paradigm of language teaching that broadens its content range significantly forges ahead.

Design of the Study

The study reported in this section was designed to determine if JFL teacher raters would be influenced by grammatical errors in the Japanese essays written by JFL college students. To determine this, two versions—one exactly as originally written and the other with surface-level morphosyntactic errors corrected—of 23 JFL essays were given to two JFL teacher raters using a multiple-trait scoring instrument.

Participants and the Writing Task

A group of 23 students enrolled in the fourth-semester Japanese course (or Intermediate Japanese II) were asked to write a composition in Japanese on the most memorable vacation or trip they had had in recent years. They were encouraged to give as detailed a description as possible and explain what made the vacation or trip memorable. They were told that their compositions would not be graded but read for the purpose of diagnosing their Japanese writing abilities and that results of the diagnosis would be provided to them individually together with advice for improving their Japanese writing skills. The entire 50-minute class period in the first week of the semester was devoted to this diagnostic writing test. The use of dictionaries or reference books was not permitted in this writing task. One sheet of legal-size paper with horizontal lines from the top to the bottom on both sides was provided for the student to write on. Most students used a pencil to write and wrote the entire front page and some portion of the back page. No one left the classroom before the class ended and all worked on the task until the last minute.

In the Japanese program that offers the course in question, language courses become progressively content-based from elementary- to advanced-level and the acquisition of spoken as well as written language skills are emphasized from the very beginning. Intermediate Japanese II can be viewed as a transitional course whose instructional focus moves gradually from language to content so that students may be sufficiently prepared for the next level of more content-centered course. This is also the course where teachers must be able to assess learners' development in language use and content generation separately so as to maximize the effect of instruction. Students' texts written at different points in time during the course would be examined employing the same methodology; however, the present report concerns only the ones written at the very beginning of the course.

Raters and the Instrument

Two independent raters were selected who possess characteristics typical of instructors often found in Japanese language classrooms in North America. Both Yuka and Kyoko (both pseudonyms), native female speakers of Japanese, received undergraduate education in Japan; Yuka studied Japanese literature and Kyoko early childhood education. Yuka, in her late thirties, had taught Japanese to nonnative speakers in Japan for several years before moving to the United States for a family reason. Yuka had just begun teaching one of the advanced-level courses in the Japanese program of the present research site when she agreed to participate in the study as a rater. Kyoko, in her late twenties, lacked the teaching experience that Yuka had. However, Kyoko's enthusiasm about teaching JFL was impressive. Upon her arrival in the United States, she enrolled in a couple of graduate courses on FL teaching, often observed JFL classes in the aforementioned program, participated in a JFL research project as an assistant, and volunteered frequently to assist or teach college and high school JFL classes when she was needed. The raters had had no personal contact with any of the students involved and no information on the students was disclosed for ethical and halo effect considerations. Neither Yuka nor Kyoko received any training in writing instruction or assessment.

The writing assessment scale for the MELAB (Hamp-Lyons, 1991b, pp. 268–269), which was used to assess the students' JFL compositions to obtain diagnostic information, was adopted for the purpose of the present study. The MELAB (Michigan English Language Assessment Battery) was developed to test the level of English proficiency of nonnative speakers wishing to attend college or university in the United States. Considering apparent differences (in languages involved, purposes, tasks, writing conditions, etc.) between the MELAB and my research context, the application of the MELAB scale to the assessment of intermediate-level JFL essays may seem problematic. On my examination of the instrument, however, I found the criteria or scoring guides fairly general and appropriate for the assessment of the JFL compositions used for the present study. It certainly remains to be seen if the MELAB writing scale is a valid measure in assessment contexts different from that for which the instrument was designed.

The MELAB contains six component scales, each focusing on an important aspect of composition and weighted a maximum of 10 points: topic development, organization, connections, sentence structure, vocabulary, and mechanics. The total weight of 10 points for each dimension is broken down into 10 levels from 1 point (the poorest) to 10 points (the best). These levels are characterized and differentiated by descriptors representing specific criteria of mastery levels. The component of mechanics was disregarded because the essays in both versions were typewritten before they were given to the raters to avoid the possibility of confusing textual appearance with the quality of what is said and how it is said in the text (Carlson, 1991, p. 308).

Procedures

The assessment took place at two different times, rating the edited version first then the unedited version four and a half months later. Prior to the first assessment, I met with Yuka and Kyoko separately for about an hour each time, handing them a packet containing the coded and randomly-sequenced essays to be assessed and copies of the rating scale, explaining the rating scale and procedure, doing a practice assessment with an intermediate-level JFL composition not included in the packet, and answering any questions posed by the rater. I made certain that both raters had the same understanding and interpretation of such terms as "simple sentence structure," "complex sentence structure," and "connection" and such descriptors as "awkward," "many errors," and "broad vocabulary" as they appear in the rating scale. Only when I could be sure of the rater's relatively high level of confidence in carrying out this task, was she dismissed from the meeting.

The raters were encouraged to contact me for any further questions as they might arise; however, no such contact was made. Yuka and Kyoko proceeded to assess the given essays independently and without my presence. They did not know each other, nor were they told that the two raters were involved in the study. Thus, it is fair to believe that no discussion took place between the two concerning the rating. Furthermore, they were not informed of the purpose of this study until both assessment tasks were completed for fear that the raters' knowledge of it would affect their approach to the assessment tasks negatively.

When they were done with the first assessment, all the materials including unused extra sheets of scoring paper were returned to me personally and a brief meeting was held at which they shared with me their feelings and experience with the assessment task. I was assured of their competence in doing this task through the meeting. The packet for the second assessment was not given to them until the scheduled time. Yuka and Kyoko followed the same steps to carry out the second assessment. Between the two tasks they were much occupied with many other daily commitments. I hoped that this would leave little room in their memory capacities for them to remember any parts of the essays they had read in the edited version and that it would eliminate the possibility of the rater carrying over her judgment on the quality of an edited version to that of an unedited version of the same essay.

Analysis and Results

Table 3 shows means and standard deviations of the scores given to the five dimensions by the two raters. Once the general picture—indicating slightly higher scores for most of the dimensions of the edited essays—is obtained with these descriptive statistics, I decided to subject the rating data to two sets of paired *t*-tests—one for edited and unedited essays separately, comparing the two readers, and the other for the two readers separately, comparing edited and unedited essays.

Table 3.   Means and Standard Deviations of the Two Readers' Scores for Edited and Unedited Essays

Dimension		Edited Essays[a]		Unedited Essays[a]	
		Yuka	Kyoko	Yuka	Kyoko
Topic Development					
	M	6.09	5.98	5.76	5.85
	SD	1.25	.96	1.25	1.00
Organization					
	M	5.87	6.09	6.00	6.00
	SD	.92	.90	.90	1.10
Connections					
	M	6.09	5.91	5.87	6.00
	SD	1.08	.89	.87	.95
Sentence Structure					
	M	5.30	6.15	5.11	5.83
	SD	.93	1.21	.78	1.21
Vocabulary					
	M	5.52	6.26	5.35	5.93
	SD	1.16	.69	.98	.84

Note. The maximum score for each dimension is 10 points.
[a] $n = 23$.

Results of the *t*-tests comparing Yuka and Kyoko's scores for the edited and unedited essays, shown in Table 4, conclude that the two readers differ significantly on their ratings of *sentence structure* and *vocabulary* of both edited and unedited essays but not on the other measures. Differences in their scores for the aspects of language use may have something to do with different degrees of familiarity that Yuka and Kyoko have with nonnative speakers' use of language (cf. Schoonen, Vergeer, & Eiting, 1997). In rating the quality of nonnative speakers' language use, readers have to have explicit intuitions on what is appropriate and expectable language. Yuka, an experienced JFL teacher, might possess this kind of metalinguistic awareness, which could guide her rating process. Kyoko, on the other hand, lacking in such experience, might have looked at JFL students' use of language quite differently than Yuka.

The rating of content-related elements was probably less disputable because texts the students had to write were relatively simple, limited, and more or less countable, thus leaving little room for any obvious discrepancies to occur between the more and less experienced JFL teachers' ratings.

Table 4.   Paired *t*-Test Statistics Comparing the Two Readers' Scores for Edited and Unedited Essays

Dimension	Edited Essays[a]	Unedited Essays[a]
Topic Development	−.43	.40
Organization	1.02	.00
Connections	−.58	.60
Sentence Structure	3.53[**]	3.45[**]
Vocabulary	3.68[**]	2.93[**]

Note. [a]$n = 23$. [**]$p < .01$.

At any rate, similar results obtained for the edited and unedited essays attest to the consistent patterns of the two readers' rating behavior unaffected by the presence or absence of surface errors in language use.

Table 5 shows results of the *t*-tests comparing each reader's scores for the edited and unedited essays. None of Yuka's or Kyoko's scores for the edited and unedited essays differed significantly. Thus, it can be concluded that for both Yuka and Kyoko, editing made no difference in the evaluations. The readers rating intermediate-level JFL compositions were not unduly influenced by the presence of surface errors. Similar findings have been reported in other assessment studies with academic essays written by ESL students matriculated in American colleges or universities (Carlisle & McKenna, 1991; Santos, 1988).

Table 5.   Paired *t*-Test Statistics Comparing Each Reader's Scores for Edited and Unedited Essays

Dimension	Yuka	Kyoko
Topic Development	1.57	.67
Organization	−.83	.43
Connections	1.00	−.36
Sentence Structure	1.04	1.57
Vocabulary	.75	1.74

Note. Twenty-three edited and 23 unedited essays were rated by each rater.

CONCLUSIONS

The two studies reported in this chapter are necessarily exploratory, rather than confirmatory, by nature and due to their limited sample size. Colin's case suggests that FL writing can be more than just writing a foreign language. Colin, despite his limited proficiency in Japanese, was able to demonstrate many of the competent writing behaviors characteristic of FL writers with near-native proficiency (So, 1997) or FL writers with professional writing expertise in L1 (Cumming, 1989). His compositions were highly evaluated for the depth of thinking underlying the content. This particular case dismisses the "foreign language effect" that "refers to a temporary decline in the thinking ability of people who are using a foreign language in which they are less proficient than in their own native language" (Takano & Noda, 1995, p. 658). According to Takano and Noda, because working memory is limited, one cannot easily concentrate on the more abstract levels of meaning or semantic integrity until the processing of the lower, subordinate levels (e.g., orthographics, word choice, within-sentence grammar) of discourse production has become automated (cf. automatic processing vs. controlled processing; see McLaughlin, 1987). This is to say, lack of skill in linguistic processing reduces one's capacity for ideational thinking.

While the presence of foreign language effect cannot be denied in any activity of FL discourse production, a case like Colin's lends support to the current movement of FL teaching that emphasizes meaning-making from early on. Colin's unique and sophisticated view of writing and his attitude toward the process of learning Japanese may be translated into elements of instruction in the effort to improve students' perceptions of FL writing and learning.

The major finding of the assessment study relevant to the present inquiry was: The FL teacher raters, regardless of their experiences, were able to discriminate the two general subscales of *content* and *language use* of FL texts without being unduly affected by surface-level, morphosyntactic errors. Judgment about *language use* appears to be more complex and may require experience and training if high reliability is desired. At any rate, the fact that the readers were able to focus on content despite the conspicuous presence of surface errors is encouraging as the new paradigm of meaning-focused FL pedagogy emerges.

Obviously more studies need to be done in order to link assessment research and pedagogy. One promising line of research would be documentation of "effective" teacher raters' thought processes in interpreting scoring criteria and evaluating essays (e.g., Carlisle & McKenna, 1991; Cumming, 1990; Vaughan, 1991). Also the research that takes into consideration such factors as the types of writing and rating tasks and the aspects of the text to be rated would be useful. Concurrently there must be an effort to create, examine, and revise a definition of "good writing" for a specific FL context. It is my hope that as research on FL writing assessment increases, it would inform us more about the way to improve teaching practices and their effects on students' learning to write meaningful content in the target language.

AUTHOR NOTE

I am grateful to Nicole Nazar for her expert assistance with the statistical analysis and the two readers who rated compositions for the assessment study reported here. I also thank "Colin," a participant in the case study also reported in this chapter, for his participation and kind permission to report his case.

Correspondence concerning this article should be addressed to Sufumi So, Department of Modern Languages, Baker Hall 160, Carnegie Mellon University, Pittsburgh, PA 15213-3890, or e-mailed to sufumi@andrew.cmu.edu.

NOTES

1. Presently so-called *second-language writing* can be considered, in its research practice and theory building, synonymous with academic writing in English as a second language. The present inquiry, which concerns writing in non-English foreign languages taught in college and university departments of languages and literatures, is intended to contribute to broadening the scope of second-language writing research and theory.

2. See Crandall (1993) and Crandall and Tucker (1990) for a comprehensive overview of content-centered language instruction. The former includes an annotated bibliography on the subject. Practical suggestions and guidelines for the implementation of content-centered instruction can be found in Mohan (1986) especially for ESL professionals, Brinton, Snow, and Wesche (1989) for L2 specialists at postsecondary academic institutions, and Cantoni-Harvey (1987) for elementary and secondary educators dealing with minority students. See also Adair-Hauck's (1996) strategies for the practical application of a whole language approach in L2 classrooms at the secondary and university levels, as well as the recent national movement in FL education in the United States known as *Standards for Foreign Language Learning* (National Standards in Foreign Language Education Project, 1999; Phillips & Terry, 1999).

3. This and other quotes in this section were taken from the transcripts of Colin's remarks during his interviews with me in English, unless indicated otherwise. The words are minimally edited for readability.

REFERENCES

Adair-Hauck, B. (1996). Practical whole language strategies for secondary and university-level FL students. *Foreign Language Annals, 29,* 253–270.

Arndt, V. (1987). Six writers in search of texts: A protocol-based study of L1 and L2 writing. *ELT Journal, 41,* 257–267.

Bereiter, C., & Scardamalia, M. (1987). *The psychology of written composition.* Hillsdale, NJ: Erlbaum.

Biggs, J.B. (1991). Enhancing learning in the context of school. In R.F. Mulcahy, R.H. Short, & J. Andrews (Eds.), *Enhancing learning and thinking* (pp. 35–52). New York: Praeger.

Biggs, J.B., & Collis, K.F. (1982). *Evaluating the quality of learning: The SOLO Taxonomy (Structure of the Observed Learning Outcome).* New York: Academic Press.

Biggs, J.B., & Moore, P.J. (1993). *The process of learning* (3rd ed.). Sydney: Prentice-Hall.

Blok, H., & de Glopper, K. (1992). Large scale writing assessment. In L. Verhoeven & J.H.A.L. de Jong (Eds.), *The construct of language proficiency: Applications of psychological models to language assessment* (pp. 101–111). Amsterdam/Philadelphia: John Benjamins.

Brinton, D.M., Snow, M.A., & Wesche, M.B. (1989). *Content-based second language instruction.* New York: Newbury House.

Cantoni-Harvey, G. (1987). *Content-area language instruction: Approaches and strategies.* Reading, MA: Addison-Wesley.

Carlisle, R., & McKenna, E. (1991). Placement of ESL/EFL undergraduate writers in college-level writing programs. In L. Hamp-Lyons (Ed.), *Assessing second language writing in academic contexts* (pp.197–211). Norwood, NJ: Ablex.

Carlson, S.B. (1991). Program evaluation procedures: Reporting the program publicly within the political context. In L. Hamp-Lyons (Ed.), *Assessing second language writing in academic contexts* (pp. 293–320). Norwood, NJ: Ablex.

Carrell, P.L., Devine, J., & Eskey, D.E. (Eds.). (1988). *Interactive approaches to second language reading.* Cambridge: Cambridge University Press.

Center for Applied Linguistics. (1992). *Japanese Speaking Test.* Washington, DC: Author.

Connor, U. (1987). Research frontiers in writing analysis. *TESOL Quarterly, 21,* 677–696.

Crandall, J. (1993). Content-centered learning in the United States. *Annual Review of Applied Linguistics, 13,* 111–126.

Crandall, J., & Tucker, G.R. (1990). Content-based language instruction in second and foreign languages. In S. Anivan (Ed.), *Language teaching methodology for the nineties* (pp. 83–96). Singapore: SEAMEO Regional Language Centre.

Crawford-Lange, L.M., & Lange, D.L. (1987). Integrating language and culture: How to do it. *Theory Into Practice, 26,* 258–266.

Cumming, A. (1989). Writing expertise and second-language proficiency. *Language Learning, 39,* 81–141.

Cumming, A. (1990). Expertise in evaluating second language compositions. *Language Testing, 7,* 31–51.

Cummins, J. (1980). The cross-lingual dimensions of language proficiency: Implications for bilingual education and the optimal age issue. *TESOL Quarterly, 14,* 175–187.

Cummins, J., & Swain, M. (1986). *Bilingualism in education: Aspects of theory, research and practice.* London: Longman.

Davis, J.N. (1997). Educational reform and the Babel (babble) of culture: Prospects for the *Standards for Foreign Language Learning. Modern Language Journal, 81,* 151–163.

Dewey, J. (1938/1963). *Experience & education.* New York: Macmillan.

Dickson, P., & Cumming, A. (Eds.). (1996). *Profiles of language education in 25 countries: Overview of phase 1 of the IEA language education study.* Slough, England: National Foundation for Educational Research.

Freire, P. (1973). *Education for critical consciousness* (M.B. Ramos, Trans.). New York: Seabury Press.

Gaudiani, C. (1981). *Teaching writing in the foreign language curriculum.* Washington, DC: Center for Applied Linguistics.

Hamp-Lyons, L. (1991a). Reconstructing "academic writing proficiency." In L. Hamp-Lyons (Ed.), *Assessing second language writing in academic contexts* (pp. 127–153). Norwood, NJ: Ablex.

Hamp-Lyons, L. (1991b). Scoring procedures for ESL contexts. In L. Hamp-Lyons (Ed.), *Assessing second language writing in academic contexts* (pp. 241–276). Norwood, NJ: Ablex.

Jacobs, H.L., Zinkgraf, S.A., Wormuth, D.R., Hartfiel, V.F., & Hughey, J.B. (1981). *Testing ESL composition: A practical approach.* Rowley, MA: Newbury House.

Koda, K. (1993). Task-induced variability in FL composition: Language-specific perspectives. *Foreign Language Annals, 26,* 332–346.

Kubota, R. (1996). Critical pedagogy and critical literacy in teaching Japanese. *Japanese-Language Education Around the Globe, 6,* 35–48.

Lange, D.L. (1990). Sketching the crisis and exploring different perspectives in foreign language curriculum. In D.W. Birckbichler (Ed.), *New perspectives and new directions in foreign language education* (pp. 77–109). Lincolnwood, IL: National Textbook.

Lange, D.L. (1992). Foreign language education. In M.C. Alkin (Ed.), *Encyclopedia of educational research* (6th ed., pp. 521–530). New York: Macmillan.

Leaver, B.L., & Stryker, S.B. (1989). Content-based instruction in foreign language classrooms. *Foreign Language Annals, 22,* 269–275.

Littlejohn, A., & Windeatt, S. (1989). Beyond language learning: Perspectives on materials design. In R.K. Johnson (Eds.), *The second language curriculum* (pp. 155–175). Cambridge: Cambridge University Press.

Martin, J.R. (1997). Analysing genre: Functional parameters. In F. Christie & J.R. Martin (Eds.), *Genre and institutions: Social processes in the workplace and school* (pp. 3–39). London: Cassell.

McLaughlin, B. (1987). *Theories of second-language learning.* London: Edward Arnold.

Miller, J.P. (1988). *The holistic curriculum.* Toronto: OISE Press.

Miller, J.P. (1993). *The holistic teacher.* Toronto: OISE Press.

Miller, J.P., Cassie, J.R.B., & Drake, S.M. (1990). *Holistic learning: A teacher's guide to integrated studies.* Toronto: OISE Press.

Mohan, B.A. (1986). *Language and content.* Reading, MA: Addison-Wesley.

Moskowitz, G. (1978). *Caring and sharing in the foreign language class: A sourcebook on humanistic techniques.* Rowley, MA: Newbury House.

National Standards in Foreign Language Education Project. (1999). *Standards for foreign language learning in the 21st century.* Yonkers, NY: Author.

Nunan, D. (1988). *The learner-centred curriculum.* Cambridge: Cambridge University Press.

Nunan, D. (1992). *Research methods in language learning.* Cambridge: Cambridge University Press.

Phillips, J., & Terry, R.M. (Eds.). (1999). *Foreign language standards: Linking research, theories, and practices.* Lincolnwood, IL: National Textbook.

Raimes, A. (1985). What unskilled ESL students do as they write: A classroom study of composing. *TESOL Quarterly, 19,* 229–258.

Reichelt, M. (1999). Toward a more comprehensive view of L2 writing: Foreign language writing in the U.S. *Journal of Second Language Writing, 8,* 181–204.

Richards, J.C., & Nunan, D. (1992). Second language teaching and learning. In M.C. Alkin (Ed.), *Encyclopedia of educational research* (6th ed., pp. 1200–1208). New York: Macmillan.

Santos, T. (1988). Professors' reactions to the academic writing of nonnative-speaking students. *TESOL Quarterly, 22,* 69–90.

Schoonen, R., Vergeer, M., & Eiting, M. (1997). The assessment of writing ability: Expert readers versus lay readers. *Language Testing, 14,* 157–184.

Schubert, W.H. (1986). *Curriculum: Perspectives, paradigm, and possibility.* New York: Macmillan.

Smith, F. (1994). *Writing and the writer* (2nd ed.). Hillsdale, NJ: Erlbaum.

Snow, M.A., Met, M., & Genesee, F. (1989). A conceptual framework for the integration of language and content in second/foreign language instruction. *TESOL Quarterly, 23,* 201–217.

So, S. (1994). A holistic approach to foreign language curriculum. Unpublished manuscript, Ontario Institute for Studies in Education of the University of Toronto.

So, S. (1997). *Writing to make meaning or to learn the language? A descriptive study of multi-ethnic adults learning Japanese-as-a-foreign-language.* Unpublished doctoral dissertation, University of Toronto.

Stern, H.H. (1983a). *Fundamental concepts of language teaching.* Oxford: Oxford University Press.

Stern, H.H. (1983b). Toward a multidimensional foreign language curriculum. In R.G. Mead (Ed.), *Foreign languages: Key links in the chain of learning* (pp. 120–146). Middlebury, VT: Northeast Conference on the Teaching of Foreign Languages.

Stern, H.H. (1992). *Issues and options in language teaching* (edited by P. Allen & B. Harley). Oxford: Oxford University Press.

Stevick, E.W. (1990). *Humanism in language teaching.* Oxford: Oxford University Press.

Sudermann, D.P., & Cisar, M.A. (1992). Foreign language across the curriculum: A critical appraisal. *Modern Language Journal, 76,* 295–308.

Takano, Y., & Noda, A. (1995). Interlanguage dissimilarity enhances the decline of thinking ability during foreign language processing. *Language Learning, 45,* 657–681.

Van Maanen, J. (1988). *Tales of the field: On writing ethnography.* Chicago: University of Chicago Press.

Vaughan, C. (1991). Holistic assessment: What goes on in the rater's mind? In L. Hamp-Lyons (Ed.), *Assessing second language writing in academic contexts* (pp. 111–125). Norwood, NJ: Ablex.

Willows, D. (1996, November). The balanced and flexible literacy diet: A teacher education system for improving literacy levels. Paper presented at the Human Development and Applied Psychology Research Colloquium, Ontario Institute for Studies in Education of the University of Toronto.

CHAPTER 7

ELECTRONIC MESSAGE BOARDS IN THE FOREIGN LANGUAGE CLASSROOM:

LINKING LEARNERS AND LITERACY

Rebecca L. Chism

ABSTRACT

The goal of the present study is to investigate the use of the electronic message board and its potential for the foreign language classroom. This study finds its theoretical basis in sociocultural theory, which holds that learning occurs through meaningful interactions with one's environment and the people within it (Wertsch, 1998).

The present study considers the research question: does the electronic message board provide a viable alternative to face-to-face conversation? Students from a third-semester French class discussed short stories in the L2 via the electronic message board as well as face-to-face. A comparison of recall protocol scores from both formats was used to ascertain the effectiveness of the board regarding the comprehension of foreign language literary text. The study then draws conclusions based on the scores and offers recommendations for the use of the electronic message board in the foreign language classroom.

INTRODUCTION

The use of technology in the foreign language curriculum has been a central theme amongst educators and researchers in the latter half of the twentieth century and at the beginning of the twenty-first. As a result, contemporary foreign language classrooms have the opportunity to incorporate a variety of software tools designed to enhance various methods of instruction and provide immediate access to information and interaction.

The possible uses of computer technology in foreign and second language learning have been documented in studies on interactive and assistant software (Chávez, 1997; Masters-Wicks, Postlewate, & Lewental, 1996; Nagata, 1993), authoring software (Arneil & Holmes, 1999; Martínez-Lage, 1997), multimedia software (Borrás & Lafayette, 1994; Hong, 1997; Lyman-Hager, 1995; Vignola, Kenny, Schilz, Andrews, & Covert, 1998), the Internet and the World Wide Web (Beaudoin, 1998; Charrière & Magnin, 1998; Lee, 1997; Oliva & Pollastrini, 1995; Walz, 1998), distance learning (Davis, 1988; Glisan, Dudt, & Howe, 1998; Moore & Thompson, 1997; Warriner-Burke, 1990; Yi & Magima, 1993), and web pages and hyperlinks (Davis & Lyman-Hager, 1997; Feustle, 1997).

More recently, researchers are focusing on the potential of computer technology as a means of communication in the second and foreign language classroom. Computer mediated communication research first emerged in the mid-1980s and continues to grow in light of the overwhelming use and popularity of such technologies in everyday life. More and more, researchers are considering how best to implement these tools in the classroom. For instance, Oliva and Pollastrini (1995) and Warschauer, Turbee, and Roberts (1996) reported findings of greater student autonomy, greater equality in the classroom, a movement from teacher-centered to student-centered learning activities, and improved learning skills with the use of computer mediated communication in the second and foreign language classroom.

The most popular, and most researched, of the computer mediated forums used in the second and foreign language classroom is electronic mail, or e-mail. Electronic mail provides a means for students to exchange correspondence and develop relationships with teachers, peers, and native speakers. Barson, Frommer, and Schwartz (1993) described and analyzed their five-year inter-university experiment using electronic mail for communication purposes in intermediate college French courses. In their study, they noticed the development of real interpersonal relationships that first began via electronic mail but continued well beyond the end of the academic year. This suggests that online communication can serve as an authentic and meaningful forum for the development of interpersonal relationships.

Electronic mail can be accessed either synchronously or asynchronously, with the latter being the most common. Another means of synchronous communication is electronic conferencing, also referred to as a chat. Synchronous communication permits students to participate in virtual conversations, or what Beauvois (1992) calls "conversation in slow motion" (p. 455). While these conversations occur in real time, they also afford users an opportunity to contemplate their message before sending it. Kroonenberg (1994/1995) found this to be the case when using electronic mail synchronously for high school French students as a discussion forum. Students were able to practice and reflect on their interaction and their discourse was found to be more expressive and enriched (pp. 26–27).

Electronic communication also has the particular feature of alleviating the immediate demands of face-to-face conversations, reducing what MacIntyre and Gardner (1991) refer to as "communication apprehension anxiety" (p. 103). Chun (1994), Kern (1995), and Warschauer (1996) noted that students produce more target language output in computer mediated communications environments than in traditional oral classroom discussions.

While most of the research has focused on electronic mail, other forms of computer mediated communication have been largely ignored, particularly the electronic message board. The electronic message board allows multiple users to engage in either synchronous or asynchronous conversation while retaining the text as discussion threads, a unique feature that may prove to be a useful pedagogical tool for the second and foreign language classroom.

Given the possible uses of the electronic message board, the goal of this study is to investigate how the electronic message board can be applied for the purpose of reading comprehension. For this study, students were asked to construct the meaning of the text either via the message board or, as a point of comparison, through face-to-face discussion. They then were asked to reconstruct the story individually through a recall protocol. A recall protocol consists of participants either writing or verbalizing in their first language everything that they are able to remember of the second language text after having read it. The recall protocol is considered a standard means of measuring reading comprehension and is often used in second and foreign language research (Bernhardt, 1991; Horiba, Van Den Broek, & Fletcher, 1993; Lee, 1986; Swaffar, Arens, & Byrnes, 1991). In this manner, the recall protocol will be used as a means by which to measure comprehension of the literary passage and will add to the overall evaluation of the effectiveness of the electronic message board.

The activity of having students discuss and construct the meaning of foreign language literary texts was selected for several reasons. First, reading comprehension is an activity that warrants continuous study, particularly at the beginning levels of second and foreign language learning. Also, given the interpretive nature of reading comprehension, the activity would provide many opportunities for meaning construction on the part of the participants. In addition, since many foreign language learners may be intimidated by foreign language reading, the social forum offered by the electronic message board could provide an opportunity for learners to work together.

Allowing learners to engage actively in meaningful discussions of literary text via the electronic message board may have profound implications for the way reading is taught in the foreign language classroom. With the opportunities that technology provides, group discussions that once occurred face-to-face are now able to occur in an electronic format. Given this potential, it is the goal of the present study to determine if the electronic format constitutes a real and viable alternative to face-to-face discussions for the purposes of comprehending foreign language literary text. While the discussions themselves offer insights into the activity of meaning construction, the present study will concentrate primarily on measuring the level of comprehension as determined by recall protocols. The nature of the discourse itself and how it was used by the participants during the activity is intended for a future study.

THEORETICAL FRAMEWORK

The present study is grounded in sociocultural theory which posits that learning is a socially-constructed phenomenon and that it is singular and unique to its participants (Donato & Adair-Hauck, 1992; Rogoff, 1990; Tharpe & Gallimore, 1988; Wertsch, 1985). Through interaction and communication, a community of learners construct meaning that is relevant to their particular situation. Sociocultural theory acknowledges the construction of meaning as a process, thus providing a more comprehensive understanding of the use of the electronic message board as a forum of discussion. Unlike other forms of computer technologies in the second and foreign language classroom, computer mediated communication is inherently a social tool; thus, sociocultural theory provides the appropriate framework from which to investigate the electronic message board as a forum of negotiation between learners.

THE STUDY

The present study explores the overriding research question: how does the use of the electronic message board compare to the use of face-to-face discussion? More specifically, what do the recall protocols reveal about comprehension attained through use of the electronic message board as compared to comprehension attained through the use of face-to-face discussion? By examining the recall protocols as a measure of comprehension, the present study will provide detailed evidence of the effectiveness of the electronic message board as a forum of meaning construction.

Subjects and Materials

The subjects were approximately sixteen undergraduates from a third-semester introductory French language course taught during a six-week summer session at a large state university. A series of surveys was used to determine the profile of the participants in the study. These surveys consisted of modified Likert scale questions as well as open-ended questions. These surveys addressed language background and experience, reading and memory skills, attitudes toward and use of computers, and familiarity with French literature. After the subjects had the opportunity to participate in both the face-to-face and electronic message board discussions, they filled out an exit survey to express their reaction to the use of the electronic message board as a forum for discussing foreign language literary passages.

The material used for discussion consisted of two different authentic literary texts. The two passages are from an anthology titled *Nouvelles lectures libres*. This anthology is commonly used in both third and fourth year high school French courses as well as by introductory and intermediate college French courses. The two passages selected from the anthology were *La Vierge aux oiseaux* by Jérôme and Jean Tharaud (Appendix A) and Part One of *La parure* by Guy de Maupassant (Appendix B). *La Vierge aux oiseaux*, tells the story of the Virgin Mary who, with her infant, is fleeing the soldiers of King Herod. The second passage, Part One of *La parure*, tells the story of a pretty and charming girl who marries a clerk, but aspires to an upper class life. These texts, although varied in length, were determined to be fairly equal in difficulty as corroborated by the mean average analysis, which will be discussed later in this study.

The group using the electronic message board for discussion purposes accessed the literary material on a private access web site. This was done as a matter of convenience for the participants since they were able to access both the web site and the electronic message board at the same time and in the same manner. For those discussing the literary passage face-to-face, the literary text was presented in a paper format, which was collected at the end of the exercise.

The electronic message board discussions took place at the computer facility located in the Language Learning Centre of the Department of Modern Languages and Linguistics. The Language Learning Centre consists of two labs with thirty computers each. The computers used by the students were upgraded three years ago to accommodate multimedia software. Every student had individual access to a computer and was able to select his or her seating within the facility. The electronic message board was established by using *Discus*, a free World Wide Web discussion board software package. More than 30,000 Internet sites are currently using *Discus*. Its zero cost, accessibility, management capacities, and popularity were factors in its selection for this study. Also, the simple installation and easy use of *Discus* minimized any technical concerns about its implementation and use.

Procedure

The participants gave permission for their involvement in the study with an informed consent form, which indicated that they had the option to stop participation at any time during the course of the project. They were told that while their participation would be valuable for the purposes of the study, it would have no effect on their grade. The subjects completed a background information form which elicited information regarding language background and experience as well as reading and memory skills. The subjects also completed surveys detailing their attitudes toward and use of computers and familiarity with foreign language text. In addition, the participants also filled out a form to indicate their preferred user name and password in order to establish a confidential account for the electronic message board.

After the subjects completed the surveys, the researcher/instructor, a nonnative speaker of French with native-like fluency and extensive teaching and research experience, gave the students an orientation session on the computer lab and the use of the electronic message board. First, students received a handout describing how to create French accents on the computer and were given an opportunity to experiment with this. This portion of the orientation was included in order to assist anyone who chose to use French for the activity. However, it is important to note that, although the orientation was conducted in English, no attempt was made to enforce the use of French or of English as the dialogue tool in this exercise. This decision was made in accordance with the definition of activity theory, which stipulates that all decisions regarding the course of the activity are to be made by the subjects (Wertsch, 1979). Activity, within the constructs of sociocultural theory, provides the context for how language is used. Thus, since the activity used for this study focused primarily on comprehension, language serves as the tool to orient to the activity, to engage in negotiation of meaning, and to complete the exercise.

The next portion of the orientation session introduced the subjects to the message board itself. The researcher/instructor demonstrated how to access the board, how to initiate a new conversation, and how to respond to a posting. In addition, the researcher/instructor showed the subjects how to manipulate the screen so they could simultaneously view multiple windows in a half-screen format. The subjects then had the opportunity to engage in a non-academic discussion in order to become accustomed to the operations of the board as well as to resolve any difficulties involved with its use. This discussion began with the question, "What do you think of this message board?" All participants had the opportunity to post responses and engaged in the discussion until they were able to post and respond with no difficulty and did not require any assistance from the researcher/ instructor or the staff throughout the exercise.

The day after the computer orientation, the discussion of the first literary text, *La Vierge aux oiseaux* took place. The researcher/instructor divided the group of sixteen into four subgroups, each with four members. These groups were identified as Group 1, Group 2, Group 3, and Group 4. Students were assigned to groups based on information gleaned from the surveys intended to evenly distribute skills and abilities across the four groups. This division can be characterized as purposeful, since the formation of groups was considered essential for the exploration of the collective use of the electronic message board (Krathwohl, 1998, p. 173). The composition of the groups remained the same throughout the course of the study.

Two of the subgroups were assigned to use the electronic message board for their discussion while the other two subgroups were assigned to engage in face-to-face discussion. Both the face-to-face and the message board groups were instructed to ascertain the meaning of the given literary passage. The question posed to the message board users consisted of the following: "What is your understanding of this story? Working with your classmates, please post your reconstruction of the story to your assigned message board. Feel free to post as many responses as you would like." The question posed to the face-to-face groups was similar in context: "What is your understanding of this story? Working with your classmates, please discuss your reconstruction of the story."

Both the face-to-face and the message board groups were also asked not to use any additional resources other than their classmates, to use any outside material, or to take notes. The researcher/instructor gave this instruction in order to observe how students would discuss and collaboratively construct the meaning of a given text. Each of the two face-to-face subgroups used audiotape recorders to record their discussions, which were later transcribed. The computer retained the discussion from each of the two subgroups using the message board; therefore, no transcription was necessary. Both the face-to-face and the message board subgroups had approximately a half hour to engage in the activity.

After all the subgroups had the opportunity to discuss the literary passage, they were asked to individually write a recall protocol in English detailing their understanding of the story. The recall protocol was used to measure the students' overall comprehension of the literary passage.

The following week, the same procedure was used for a discussion of *La parure*, only this time the two subgroups who had engaged in a face-to-face discussion of the first literary passage were assigned to the electronic message board, and vice versa. The use of an intersubject alternating design was adopted for several reasons. First, it ensured a more realistic comparison of the use of the electronic message board with face-to-face conversation and was employed to help answer the research question: what do the messages reveal about comprehension attained through use of the electronic message board as compared to the use of face-to-face discussion? Also, the use of an intersubject alternating design enabled the researcher/ instructor to better observe how the same groups comprehended using either the message board or the face-to-face forum. In addition, this design gave subjects the opportunity to participate in both discussion formats, thus allowing them to better assess the use of the electronic message board as a medium with which to discuss foreign language literary text. The discussion of the text and the recall protocol activity proceeded as previously described, with Table 1 explaining the overall procedure.

Table 1.   Procedure

Text	Face-to-Face	Message Board
La Vierge aux oiseaux	Group 1, 2	Group 3, 4
La parure	Group 3, 4	Group 1, 2

After the two sessions, all participants completed an exit survey that was used to assess student attitudes and commentary on the activity and the two formats in which it took place. The results of this assessment will be reported in a subsequent study.

The Results

For each of the two stories, the subjects of both the face-to-face and the message board groups participated in a recall protocol immediately after their discussion. For the recall protocols, the subjects wrote everything that they were able to remember of the French language text in English. Through recall protocols, that which has been understood on the part of the reader can be measured and analyzed. The present study used descriptive statistics to measure the level of comprehension attained by those who used the electronic format for discussion purposes and those who engaged in face-to-face conversation.

The stories themselves were divided into idea units by the researcher/instructor and a nonnative speaker of French with extensive teaching and research experience. Idea units were identified in the story according to a definition provided by Bransford and Johnson (1973), that idea units "correspond either to individual sentences, basic semantic propositions, or phrases" (p. 393). The interrater reliability; that is, the rate of consistency between the researcher/instructor and the other observer in their division of idea units, was 0.98. In other words, they reached the same conclusions 98% of the time. Any questions regarding the division were discussed and mutually resolved. A high interrater reliability lends itself to the overall reliability of the findings. The message from the two face-to-face and the two message board groups were analyzed according to the number of idea units they contained. The total number of idea units is listed below under the category of "Total." Then, the number of contributors (n) was divided into the "Total" number to obtain the average number of idea units for each discussion mode. In addition, a standard deviation and a mean average were also calculated. The standard deviation indicates the measure of the variability, or spread, of scores whereas the mean average, or an average of the average, provides an additional way of comparing the number of idea units expressed by the face-to-face and the message board groups. These findings are summarized in Table 2.

Table 2. Descriptive Statistical Analysis of Modes

Story 1				Story 2			
Mode	F2F		MB		F2F		MB
Total	59.00		52.00		62.00		69.00
N		7.00		8.00		8.00		7.00
Avg.	8.43		6.50			7.75		9.86
Std. Dev.	4.24		2.87		3.60		1.46	
Mean Avg.		7.46				8.80		

The data revealed that the face-to-face groups in Story 1 had 59 idea units while the message board groups had 52. For Story 2, the face-to-face groups had a total of 62 idea units while the message board groups had 69.

With Story 1, the data showed that the face-to-face groups had a slightly higher number of idea units as compared to the message board groups. However, with Story 2, it was the message board groups who had a slightly higher number of idea units, as illustrated in Figure 1.

Based on these results, the message board format is similar to the face-to-face format in terms of the level of comprehension attained by the participants. This conclusion is further corroborated by the information provided by the average. The data revealed that the face-to-face groups in Story 1 averaged 8.43 idea units while the message board groups averaged 6.50. For Story 2, the face-to-face groups averaged 7.75 idea units while the message board groups had 9.86. With Story 1, the data showed that the face-to-face groups averaged a higher number of idea units as compared to the message board groups. However, with Story 2, it was the message board groups who averaged a higher number of idea units. This corroborates that in Story 1 the face-to-face groups fared better than the message board groups, while the reverse was true for Story 2. In addition, the low standard deviations of the face-to-face groups (4.24) and the message board groups (2.87) in Story 1, and of the face-to-face groups (3.60) and the message board groups (1.46) in Story 2 illustrate that the scores are close to the mean. The mean average of 7.46 for the face-to-face groups and of 8.80 for the message board groups provide evidence to compare the level of difficulty of the stories for the groups. The slight discrepancy in scores in the face-to-face and the message board groups does not appear to indicate a

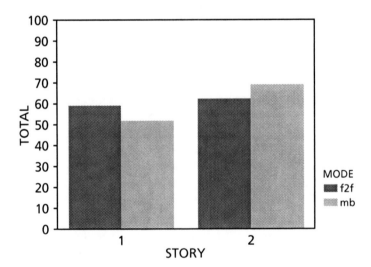

Figure 1.   Graph of total scores.

large enough difference in levels of comprehension, thus suggesting that the same groups comprehended to the same degree, regardless of discussion mode. This additional analysis suggests that the levels of comprehension attained by the face-to-face and the message board groups are comparable, and that there is no discernable difference between the discussion formats toward this end.

Limitations

Despite these encouraging findings, there are some limitations to note. First, a longer study would have produced more information on how students used the electronic medium for discussion and would have possibly influenced the conclusions of this study. In addition, a longer study would have given students more time to become accustomed to discussing foreign language literature via an electronic format. Also, for the present study, the electronic message board was used in a synchronous manner; use in an asynchronous manner may produce different results that may or may not concur with the findings presented here.

IMPLICATIONS AND CONCLUSION

Technological developments during the second half of the twentieth century have given students unprecedented access to information and increased opportunities for communication. However, the increase of technological advances, particularly of computer mediated communications, warrants careful consideration of their intrinsic advantages and limitations.

It was the goal of the present study to add to the comprehensive body of research on the use of computer mediated technologies and to gain a practical understanding of its use by investigating its application to a foreign language classroom. Recall protocols revealed that both the face-to-face and the message board groups attained similar comprehension levels, regardless of the forum used for discussion. The results of the present study suggest that the electronic message board can indeed act as a surrogate or as a supplement for face-to-face conversation when such conversations cannot take place. These findings are especially pertinent in light of the increased use of technology in the face-to-face classroom as well as the growing development of distance learning and other non-traditional learning situations.

The electronic message board offers many of the same advantages as other forms of computer mediated communication. For example, the features of the electronic message board allowed its users the opportunity to

reflect upon and modify postings as needed, thus giving them more control over their contributions and more opportunities for success. In addition, the features of the board discouraged users from dominating the
conversation and from interrupting one another, thus encouraging more
active participation vis-à-vis the others. However, the electronic message
board also offers advantages not found with other types of computer mediated communication technologies. For instance, the combination of synchronous and asynchronous features provides a number of possibilities for
application to the second and foreign language classroom. This type of
technology can be used either in class or outside of class, thus increasing
the opportunities for students to interact with one another, offering a
unique forum in which to engage in discussions. Unlike electronic mail or
electronic conferencing, the threads of postings and responses are immediately available and easily accessed by users, enabling them to read the
entire progression from inception to conclusion. Nevertheless, further
investigation into the use of the electronic message board is needed to provide additional information regarding the options available for applications to the second and foreign language classroom.

APPENDIX A

Story 1: *La vierge aux Oiseaux*

From *Les contes de la vierge* by Jérome and Jean Tharaud. Reprinted by permission of Librairie Plon, Paris, 1940.

La Vierge fuyait avec l'enfant devant les soldats du roi Hérode.

En chemin elle rencontra la colombe, et la colombe lui demanda:
   —Où vas-tu avec ton enfant?

La Vierge alors lui répondit:
   —Je fuis les soldats du roi Hérode.

Mais déjà on apercevait la poussière que faisaient les cavaliers, et la
colombe s'envola.

La Vierge continuait de fuir devant les soldats du roi Hérode.

En chemin elle rencontra la caille, et la caille lui demanda:
   —Où vas-tu avec ton enfant?

La Vierge alors lui répondit:
 —Je fuis les soldats du roi Hérode.

Mais déjà on entendait le galop des chevaux, et la caille aussi s'envola.

La Vierge s'enfuyait toujours devant les soldats du roi Hérode.
En chemin elle rencontra l'alouette, et l'alouette lui demanda:
 —Où vas-tu avec ton enfant?

La Vierge alors lui répondit:
 —Je fuis les soldats du roi Hérode.

Mais déjà on entendait les jurons des soudards, et l'alouette fit cacher la Vierge derrière une touffe de sauges.

Les soldats d'Hérode ont rencontré la colombe, et ils ont dit à la colombe:
 —Colombe, as-tu vu passer une femme avec son enfant?

La colombe leur a répondu:
 —Soldats, elle a passé par ici.

Et elle leur montra, à son tour, le chemin que la Vierge avait suivi.

Les soldats d'Hérode ont rencontré l'alouette, et ils ont dit à l'alouette:
 —Alouette, as-tu vu passer une femme avec son enfant?

L'alouette leur a répondu:
 —Soldats, elle a passé par ici.

Mais elle les conduisit très loin de la sauge, de la Vierge et de l'enfant.
Or, sachez à présent ce qu'il advint des trois oiseaux.
Dieu a condamné la colombe à roucouler une plainte sans fin, et la caille à raser la terre d'un vol qui la livre au chasseur.
Quant à l'alouette, sa récompense est de porter, chaque matin, le salut de la Vierge au soleil.

APPENDIX B

Story 2: *La parure: première partie* by Guy de Maupassant.

From *Nouvelles lectures libres*, edited by Rebecca M. Valette, copyright © 1982 by D.C. Heath and Company. Reprinted with permission of Houghton Mifflin Company.

C'était une de ces jolies et charmantes filles, nées, comme par une erreur du destin, dans une famille d'employés. Elle n'avait pas de dot, pas d'espérance, aucun moyen d'être connue, comprise, aimée, épousée par un homme riche et distingué; et elle se laissa marier avec un petit commis du Ministère de l'instruction publique. Elle fut simple ne pouvant être parée, mais malheureuse comme une déclassée, car les femmes n'ont point de caste ni de race, leur beauté, leur grâce et leur charme leur servant de naissance et de famille. Leur finesse native, leur instinct d'élégance, leur souplesse d'esprit, sont leur seule hiérarchie, et font des filles du peuple les égales des plus grandes dames. Elle souffrait sans cesse, se sentant née pour toutes les délicatesses et tous les luxes. Elle souffrait de la pauvreté de son logement, de la misère des murs, de l'usure des sièges, de la laideur des étoffes. Toutes ces choses, dont une autre femme de sa caste ne se serait même pas aperçue, la torturaient et l'indignaient.

La vue de la petite Bretonne qui faisait son humble ménage éveillait en elle des regrets désolés et des rêves éperdus. Elle songeait aux antichambres muettes, capitonnées avec des tentures orientales, éclairées par de hautes torchères de bronze, et aux deux grands valets à culotte courte qui dorment dans les larges fauteuils, assoupis par la chaleur lourde du calorifère. Elle songeait aux grands salons vêtus de soie ancienne, aux meubles fins portant des bibelots inestimables, et aux petits salons coquets parfumés, faits pour la causerie de cinq heures avec les amis les plus intimes, les hommes connus et recherchés dont toutes les femmes envient en désirent l'attention. Quand elle s'asseyait, pour dîner, devant la table ronde couverte d'une nappe de trois jours, en face de son mari qui découvrait la soupière en déclarant d'un air enchanté: "Ah! Le bon pot-au-feu!" je ne sais rien de meilleur que cela ... elle songeait aux dîners fins, aux argenteries reluisantes, aux tapisseries peuplant les murailles de personnages anciens et d'oiseaux étranges au milieu d'une forêt de féerie; elle songeait aux plats exquis servis en des vaisselles merveilleuses, aux galanteries chuchotées et écoutées avec un sourire de sphinx tout en mangeant la chair rose d'une truite ou des ailes de gelinotte. Elle n'avait pas de toilettes, pas de bijoux, rien. Et elle n'aimait que cela; elle se sentait faite pour cela.

Elle eût tant désiré plaire, être enviée, être séduisante et recherchée. Elle avait une amie riche, une camarade de couvent qu'elle ne voulait plus aller voir, tant elle souffrait en revenant. Et elle pleurait pendant des jours entiers, de chagrin, de regret, de désespoir et de détresse.

Or, un soir, son mari rentra, l'air glorieux, et tenant à la main une large enveloppe. "Tiens, dit-il, voici quelque chose pour toi." Elle déchira vivement le papier et en tira une carte imprimée qui portait ces mots: "Le Ministre de l'instruction publique et Mme Georges Ramponneau prient M. et Mme Loisel de leur faire l'honneur de venir passer la soirée à l'hôtel du Ministère, le lundi 18 janvier." Au lieu d'être ravie, comme l'espérait son mari, elle jeta avec dépit l'invitation sur la table, murmurant: "Que veux-tu que je fasse de cela ? —Mais, ma chérie; je pensais que tu serais contente. Tu ne sors jamais, et c'est une occasion, cela, une belle! J'ai eu une peine infinie à l'obtenir. Tout le monde en veut; c'est très recherché et on n'en donne pas beaucoup aux employés. Tu verras là tout le monde officiel."

Elle le regardait d'un oeil irrité, et elle déclara avec impatience:

Que veux-tu que je me mette sur le dos pour aller là?

Il n'y avait pas songé, il balbutia:

Mais la robe avec laquelle tu vas au théâtre. Elle me semble très bien, à moi…

Il se tut, stupéfait, éperdu, en voyant que sa femme pleurait. Deux grosses larmes descendaient lentement des coins des yeux vers les coins de la bouche; il bégaya:

Qu'as-tu? Qu'as-tu?

Mais, par un effort violent, elle avait dompté sa peine et elle répondit d'une voix calme en essuyant ses joues humides:

Rien. Seulement je n'ai pas de toilette et par conséquent je ne peux aller à cette fête. Donne ta carte à quelque collègue dont la femme sera mieux nippée que moi.

Il était désolé. Il reprit:

Voyons, Mathilde. Combien cela coûterait-il, une toilette convenable, qui pourrait te servir encore en d'autres occasions, quelque chose de très simple?

Elle réfléchit quelques secondes, établissant ses comptes et songeant aussi à la somme qu'elle pouvait demander sans s'attirer un refus immédiat et une exclamation effarée du commis économe. Enfin, elle répondit en hésitant:

Je ne sais pas au juste, mais il me semble qu'avec quatre cents francs je pourrais arriver.

Il avait un peu pâli, car il réservait juste cette somme pour acheter un fusil et s'offrir des parties de chasse, l'été suivant, dans la plaine de Nanterre avec quelques amis qui allaient tirer des alouettes, par là, le dimanche. Il dit cependant:

Soit. Je te donne quatre cents francs. Mais tâche d'avoir une belle robe.

REFERENCES

Arneil, S., & Holmes, M. (1999). Juggling hot potatoes: Decisions & compromises in creating authoring tools for the web. *ReCall, 11*(2), 12–19.

Barson, J., Frommer, J., & Schwartz, M. (1993). Foreign language learning using e-mail in a task-oriented perspective: Inter-university experiments in communication and collaboration. *Journal of Science Education and Technology, 2*(4), 565–584.

Bernhardt, E. (1991). *Reading development in a second language.* Norwood, NJ: Ablex.

Beaudoin, M. (1998). De l'enseignement de la grammaire par l'internet. *The Canadian Modern Language Review/La revue canadienne des langues vivantes, 55*(1), 61–75.

Beauvois, M.H. (1992). Computer-assisted classroom discussion in the foreign language classroom: Conversation in slow motion. *Foreign Language Annals, 25,* 455–463.

Borrás, I., & Lafayette, R. (1994). Effects of multimedia courseware subtitling on the speaking performance of college students of French. *Modern Language Journal, 78,* 61–75.

Bransford, J., & Johnson, M. (1973). Consideration of some problems of comprehension. In W. Chase (Ed.), *Visual information processing* (pp. 383–438). New York: Academic Press.

Charrière, P., & Magnin, M. (1998). Simulations globales avec internet: un atout majeur pour les départments de langues. *French Review, 72,* 320–328.

Chávez, C. (1997). Students take flight with Daedalus: Learning Spanish in a networked classroom. *Foreign Language Annals, 30,* 27–37.

Chun, D. (1994). Using computer networking to facilitate the acquisition of interactive competence. *System, 22,* 17–31.

Davis, J. (1988). Distance education & foreign language education: Towards a coherent approach. *Foreign Language Annals, 21*, 547–50.

Davis, J., & Lyman-Hager, M. (1997). Computers and L2 reading: Student performance, student attitudes. *Foreign Language Annals, 30*, 58–71.

De Maupassant, G. (1982). La Parure. In R. Vallette (Ed.), *Nouvelles lectures libres* (pp. 112–114). Lexington: Heath.

Donato, R., & Adair-Hauck, B. (1992). Discourse perspectives on formal instruction. *Language Awareness, 1*, 73–89.

Feustle, J.A., Jr. (1997). Literature in context: Hypertext and teaching. *Hispania, 80*(2), 216–226.

Glisan, E., Dudt, K., & Howe, M. (1998). Teaching Spanish through distance education: Implications of a pilot study. *Foreign Language Annals, 31*, 48–66.

Hong, W. (1997). Multimedia computer-assisted reading in business Chinese. *Foreign Language Annals, 30*, 335–409.

Horiba, Y., Van Den Broek, P., & Fletcher, C. (1993). Second language readers' memory for narrative texts: Evidence for structure-preserving top-down processing. *Language Learning, 43*, 345–372.

Kelm, O. (1992). The use of synchronous computer networks in second language instruction: A preliminary report. *Foreign Language Annals, 25*, 441–54.

Kern, R. (1995). Restructuring classroom interaction with networked computers: Effects of quantity and quality of language production. *Modern Language Journal, 79*, 457–476.

Krathwohl, D. (1998). *Methods of educational & social science research: An integrated approach.* New York: Longman.

Kroonenburg, N. (1994/5). Developing communicative and thinking skills via electronic mail. *TESOL Journal, 4*(2), 24–27.

Lee, J. (1986). On the use of the recall task to measure L2 reading comprehension. *Studies in Second Language Acquisition, 8*, 201–212.

Lee, L. (1997). Using internet tools as an enhancement of C2 teaching and learning. *Foreign Language Annals, 30*, 411–27.

Lyman-Hager, M. (1995). Multitasking, multilevel, multimedia software for intermediate-level French language instruction: *Ça continue... Foreign Language Annals, 28*, 181–192.

MacIntyre, P., & Gardner, R. (1991). Methods and results in the study of anxiety and language learning: A review of the literature. *Language Learning, 41*, 85–117.

Martínez-Lage, A. (1997). Hypermedia technology for teaching reading. In M. Bush & R. Terry (Eds.), *Technology-enhanced language learning* (pp. 121–163). Lincolnwood: National Textbook.

Masters-Wicks, K., Postlewate, L., & Lewental, M. (1996). Developing interactive instructional software for language acquisition. *Foreign Language Annals, 29*, 217–222.

Moore, M., & Thompson, M. (1997). The effects of distance learning. *ACSDE Research Monograph, 15.* University Park: The Pennsylvania State University.

Nagata, N. (1993). Intelligent computer feedback for second language instruction. *Modern Language Journal, 77*, 330–339.

Oliva, M., & Pollastrini, Y. (1995). Internet resources and second language acquisition: An evaluation of virtual immersion. *Foreign Language Annals, 28,* 552–563.

Paulisse, K.W., & Polik, W.F. (1998/1999). *DiscusWare.* Department of Chemistry, Hope College. http://www.chem.hope.edu/discus/.

Rogoff, B. (1990). *Apprenticeship in thinking: cognitive development in social context.* Cambridge: Cambridge University Press.

Swaffar, J., Arens, K., & Byrnes, H. (1991). *Reading for meaning: An integrated approach to language learning.* Englewood Cliffs, NJ: Prentice-Hall.

Tharpe, R., & Gallimore, R. (1988). *Rousing minds to life: Teaching and learning in social contexts.* Cambridge: Cambridge University Press.

Tharaud, J. & Tharaud, J. (1940). *Les contes de la vierge.* Paris: Librairie Plon.

Tharaud, J., & Tharaud, J. (1982). La vierge aux oiseaux. In R. Vallette (Ed.), *Nouvelles lectures libres* (pp. 8–9). Lexington: Heath.

Vignola, M., Kenny, R.F., Schilz, M., Andrews, B.W., & Covert, J. (1998). Multimédia interactif et formation des maîtres en français langue seconde: un outil pour l'enseignement réflexif. *The Canadian Modern Language Review/La revue canadienne des langues vivantes, 55* (1), 166–171.

Walz, J. (1998). Meeting standards for foreign language learning with world wide web activities. *Foreign Language Annals, 31,* 103–114.

Warriner-Burke, H. (1990). Distance learning: What we don't know can hurt us. *Foreign Language Annals, 23,* 129–133.

Warschauer, M. (1996). Motivational aspects of using computers for writing & communication. In M. Warschauer (Ed.), *Telecollaboration in foreign language learning* (pp. 29–46). Manoa: Second Language Teaching & Curriculum Center.

Warschauer, M., Turbee, L., & Roberts, B. (1996). Computer learning networks and student empowerment. *System, 24,* 1–14.

Wertsch, J. (1979). The regulation of human interaction and the given-new organization of private speech. In G. Ziven (Ed.), *The development of self-regulation through private speech* (pp. 79–98). New York: Wiley.

Wertsch, J. (1985). *Culture, communication, & cognition: Vygotskian perspectives.* New York: Cambridge University Press.

Yi, H., & Magima, J. (1993). The teacher-learner relationship and classroom interaction in distance learning: A case study of the Japanese language classes at an American high school. *Foreign Language Annals, 26,* 21–30.

CHAPTER 8

THE EFFECTS OF PASSAGE CONTENT ON SECOND LANGUAGE READING COMPREHENSION BY GENDER ACROSS INSTRUCTION LEVELS

Cindy Brantmeier

ABSTRACT

At the university level, Brantmeier (2000) found significant interactions between readers' gender and passage content with comprehension among intermediate second language (L2) learners of Spanish. In that study, participants read passages of approximately 600 words, one about boxing and the other about a frustrated housewife. Both written recall and multiple-choice assessment tasks were utilized to measure reading comprehension. Brantmeier suggested that at the intermediate level of instruction it may not be the Spanish language (a linguistic factor) that impedes second language reading comprehension but rather the unfamiliar content of the text. The present investigation used the same research design and procedures with two groups of participants from higher levels of instruction in order to determine the level at which passage content no longer impedes L2 reading comprehension. Participants were 76 students from advanced grammar courses and 56 students from advanced literature courses. Scores were submitted to an analysis of variance (ANOVA). Results revealed no significant interaction between readers' gender and passage content with comprehension. These results provide evidence that while degrees of topic familiarity maintain across instruction levels, the effects of passage content on L2 reading comprehension by gender do not maintain when the intermediate level text is read by more advanced learners.

GENDER AND LANGUAGE LEARNING

Some second language (L2) research has documented significant gender differences in learning with relation to listening comprehension (Farhady, 1983), aural bias and prestige of dialects (Eisentstein & Berkowitz, 1982), and aural vocabulary knowledge (Boyle, 1987). Gender differences were also found with motivation in foreign language learning. Chavez (1995) found that females reported that attitude and interest were integral to successful language learning, and males did not agree. Studies have also reported differences between male and female strategy use in oral situations such as: women's greater use of social behaviors, women's more frequent use of conversation, and women's greater willingness to initiate and communicate meaning (Bacon & Finnemann, 1990; Ehrman & Oxford, 1989; Nyikos & Oxford, 1989). On the contrary, other language researchers reported no differences between males and females. For example, Bacon (1992) reported no significant differences between males and females in listening comprehension levels, and in an examination of reading strategies, Young and Oxford (1997) found no significant gender differences for frequency of use of specific strategies or of strategy type. In a recent book devoted specifically to gender in the language classroom, Chavez (2001) reviewed studies that reveal no gender-linked differences and those that do show gender differences. She reminds readers that many studies to date have not considered gender as a variable in analysis. Overall, the lack of second language research where gender is a key variable in the procedures and analysis coupled with the contrasting findings in existing studies of this type warrant the need for further investigations.

GENDER AND TOPICS

Gender and Topic Preference

Since the early 1970s gender has been a variable in first language (L1) studies that focus on styles and strategies in oral/communicative settings (Brown, 1980; Edelsky, 1976; Fishman, 1982; Lakoff, 1975; West & Zimmerman, 1977). Some L1 studies have also been conducted on the topics of conversation within gender groups. Investigators reported that themes like sports and politics dissuaded men from revealing details of their personal lives to one another, and that women conversed on a wider variety of topics (Dabbs & Ruback, 1984; Haas & Sherman, 1982; Tannen, 1990). Jonstone (1993) examined the topics that Midwestern men and women focus on while telling stories. She concluded that men's stories were about physical and social competitions, whereas women's stories revolved around norms of community and action by groups of people.

Schema Theory and Text Topic

Research that considered gender in the silent task of reading focused primarily on the role of content schema. Schemata are organized knowledge structures in permanent memory that contain elements of related information and include plans for gathering additional information. In other words, a learner's schema is the mental framework that helps him/her organize knowledge, direct perception and attention, and guide recall (Anderson, 1984; Bruning, 1995). To examine the effects of content schemata in second language reading comprehension, researchers manipulate passage content and ask learners to process each different passage. After reading, participants might answer basic comprehension questions, inferential questions, write recalls or summaries, perform oral think-aloud recalls and more. Any differences in these measures of comprehension are correlated with the direct manipulation of content and the reader's existing knowledge of that content. Brantmeier (2001) noted disparities in research methods and procedures in the database of reading research that examines passage content, and contended that it is difficult to formulate generalizations across studies. However, these studies provide empirical support for the hypothesis that content schemata, as seen as culturally familiar and unfamiliar content, influence both first and second language reading comprehension. Table 1 provides a brief summary of this research (Brantmeier, 2001).

Table 1.   Research on Passage Content

Author	Participants	Passage Content	Results
Seffensen, Joagdev, & Anderson (1979)	Two groups—Indians and Americans (adults at different levels)	Two passages: (1) Indian wedding (2) American wedding Both passages written in English	Subjects read the native passage content: (1) faster (2) recalled more information (3) produced appropriate cultural elaborations
Johnson (1981)	Two groups—Iranians and Americans (intermediate/advanced levels)	Authentic folktales: (1) Buffalo Bill (2) Mullah Nasr-el-Din Both passages written in English	Members of cultural group showed superior performance on content of the familiar text
Carrell (1981)	Two groups—Japanese and Chinese (advanced levels)	Eight folktales from 3 different cultures: (1) native culture—Chinese or Japanese (2) second culture—Western European (3) unfamiliar culture—Apache Native Americans	Different cultural origin of text affected the recall of information and the judgment of level of difficulty
Carrell (1987)	Two groups—Muslims and Roman Catholics (high intermediate level)	Two fictionalized religion-based texts of historical biographies	When content was familiar, reading was relatively easy; Content was more important than form
Pritchard (1990)	Two groups—Americans and Palauans	Two letters written in native language (1) an American funeral (2) a Palauan funeral	When content of reading materials changed, processing behavior changed as well

Source: Brantmeier (2001).

Recently, Chavez (2001) claimed that the topic of reading comprehension tests may affect male and female performance on reading comprehension scores. She claimed that:

> Both the greater likelihood of prior familiarity with a topic which one finds truly interesting and the added incentive for comprehension when one reads something of personal relevance may raise test scores... (p. 41)

Reading research that utilized male/female content-oriented passages with male and female readers of the same national background has shown gender differences in both L1 and L2 comprehension (Bügel & Buunk, 1996; Doolittle & Welch, 1989; Hyde & Lynn, 1988).

More specifically, Brantmeier (2000) examined the relationship between four key variables in the study of L2 reading: reader's gender, passage content, comprehension, and strategy use. A total of 78 subjects (29 men and 49 women) from a large, Midwestern university participated in the investigation, and all were enrolled in fifth-semester Spanish, an Introduction to Hispanic Culture course. The main goal of the course was to prepare learners for the level of reading, writing, and speaking necessary to be successful in the advanced language, literature, and civilization courses. All of the participants had previously taken Spanish 250, a second year course, and all participants were native English speakers. The results of the study revealed that gender-oriented passage topic did indeed affect second language reading achievement by gender with students in an intermediate level course. At this level of instruction, lack of relevant topic familiarity inhibited comprehension, and men and women were not familiar with the same topics. Subjects achieved higher comprehension scores when reading texts that contained familiar topics.

THE PRESENT STUDY

Brantmeier (2000) utilized fifth semester students in her study. The present study replicates Brantmeier (2000) but includes participants from higher ranges of target language instruction to find out if there is a point or level when gender oriented passage topic does not affect comprehension.

Research Questions

The following questions guide the present study:

1. Are there gender differences in learners' second language reading comprehension with participants from an advanced grammar course?
2. Does the gender-oriented passage content of the second language reading text affect comprehension of male and female learners from an advanced grammar course?
3. Are there gender differences in learners' second language reading comprehension with participants from an advanced literature course?
4. Does the gender-oriented passage content of the second language reading text affect comprehension of male and female learners from an advanced literature course?

METHODS

All participants read both passages and completed all measurements for both passages on two different days during regular class time. In all sections, participants received a packet that contained a consent form, a reading passage, a recall comprehension task page, a multiple-choice comprehension test, and a topic familiarity questionnaire. Students were instructed not to look back at any previous pages while reading and completing all tasks. The order of presentation of the passages was counterbalanced according to the readers' gender.

Participants

The present investigation used the same research design and procedures as Brantmeier (2000) with two groups of participants from higher levels of instruction. A total of 132 participants from a Midwestern university participated in the investigation. Seventy-six participants were enrolled in an advanced grammar course, and 56 students were enrolled in advanced literature courses. The advanced grammar course is one of the last formal grammar courses taken before students enter the literature courses. It is a practical review of Spanish grammar and syntax, and it focuses on refining written and spoken Spanish. Class activities include oral reports, compositions, class discussions, group projects, and the study of selected literary and nonliterary materials. The advanced literature courses are survey courses of major literary works written by Spanish and Latin American authors. Course activities include lectures, class discussion of the readings, exams, short and long essays, and short oral reports. Only students whose native language was English and only those who completed both tasks on both days were included in the final data analysis.

Reading Passages

Brantmeier (2000) chose the two reading passages after carefully looking at several different literary texts that are used at the intermediate level. The same passages were used in the present study. The literature courses at the intermediate level often utilize anthologies that include authentic readings, and most texts used at this level incorporate works by Elena Poniatowska and Julio Cortazar. The passage from the short story "La casita de sololoi," by Poniatowska, was taken from a volume of short stories titled *La pluma mágica*. Cortazar's passage was taken from his short story "La noche de Mantequilla," which is in a book of short stories entitled *Los relatos: Ahí y ahora*. The Cortazar passage was chosen because it centered on male spectators at a boxing match, and all of the characters are men. The Poniatowska passage was selected because it focused on a frustrated mother and wife who visits her college roommate, and all the characters are women. The stories were not used in their entirety, and each passage contained approximately 600 words. The passages were retyped and formatted so that glosses could be supplied to aid the reading process.[1] To control for authenticity of passage selection, both passages were written in their original form, and consequently there were a few ungrammatical items in the texts. The titles of both passages contained misleading and ambiguous terms, so a description of key concepts in the title was included more than half of a page length above the title of the passage. The experimental passages are presented in the Appendix.

COMPREHENSION ASSESSMENT TASKS

Previous research has shown that the tasks used to assess reading comprehension influence readers' performance (Lee, 1986; Shohamy, 1984; Wolf, 1993), and therefore two different reading comprehension assessment tasks were used: the written recall and multiple-choice questions. Prior L2 reading researchers have concluded that comprehension assessment tasks should be completed in the learner's native language. Therefore, both the instruction on the written recall and all of the multiple-choice questions were written in English (Bernhardt, 1983; Lee, 1986; Wolf, 1993).

Recall

In the written recall measure there is no tester interference that influences the reader's comprehension of the passage. The written instructions on the recall page told the learner to try to recall main ideas, as well as details, and it also indicated that the emphasis was on quantity of ideas recalled. The written recall measure was administered directly after the passages were read, and before the multiple-choice questions.

Multiple-Choice Questions

The multiple-choice questions were created to meet the two criteria set by Wolf (1991): (a) all items are passage dependent, and (b) some of the items require the reader to make inferences. In addition, a third condition was added: correct responses could not be determined by looking at the other questions on the page. For each of the 10 multiple-choice questions three possible responses were created: one correct response and two distractors. All distractors in the multiple-choice questions are plausible (Wolf, 1991). All multiple-choice questions could not be answered correctly without having read and understood relevant parts of the passages.

TOPIC FAMILIARITY QUESTIONNAIRE

The degree of topic familiarity was assessed using a 5-point scale, ranging from "I was really familiar with the topic" to "I was really not familiar with the topic at all." The wide range of choices encouraged respondents to show discrimination in their judgments. Participants filled out the topic familiarity questionnaire after completing all other tasks.

SCORING AND ANALYSIS PROCEDURES

The written recall task was scored using Riley and Lee's (1996) criteria. The text was divided into separate "units of analysis," which are ideas, propositions, or constituent structures. Both the researcher and a rater separately identified the idea units recalled correctly for each written recall, and then these units were compared to the text to ensure that the information in the written recall appeared in or was implied in the reading passage. The two raters compared results, and the percent of scoring agreement between the two raters was 98%. The "total number of units recalled correctly" was identified as one independent variable used to measure comprehension. The multiple-choice questions were scored according to the total number of correct responses out of the ten questions.

For all research questions, data were submitted to an Analysis of Variance (ANOVA) procedure. Reader's gender and passage content were the independent variables, and the dependent variables were comprehension and topic familiarity.

RESULTS

Topic Familiarity

Mean scores and standard deviations for self-reported degrees of topic familiarity for participants in both of the advanced courses are listed in Table 2. The lower the mean score the more familiar the participants were with the passage topic. Results for students from the advanced grammar course revealed the following: the male participants were more familiar with the passage on boxing than the females were, and the females were more familiar with the passage about the frustrated housewife than the males were.

Table 2.   Mean Scores and Standard Deviations (SD) for Degree of Topic Familiarity by Gender

Participants from Advanced Grammar Courses

		Passage Topic	
		Boxing	Frustrated
Housewife			
Males	M*	2.74	3.30
	(SD)	1.05	1.04
Females	M*	3.62	2.66
	(SD)	1.04	.98

Note. *n* = 76 participants, 23 males and 53 females

Participants from Advanced Literature Courses

		Passage Topic	
		Boxing	Frustrated
Housewife			
Males	M*	2.74	3.30
	(SD)	1.05	1.04
Females	M*	3.62	2.66
	(SD)	1.04	.98

Note. *n* = 56 participants, 9 males and 47 females
* The lower the mean score the more familiar with the passage topic; 1 = really familiar with the topic, 5 = really not familiar with the topic at all.

Two one-way ANOVAs were calculated to determine statistical differences by gender in the mean topic familiarity ratings. The results of the ANOVAs revealed significant main effects of readers' gender and topic familiarity with the male oriented passage (p = .00) and significant main effects of readers' gender and topic familiarity with the female-oriented passage (p = .02).

Results with students in the advanced literature courses revealed, again, that the male participants were more familiar with the passage on boxing than the females were, and the females were more familiar with the passage about the frustrated housewife than the males were (see Table 2). The results of the ANOVAs revealed significant main effects of readers' gender and topic familiarity with the male oriented passage (p = .00) and marginal main effects of readers' gender and topic familiarity with the female-oriented passage (p = .07).

Overall Comprehension

The sample means and standard deviations for the main effect of readers' gender on both comprehension tasks across passages for participants from both of the advanced courses are presented in Table 3. With the participants from the advanced grammar courses, sample mean scores indicated better performance by females on overall recall, but mean scores were exactly the same for the multiple-choice questions. The results of the ANOVA showed no significant difference between mean scores for males and females on recall ($p = .24$) and multiple-choice questions ($p = .42$). With participants from the advanced literature courses females recalled two more total idea units across passages than males did, and scores were the same for multiple-choice questions by gender. Results of the ANOVAs revealed no significant differences by gender for overall mean scores for recall ($p = .50$) and multiple-choice ($p = .74$).

Table 3.   Mean Scores and Standard Deviations (SD) for Overall Comprehension by Readers' Gender Participants from Advanced Grammar Courses

		Readers' Gender	
		Male	Female
Recall	M	27.0	30.0
	(SD)	13.4	12.4
Multiple-Choice Questions	M	14.0	14.0
	(SD)	2.9	2.8

Note. n = 76 participants, 23 males and 53 females; maximum scores possible for multiple-choice is 20.

Participants from Advanced Literature Courses

		Reader's Gender	
		Male	Female
Recall	M	27.80	30.00
	(SD)	9.35	8.86
Multiple-Choice Questions	M	15.78	15.60
	(SD)	15.55	1.85

Note. n = 56 participants, 9 males and 47 females; maximum scores possible for multiple-choice is 20.

Comprehension of Passages by Gender

To explore the interaction effect between readers' gender and passage content as they affect comprehension, four one-way ANOVAs were calculated. Table 4 lists the sample means and standard deviations of recall and multiple-choice questions for male and female-oriented passages with participants from the advanced grammar courses. Females recalled one more idea unit than the males did for the male-oriented passage, and females recalled three more idea units than the males did for the female-oriented passage. For the multiple-choice questions, males and females achieved the same scores for both passages. The results of the one-way ANOVAS revealed no significant main effects of male-oriented passage on recall ($p = .42$) and multiple-choice ($p = .60$) and no significant main effects of female-oriented passage on recall ($p = .19$) and multiple-choice ($p = .47$).

Table 4.   Mean Scores and Standard Deviations (SD) for Comprehension of Passages by Gender with Participants from Advanced Grammar Courses

| | | Male-Oriented Passages | |
		Recall	Multiple Choice
Males	M	11.35	6.09
	(SD)	5.29	2.35
Females	M	12.36	6.36
	(SD)	4.84	1.93
		Female-Oriented Passages	
		Recall	Multiple Choice
Males	M	15.65	8.09
	(SD)	9.40	1.73
Females	M	18.74	8.43
	(SD)	9.15	1.97

Note. $n = 76$ participants, 23 males and 53 females; maximum score possible for multiple-choice is 10.

The sample means and standard deviations of recall and multiple-choice questions for male and female-oriented passages with students from advanced literature are listed on Table 5. Females and males recalled the same number of idea units for the male-oriented passage, and females recalled three more idea units than the males did for the female-oriented passage. For the multiple-choice questions, male and females achieved the same scores for the male-oriented passage, and females correctly answered one more question than the males for the female-oriented passage. The results of the one-way ANOVAS revealed no significant main effects of male-oriented passage on recall ($p = .58$) and multiple-choice ($p = .18$) and no significant main effects of female-oriented passage on recall ($p = .21$) and multiple-choice ($p = .18$).

Table 5.   Mean Scores and Standard Deviations (SD) for Comprehension of Passages by Gender with Participants from Advanced Literature Courses

		Male-Oriented Passages	
		Recall	Multiple Choice
Males	M	11.89	7.33
	(SD)	5.13	1.32
Females	M	11.09	7.00
	(SD)	3.73	1.60
		Female-Oriented Passages	
		Recall	Multiple Choice
Males	M	15.89	8.56
	(SD)	4.91	1.01
Females	M	18.87	9.06
	(SD)	6.75	1.03

Note. $n = 56$ participants, 9 males and 47 females; maximum score possible for multiple-choice is 10.

SUMMARY OF RESULTS ACROSS THREE LEVELS OF INSTRUCTION: INTERMEDIATE, ADVANCED GRAMMAR, ADVANCED LITERATURE

Topic Familiarity

Mean scores for degree of familiarity with the passage topic across all three levels by gender were calculated. With all three levels of instruction males indicated a significantly higher degree of familiarity with the male-oriented topic than the females did, and the females indicated a significantly higher degree of familiarity with the female-oriented topic than the males did.

Comprehension

Mean scores across all three levels for comprehension by gender on both recall and multiple-choice for the male-oriented passage are graphically displayed in Figures 1 and 2. Mean scores across all three levels for comprehension by gender on both recall and multiple-choice for the female-oriented passage are graphically displayed in Figures 3 and 4. As displayed on the graph, with students from the intermediate courses, the interaction of readers' gender and passage content significantly affected comprehension measured by both recall and multiple-choice comprehension questions. With students in both the Advanced Grammar and Advanced Literature courses, the interaction of readers' gender and passage content did not significantly affect comprehension measured by both assessment tasks.

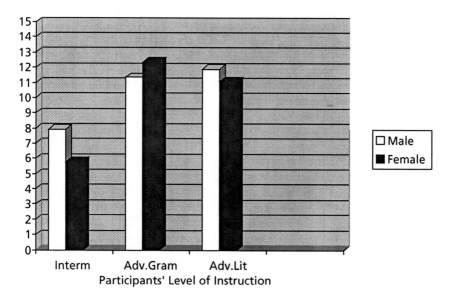

Figure 1.   Mean scores for recall of male-oriented passage content by readers' gender across instruction levels.

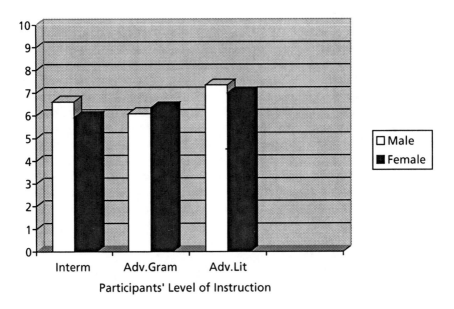

Figure 2.   Mean scores on multiple-choice for male-oriented passage content by readers' gender across instruction levels.

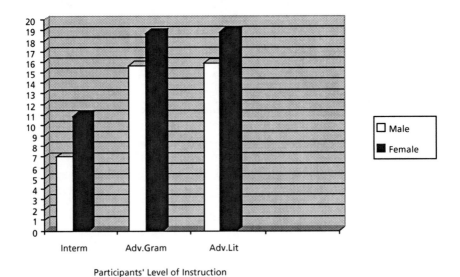

Figure 3.   Mean scores for recall with female-oriented passage content by readers' gender across instruction levels.

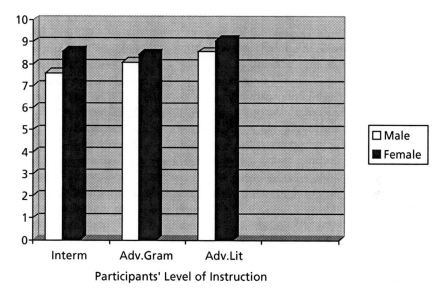

Figure 4.   Mean scores for multiple-choice with female-oriented passage content by readers' gender across instruction levels.

DISCUSSION

When examining overall results across passages with participants at the intermediate level of instruction mean scores indicated better performance by females on both recall scores and multiple-choice questions. With participants from both the advanced grammar classes and literature courses, females achieved higher recall scores across passages than males did. However, for the advanced levels mean scores for multiple-choice items across passages were the same by gender (mean score of 14 for both males and females at the advanced grammar level, mean score of 16 for both males and females from the advanced literature courses). These findings may suggest that as learners advance in their language studies differences between men and women in reading comprehension may depend on assessment tasks used to measure comprehension rather than passage content.

A meta-analysis of gender differences carried out by Hyde and Linn (1988) revealed that in the United States, females who took the American Scholastic Aptitude Test (SAT) generally had better L1 essay-writing skills than males. Perhaps females are better equipped than the males to write a narrative-like recall of the readings. With participants from the United Kingdom, Sunderland (1995) reported that girls tend to do better on essays than boys do and that boys do better on multiple-choice questions.

Feingold (1992) reports that females have an advantage over males in reading comprehension that persists through all ages, however a closer examination of the construction of literacy test instruments utilized to assess comprehension at all age levels may reveal insightful results. In a study using gender-neutral passage content with participants of second-year German, Schueller (1999) reported that only those males who had received training in global reading strategies scored higher than females on multiple-choice comprehension tests. Her findings also revealed a higher degree of reading comprehension among females for all other comprehension tests, including the recall. It can be argued that the level of comprehension depends on the type of assessment task used to measure comprehension. In all three groups, the intermediate, advanced grammar, and advanced literature, females performed better on the overall recall tasks. Perhaps the recall measure of comprehension is biased in favor of females over males. Only at the intermediate level did females outperform males on the overall scores of multiple-choice items, at the advanced levels scores on multiple-choice items were almost the same. More research of this nature needs to be conducted before making a generalization.

With participants from the intermediate level, male and female performance on both comprehension tasks was significantly affected by passage content (Brantmeier, 2000). With students from the intermediate level course, it was clear that topic selection influenced one gender to be more successful than the other. Male subjects recalled significantly more idea units from the male-oriented passage than the female-oriented passage, and female participants recalled significantly more idea units from the female-oriented passage than the male-oriented passage. The results of the multiple-choice tasks paralleled those of the recall. These findings echoed those of Bügel and Buunk (1996) who examined the reading part of the national foreign language exam in the Netherlands. They found that females achieved higher scores on readings about a housewife's dilemma, and males scored higher on a passage about sports.

With participants from the Advanced Grammar and Advanced Literature courses, male and female performance on both comprehension tasks was not significantly affected by passage content. These findings suggest that passage content ceases to affect comprehension by gender after the intermediate level of instruction. At the more advanced stages of language development, the interaction of readers' gender and passage content no longer impedes successful reading comprehension.

Male participants from all three levels of instruction were more familiar with the passage on boxing than the females were, and females from all three levels of instruction were more familiar with the passage about the frustrated housewife than the males were. However, only at the intermediate level of instruction did the interaction of reader's gender and passage content significantly affect performance on reading comprehension tasks. This finding may suggest that as participants gain more exposure to L2 reading and become better L2 readers that topic familiarity does not affect successful comprehension. Another possible explanation for this finding is that perhaps in the more advanced courses the students have developed metacognitive reading strategies that make it easier for them to learn new information from the text. L2 readers in the intermediate level courses may depend more strongly on their pre-existing knowledge about a topic rather than gaining new knowledge through reading. If this is the case, perhaps gender is not as important as learners become more proficient readers.

The results of the present study provide evidence that while degrees of topic familiarity maintain across instruction levels, the effects of passage content on L2 reading comprehension by gender do not maintain when the intermediate level text is read by more advanced learners. Perhaps this is due to level of text difficulty. The same two passages were read by groups of students from three different levels of course instruction. With the students in the more advanced courses, if the level of text difficulty increased, perhaps passage content would have had a greater effect on comprehension. Given texts of greater difficulty, men and women might be more affected by passage content while reading at the advanced levels of instruction.

The Intermediate Level of Instruction

Generally, the first and second year language courses are degree requirements at many colleges and universities across the nation. These language classes, especially the more commonly taught language courses such as Spanish, French and German, are communication driven with a focus on the development of speaking and listening skills. The instructor is seen as a facilitator and model of the language, and the classes are student-centered. Much second language acquisition research focuses on these beginning levels of instruction. In the advanced literature courses, class time is more teacher-centered with the instructor lecturing about literary works that students are assigned to read before coming to class. When discussing classroom participation at the advanced levels, some instructors contend that students are not prepared to critically analyze literature, and some claim that linguistic difficulties are the barrier.

In preparation for the advanced literature courses, most universities teach culture, composition, and grammar classes where the primary emphasis shifts from the improvement of speaking and listening skills to the development of reading and writing skills. At the intermediate level, longer, authentic cultural input samples are utilized (Rava, 2000). Many university level institutions are currently reexamining the intermediate curriculum, and consequently it is crucial for L2 reading researchers to conduct experiments at this level (Brantmeier, 2001). For some students, the first reading of lengthy L2 authentic texts begins at this bridge level, and therefore the selection of reading materials is of principal significance. The results of the previous study (Brantmeier, 2000) provided evidence on the importance of passage content at the intermediate level of instruction. In the present study, with students from more advanced levels of instruction, passage content did not affect reading comprehension. More research of this kind and studies focusing on the corresponding implications for instruction at the intermediate level are needed.

IMPLICATIONS FOR TEACHING

It is important to note that the present study did not test the effects of any instructional practices on second language reading comprehension, and therefore the following suggestions need to be examined in classroom-based studies in order to ascertain their efficacy.

Selection of reading materials is important. Studies have shown that the majority of students in intermediate and advanced courses of Spanish are female. Chavez (2001) found that in Spanish and French courses female students outnumber males at all levels with the numeric gap widening at the more advanced course levels. The instructor needs to keep this in mind when selecting reading materials. Of course this does not mean that male authors should be excluded. Rather, it means that when instructors select reading materials, they should consider the gender of the reader and should try to include a balance of reading topics, both male and female-oriented.

Reading is a complex process that involves many complicated, interacting variables. Hammadou (1991) affirmed that comprehension of a second language is not just understanding words, sentences, and paragraphs, but that it entails building a model within the mind of the learner. To account for the effects of passage content on comprehension, instructors can build a model within the existing cognitive domain of the learner by anchoring pre-reading activities to relevant schemata. Instructors can provide explanations about the topics and offer relevant background knowledge about the cultural orientation of reading passage before reading so that both male and female readers are familiar with content. Background information can be effectively taught in the L2 classroom with consequential improvement in reading comprehension (Floyd & Carrell, 1987; Hudson, 1982).

During the two years of basic level language courses, students become accustomed to a more communicative classroom that is student focused. As discussed earlier, communicative language teaching emphasizes authentic, social interactions where the teacher is the facilitator (Lee & VanPatten, 1995). At the intermediate level, the development of reading and writing skills is frequently the primary goal, and the task of reading is commonly viewed as a silent task. Females tend to use more social and interactive strategies to communicate than males do. Instructors at the intermediate level should consider these facts when planning classroom-based activities for the intermediate level by incorporating interactive pre-reading and post-reading activities that enhance topic familiarity. This interaction should include activities that provide opportunities for students to share past experiences and existing knowledge to augment topic familiarity.

SUGGESTIONS FOR FURTHER RESEARCH

A future investigation could manipulate text difficulty as well as passage content to examine whether the effects observed for intermediate level learners will maintain if text difficulty is sufficiently increased. Furthermore, a future study may include different comprehension assessment tasks such as open-ended questions, true/false statements, or cloze tests. The present study used the multiple-choice and recall tasks in order to conduct a large-scale comparison of male and female readers' comprehension. With a smaller population size perhaps an immediate oral recall protocol may provide valuable insight about gender differences in L2 comprehension across levels.

The present study utilized gender-oriented passage content. A future study could include text topics that are not oriented toward gender, but that are topics universal to the literary canon. Would common passage topics, such as violence and humor, yield different results in comprehension by gender across instruction levels? Would a gender-neutral passage topic yield different results?

Because females consistently recalled more overall idea units, perhaps a closer examination of the quality of idea units rather than quantity is necessary. A qualitative inquiry might reveal interesting gender differences in the types of ideas recalled across language development levels, and could aid instructors in the creation of pre-reading classroom activities.

Finally, researchers should be cautious when examining males and females as dichotomous constructs. Future studies of this type could examine the degree of variation within as well as between gender groups. Feingold (1992) contends that men show greater degrees of variation within their own gender group in academic achievement than do women. Would this hold true for L2 reading comprehension across instruction levels?

CONCLUSION

Successful second language reading comprehension depends on a variety of variables, and with students from the intermediate courses of Spanish results indicated that two important interacting factors are the readers' gender and gender-oriented passage content. In these courses male and female readers comprehend familiar passage content better than unfamiliar passage content. At more advanced ranges of language experience, male and female topic familiarity levels are maintained, but male and female performance on second language reading comprehension tasks is no longer affected by gender-oriented passage content. The reading of lengthy, authentic texts begins at the intermediate level, and therefore instructors need to select texts that are relevant and interesting. Instructors should also address topic familiarity differences through pre-reading activities. Finally, instructors at all levels should keep in mind that the tasks they use to measure reading comprehension may be biased in favor of males or females.

ACKNOWLEDGEMENTS

I would like to express my sincere gratitude to Jim Lee for his guidance during the first study that I conducted with the intermediate level participants. I would like to thank Joe Barcroft, Chris Brown, and Ho Sang Yoon for their assistance in the follow-up studies. I would also like to express my appreciation to the anonymous reviewers for their valuable suggestions.

NOTE

1.   To determine which words needed to be glossed, both passages were given to students in an introduction to literature course to identify words that caused them difficulty. Instructors and supervisors at the intermediate level of instruction were also consulted about the glossed words.

REFERENCES

Anderson, R.C. (1984). A schema-theoretic view of basic processes in reading comprehension. In P.D. Person (Ed.), *Handbook of reading research* (pp. 255–291). New York: Longman.

Bacon, S.M. (1992). The relationship between gender, comprehension, processing strategies, and cognitive and affective response in foreign language listening. *Modern Language Journal, 76,* 160–178.

Bacon, S.M., & Finneman, M. (1990). A study of the attitudes, motives, and strategies of university foreign-language students in relation to authentic oral and written input. *Modern Language Journal, 74,* 459–472.

Bernhardt, E.B. (1983). Syntactic and lexical/semantic skill in foreign language reading comprehension: The immediate recall protocol. *Die Unterrichtspraxis, 16,* 27–33.

Boyle, J.P. (1987). Sex differences in listening vocabulary. *Language Learning, 37,* 273–284.

Brantmeier, C. (2000). *The relationship between readers' gender, passage content, comprehension and strategy use in reading Spanish as a second language.* Unpublished doctoral dissertation. Indiana University at Bloomington.

Brantmeier, C. (2001). Second language reading research on passage content and gender: Challenges for the intermediate level curriculum. *Foreign Language Annals, 34,* 325–333.

Brown, P. (1980). How and why are women more polite: some evidence from a Mayan community. In S. McConnell-Ginet, R. Borker, & N. Furman, (Eds.), *Women and language in literature and society* (pp. 111–136). New York: Praeger.

Bruning, R.H. (1995). The college classroom from the perspective of cognitive psychology. In K. Prichard, R.M. Sawyer, & K. Hostetler (Eds.), *Handbook of college teaching: Theory and applications.* Westport, CT: Greenwood.

Bügel, K., & Buunk, B.P. (1996). Sex differences in foreign language text comprehension: The role of interests and prior knowledge. *Modern Language Journal, 80,* 15–31.

Carrell, P.L. (1981). Culture-specific schemata in L2 comprehension. In R. Orem, & J.F. Haskell, (Eds.), *Selected papers from the ninth Illinois TESOL/BE* (pp. 123–132). Chicago: Illinois TESOL/BE.

Carrell, P.L. (1987). Content and formal schemata in ESL reading. *TESOL Quarterly, 21,* 462–481.

Chavez, M. (1995). Demographically induced variation in students' beliefs about learning and studying German. *Die Unterrichtspraxis/Teaching German, 28* (2), 165–175.

Chavez, M. (2001). *Gender in the language classroom.* New York: McGraw Hill.

Dabbs, J.M., Jr., & Ruback, R.B. (1984). Vocal patterns in male and female groups. *Personality and Social Psychology Bulletin, 10,* 518–25.

Doolittle, A., & Welch, C. (1989). *Gender differences in performance on a college-level achievement test* (ACT Research Rep. Series 89-9). Iowa City, IA: American College Testing Program.

Edelsky, C. (1976). Subjective reactions to sex-linked language. *Journal of Social Psychology, 99,* 97–104.

Ehrman, M.E., & Oxford, R. (1989). Effects of sex differences, career choice, and psychological type on adult language learning strategies. *Modern Language Journal, 72,* 253–265.

Eisentstein, M., & Berkowitz, D. (1981). The effect of phonological variation on adult learner comprehension. *Studies in Second Language Acquisition, 4,* 75–80.

Farhady, H. (1983). New directions for ESL proficiency testing. In J.W. Oller (Ed.), *Issues in language testing research* (pp. 253–269). Rowley, MA: Newbury House.

Feingold, A. (1992) Cognitive gender differences: A developmental perspective. *Sex Roles, 29*(2), 91–112.

Fishman, W.K. (1982). *The new right: Unraveling the opposition to women's equality.* New York: Praeger.

Floyd, P., & Carrell, P.L. (1987). Effects on ESL reading of teaching content schemata. *Language Learning, 37,* 89–108.

Haas, L., & Sherman, M.A. (1982). Reported topics of conversation among same-sex adults. *Communication Quarterly, 30*, 341.

Hammadou, J. (1991). Interrelationships among prior knowledge, inference, and language proficiency in foreign language reading. *Modern Language Journal, 75*, 27–38.

Hudson, T. (1982). The effects of induced schemata on the short circuit in L2 reading: Non-decoding factors in L2 reading and performance. *Language Learning, 32*, 3–31.

Hyde, J.S., & Linn, M.C. (1988). Gender differences in verbal activity: A meta-analysis. *Psychological Bulletin, 104*, 53–69.

Johnson, P. (1981). Effects on reading comprehension of language complexity and cultural background of a text. *TESOL Quarterly, 15*, 169–181.

Jonstone, B. (1993). Community and contest: Midwestern men and women creating their world in conversation storytelling. In D. Tannen (Ed.), *Gender and conversational interaction* (pp. 62–82). Oxford: Oxford University Press.

Lakoff, R. (1975). *Language and women's place.* New York: Harper and Row.

Lee, J.F. (1986). On the use of the recall task to measure L2 reading comprehension. *Studies in Second Language Acquisition, 8*, 201–12.

Lee, J.F., & VanPatten, B. (1995). *Making communicative language teaching happen.* New York: McGraw-Hill.

Oxford, R., & Nyikos, M. (1989). Variables affecting choice of language learning strategies by university students. *Modern Language Journal, 73*, 291–300.

Rava, S. (2000). The changing face of the intermediate curriculum. *Foreign Language Annals, 33*, 342–348.

Riley, G.L., & Lee, J.F. (1996). A comparison of recall and summary protocols as measures of second language reading comprehension. *Language Testing, 1*, 173–187.

Schueller, J. (1999). *The effect of two types of strategy training on foreign language reading comprehension. An analysis by gender and proficiency.* Unpublished doctoral dissertation. The University of Wisconsin, Madison.

Shohamy, E. (1984). Does the testing method make the difference? The case of reading comprehension. *Language Testing, 1*, 147–70.

Sunderland, J. (1995). "We're boys, miss!": Finding gendered identities and looking for gendering of identities in the foreign language classroom. In S. Mills (Ed.), *Language and gender: Interdisciplinary perspectives.* Harlow: Longman.

Tannen, D. (1990). *You just don't understand: Women and men in conversation.* New York: William Morrow.

West, C., & Zimmerman, D.H. (1977). Women's place in everyday talk: Reflections on parent-child interaction. *Social Problems, 24*, 521–529.

Wolf, D. (1991). *The effects of task, language of assessment, and target language experience on foreign language learners performance on reading comprehension.* Unpublished doctoral dissertation. University of Illinois at Urbana-Champaign.

Wolf, D. (1993). A comparison of assessment tasks used to measure FL reading comprehension. *Modern Language Journal, 77*, 473–89.

Young, D.J., & Oxford, R. (1997). A gender-related analysis of strategies used to process input in the native language and a foreign language. *Applied Language Learning, 8*, 43–73.

APPENDIX

In order to understand the following passage, you need to know that Jose "Mantequilla" Napoles is the name of a Mexican boxer.

La Noche de Mantequilla

ropes; whip quarrel	En la tercera vuelta Mantequilla salió con todo y entonces lo esperable, pensó Estévez, Monzón contra las cuerdas°, un uno-dos de látigo°, el clinch fulminante para salir de las cuerdas, una agarrada° mano a mano hasta el final del round.
lighter	Sacaron cigarillos al mismo tiempo, los intercambiaron sonriendo, el encendedor° de Walter llegó antes. Cuando sonó el gong, Estevez miró a Walter que sacaba otra vez los cigarillos.
fans; cheered	Era difícil hablarse en el griterío, el público sabía que el round siguiente podía ser el decisivo, los hinchas° de Nápoles lo alentaban° casi como despidiéndolo, pensó Estévez con una simpatía que ya no iba en contra de su deseo ahora que Monzón buscaba la pelea y la encontraba y a lo largo de veinte interminables segundos entrando en la cara y el cuerpo
finished endure towel	mientras Mantequilla apuraba° el clinch come quien se tira al agua, cerrando los ojos. No va a aguantar° más, pensó Estévez, y con esfuerzo sacó la vista del ring para mirar la cartera de tela° en el tablón, habría que hacerlo justo en el descanso cuando todos se sentaran, exactamente en ese momento porque después volverían a pararse y otra vez la cartera de tela en el tablón, habría que hacerlo justo en el descanso cuando todos se sentaran, exactamente en ese momento porque después volverían a pararse y otra vez la cartera sola en el tablón, dos izquierdas seguidas en la cara de Nápoles que volvía a buscar el clinch, Monzón fuera de distancia, esper-
hook expert	ando apenas para volver con un gancho° exactísimo en plena cara, ahora las piernas, había que mirar sobre todo las piernas, Estévez ducho° en eso veía a Mantequilla pesado, tirándose adelante sin ese ajuste tan suyo mien-
slipped carried	tras los pies de Monzón resbalaban° de lado o hacía atrás, la cadencia perfecta para que esa última derecha calzara° con todo en pleno estómago, muchos no oyeron el gong en el clamoreo histérico pero Walter y Estévez
putting	sí, Walter se sentó primero enderezando° la cartera sin mirarla y Estévez, siguiéndolo más despacio, hizo resbalar el paquete en una fracción de Segundo y volvió a levanter la mano vacía para gesticular su entusiasmo en las narices del tipo de pantalón azul que no parecía muy al tanto de lo que estaba sucediendo.
who cares	-Eso es un campeón–le dijo Estévez sin forzar la voz porque de todos modos el otro no lo escucharía en ese clamereo-. Carlitos, carajo°.
canvas	Miró a Walter que fumaba tranquilo, el hombre empezaba a resignarse, que se le va a hacer, si no se puede no se puede. Todo el mundo parado en la espera de la campana del séptimo round, un brusco silencio incrédulo y después el alarido unanime al ver la toalla en la lona°, Nápoles siempre en su rincón y Monzón avanzando con los guantes en alto, más campeón que nunca, saludando antes de perderse en el torbellino de los abrazos y los flashes. Era un final sin belleza pero indiscutible, Mantequilla abandonada para no ser el punchingball de Monzón, toda esperanza perdida ahora que se levantaba para acercarse al vencedor y alzar los

	guantes hasta su cara, casi una caricia mientras Monzón le ponía los suyos en los hombros y otra vez se separaban, ahora sí para siempre, pensó Estevez, ahora para ya no encontrarse nunca más en un ring.
cramped	-Fue una linda pelea–le dijo a Walter que se colgaba la cartera del hombro y movía los pies como si se hubiera acalambrado°.
	-Podría haber durado más–dijo Walter–seguro que los segundos de Nápoles no lo dejaron salir.
	-¿Para qué? Ya viste como estaba sentido, che, demasiado boxeador para no darse cuenta.
one is like	-Sí, pero cuando se es como° él hay que jugarse entero, total nunca se sabe.

Recall

Without looking back at the passage, recall in English as much as you can of what you have just read. Try to recall main ideas as well as details. The emphasis is on quantity of ideas recalled.

Comprehension Questions for *La Noche de Mantequilla*

1. The passage begins:
   a. in the first round of the boxing match.
   b. in the third round of the boxing match.
   c. in the final round of the boxing match.

2. Walter and Estévez are
   a. the boxers that are competing.
   b. The spectators at the boxing match.
   c. The referees at the boxing match.

3. During the boxing match Walter and Estévez:
   a. smoke cigarettes.
   b. eat popcorn.
   c. eat hotdogs.

4. During the fight, Estévez thought that
   a. Mantequilla Nápoles would not endure the fight.
   b. Mantequilla would knock out Monzón.
   c. Monzón would knock out Mantequilla.

5. Toward the end of the fight:
   a. Monzón hit Mantequilla with two to the left and a final blow to the right.
   b. Monzón hit Mantequilla with a final big blow to the left.
   c. Monzón knocked out Mantequilla.

6. At the end of the boxing match:
   a. the gong was heard loudly and clearly by all the spectators.
   b. many spectators did not hear the gong.
   c. the gong did not ring.

7. After the match was over:
   a. Monzón saluted the spectators.
   b. Monzón fell down from exhaustion.
   c. Monzón immediately left the ring.

8. Estévez thought that:
   a. it was a great fight.
   b. it was a short fight.
   c. the match was a waste of his time.

9. The winner of the boxing match was:
   a. Monzón.
   b. Mantequilla Nápoles.
   c. Estévez.

10. Walter thought that:
   a. Monzón was not tough enough.
   b. the match could have lasted longer.
   c. it was a great fight.

Questionnaire

1. Indicate your degree of familiarity with the topic of the text.
   1. I was really familiar with it.
   2. I was familiar with most of it.
   3. I was familiar with some and unfamiliar with some.
   4. I was not familiar with very much of it.
   5. I was really not familiar with it at all.

In order to understand the following passage you need to know that sololoi refers to Hollywood films and the images they project of the "dream house."

La Casita de Sololoi

"Yo te había dicho que una vida así no era para tí, una mujer con tu talento, con tu belleza. Bien me acuerdo cómo te sacabas los primeros lugares en los 'Essay Contests.' Escrbías tan bonito. Claro, te veo muy cansada y no es para menos con esa vida de perros que llevas, pero un buen corte de pelo y una mascarilla° te harán sentirte como nueva, el azul siempre te ha sentado, hoy precisamente doy una comida y quiero presentarte a mis amigos, les vas a encantar, ¿te acuerdas de Luis Morales? El me preguntó por ti mucho tiempo después de que te casaste y va a venir, así es de que tú te quedas aquí, no, no tú aquí te quedas, lástima que mandé el chofer por las flores pero puedes tomar un taxi y más tarde, cuando me haya vestido te alcanzaré° en el salón de belleza. Cógelo Laurita, por favor, ¿qué no somos amigas? Laura yo siempre te quise muchísimo y siempre lamenté tu matrimonio con ese imbécil, pero a partir de hoy vas a sentirte otra, anda Laurita, por primera vez en tu vida haz algo por ti misma, piensa en lo que eres, en lo que han hecho contigo."

Laura se había sentido bien mirando a Silvia al borde de su tina° de mármol. Desnuda frente al espejo se cepilló el pelo, sano y brillante. De hecho todo el baño era un anuncio; enorme, satinado° como las hojas del Vogue, las cremas aplíquese en pequeños toquecitos con la yema° de los dedos en movimientos siempre ascendentes, almendras dulces, conservan la humedad natural de la piel. Su amiga, en un torbellino° un sin fin de palabras verdadero rocío de la mañana, toallitas limpiadores, suavizantes, la tomó de la mano y la guió a la recámara y siguió girando frente a ella envuelta a la romana en su gran toalla espumosa°, suplemento íntimo, benzal° para la higiene femenina, cuídese, consiéntase, introdúzcase, lo que sólo nosotras sabemos: las sales, la toalla de mayor absorbencia. Y una bata° hecha bola, la carola° del desayuno, el periódico abierto en la sección de Sociales. ¿Por qué en su propia casa estaban siempre abiertos los cajones°, los roperos° también, mostrando ropa colgada quién sabe como, zapatos apilados al aventón°? En casa de Silvia, todo era etéreo, bajaba del cielo.

Llamó al primer taxi, automáticamente dio la dirección de su casa y al bajar le dejó al chofer hasta el último centavo que había en el monedero. Como siempre, la puerta de la casa estaba emparejada° y Laura tropezó con el triciclo de una de las niñas, parecieron muchos los juguetes esparcidos° en la sala, muchos y muy grandes, un campo de juguetes, de caminar entre ellos le llegarían al tobillo°.

Empezó a subir y bajar la escalera tratando de encontrarle su lugar a cada cosa. ¿Cómo pueden amontonarse en tan poco espacio tantos objetos sin uso, tanta material muerta? Mañana habría que aerear los colchones, acomodar los zapatos, cuántos de fútbol, tenis, botas de hule°, sandalias, hacer una lista, el miércoles limpiaría los roperos, solo limpiar los trasteros de la cocina le llevaría un día entero, el jueves llamada biblioteca en que ella alguna vez pretendió escribir e instalaron la televisión porque en esa pieza se veía major, otro día entero para remendar suéteres, poner elástico a los calzones, coser botones, sí, remendar° esos calcetines caídos en torno a los tobillos, el viernes para...

Marginal glosses (left column):

face mask

catch up

bathtub

shiny
fingertip

whirlwind

foam
soap

robe; tray

drawer; closet
haphazardly

leveled

scattered
ankle

rubber

mend

Comprehension Questions for *La casita de sololoi*

1. Before Laura got married she:
   a. was a good typist.
   b. was a good writer.
   c. was a good teacher.

2. Silva recommends that Laura:
   a. divorce her husband.
   b. go to college.
   c. get a hair cut and facial.

3. Laura is feeling :
   a. satisfied with her life.
   b. indifferent about her life.
   c. frustrated with her life.

4. Silvia describes Laura's husband as:
   a. a wonderful husband.
   b. a hard worker.
   c. an imbecile.

5. Silvia's bathroom is:
   a. tiny and quite empty.
   b. large and full of feminine products.
   c. large with no feminine products.

6. Laura says that her house always has:
   a. open drawers and closets.
   b. open windows.
   c. an open refrigerator door.

7. When Laura walked into her own home she :
   a. tripped over her child's tricycle.
   b. tripped over a dresser drawer.
   c. tripped over a basketball.

8. Immediately after Laura arrived home she:
   a. went up and down the stairs to put things away.
   b. sat on the couch and cried.
   c. talked to her husband.

9. Tomorrow Laura is going to:
   a. go to get her hair done.
   b. straighten up all the shoes.
   c. return to Silvia's house.

10. After arriving home Laura:
   a. listed all the household chores that she is going to do during the following week.
   b. cooked dinner for her family.
   c. watched T.V. with her family.

CHAPTER 9

READING BETWEEN THE LINES:

DETECTING, DECODING, AND UNDERSTANDING IDIOMS IN SECOND LANGUAGES

John I. Liontas

ABSTRACT

This study investigates whether understanding of vivid phrasal (VP) idioms in second languages is universal or whether the processes of VP idiom comprehension and interpretation differ depending on the specific language being learned. Three subtypes of VP idioms have been previously established: LL (identical idioms in L1 and L2), SLL (similar idioms), and PLL (dissimilar) idioms. Fifty-three adult third-year learners of Spanish, French, and German were given an Idiom Detection Task involving 45 VP idioms (15 per language group and 5 per idiom subtype). Total idiom detection was calculated for each participant, for each VP idiom subtype, and for each language group. Results showed that (1) both idiom type and the target language studied do not significantly affect the number of correct VP idiom detections made; (2) many kinds of reading strategies and inferencing techniques are used profitably in the selection of VP idioms; and, finally, (3) the gap between L2 and L1 idioms, interaction between L1 and L2 idiomatic competence, and lack of a familiarity with target vocabulary greatly influence the accurate comprehension and interpretation of VP idioms across second languages. Implications for the classroom and future research are also discussed.

INTRODUCTION

The purpose of the present study[1] is to investigate the (meta)cognitive path taken by second language learners in detecting, decoding, and understanding *Vivid Phrasal* (VP) idioms (i.e., multiword vivid phrasal lexemic units) when such idioms are presented within texts supporting their idiomatic meanings. This study stemmed from the results of a preliminary two-year inquiry using second language (L2) learners of Modern Greek, which showed that (1) the search for a text's idiom exhibits a wide systematicity across learners; (2) context influences and affects transfer of idiomatic knowledge; and (3) understanding of L2 VP idioms requires a special processing mode, yielding two alternative interpretations—a literal and an idiomatic meaning (Liontas, 1997, 2001). Despite increased scholarly emphasis on matters of idiomaticity, none of the studies to date concerning idiom comprehension and production (Arnold & Hornett, 1990; Bobrow & Bell, 1973; Botelho da Silva & Cultler, 1993; Colombo, 1993; Cronk & Schweigert, 1992; Gibbs, 1980, 1984, 1995; Irujo, 1986; Levorato & Cacciari, 1992, 1995; McGlone, Glucksberg & Cacciari, 1994; Nippold & Rudzinski, 1993; Swinney & Cutler, 1979; Titone, 1994) has attempted to identify the cognitive-psycholinguistic processes, reading strategies and inferencing techniques used in detecting, decoding, and understanding VP idioms during contextualized reading. In an attempt to fill this gap, the present study was undertaken based on the hypothesis that L2 learners, given the situational character of the idiomatic texts used in this study, will be able to "sense" successfully where an L2 VP idiom is "hiding" in a given narrative or dialog, using a number of context cues such as graphophonics, syntax, semantics, and pragmatics.

This hypothesis is based, first, on K. Goodman's (1992, 1994, 1996) *sociopsycholinguistic transactional theory of reading.* According to this theory, reading is *making sense* of text. In order to make sense, readers construct a text parallel to the author's printed text by using graphophonic, syntactic, and semantic cues from the former text. When transacting with that text, readers also produce meaning through the personal and world knowledge they bring to the act of reading. If making sense of a text involves using the cues found there, then the construction of *idiomatic meaning* must also require use of the above cueing systems in addition to the pragmatic system that L2 readers employ in order to construct the appropriate cultural meaning of a given idiom. Use of the pragmatic system is a critical component of this construction, since the meanings of most idioms are not contained solely within the individual lexemes of which idioms are composed.

It is further hypothesized that the construction of idiomatic meaning is preceded by the construction of literal meaning, as stated in Bobrow and Bell's (1973) *literal first hypothesis*, also known as the *idiom list hypothesis*. According to this hypothesis, idioms are represented in a mental idiom list; that is, in an idiom lexicon that parallels the mental word lexicon but is distinct from it. According to the authors, the literal mode, believed to be active normally, processes the literal meaning of an idiom first. Should a linguistic analysis of literal meaning fail to yield a correct interpretation, however, the figurative mode (normally inactive) becomes active and processes the idiomatic meaning.

The reader should note that Bobrow and Bell's literal first hypothesis was framed with L1 readers in mind, who, unlike L2 readers, already possess (both consciously and unconsciously) a rich idiomatic knowledge base in their native language. As a result, L2 readers do not have the same direct access to L2 idioms as they appear to have to L1 idioms. Therefore, they should not be expected to access idioms automatically that do not exist in their mental lexicon. Similarly, they should not be expected to compute idiomatic meaning before first transacting meaning from the graphophonic, syntactic, semantic, and pragmatic cues in which a given idiom is found.

This researcher believes that the computation of idiomatic meaning is a tentative, selective, and constructive process as is the act of reading *per se*. Because the process of L2 *idiom understanding* (i.e., the comprehension and interpretation of L2 idioms) is both continuous and interactive, an investigation of L2 readers' transactional behavior while reading texts containing idioms would interest second language teachers, in that it would show how L2 reading is affected during the computation of idiomatic meaning. Such an investigation would show how L2 idioms are detected and decoded in context, what textual cues and reading strategies are used during these processes, and, finally, how L2 readers mine personal and cultural background knowledge while they attempt to comprehend and interpret texts containing a range of VP idioms. The results of this study suggest that the process of comprehending and interpreting idioms during reading is universal across second languages, despite some learner variation.

THE STUDY

This investigation sought the cognitive-psycholinguistic processes, reading strategies, and inferencing techniques used in detecting, decoding, and understanding VP idioms—whether matching idioms between L1 and L2 (Lexical-Level or LL Idioms), partially-matching (Semi-lexical Level or

SLL Idioms), and non-matching (Post-lexical Level or PLL) idioms—during contextualized reading (Table 1 presents examples of each idiom subtype discussed here). The main research question examined in this study is whether there is a universal *modus operandi* in the comprehension and interpretation of VP idioms in second languages or whether the processes of VP idiom comprehension and interpretation differ depending on the specific language being learned. To answer this question, this study investigated adult L2 learners' comprehension and interpretation of VP idioms with attention to the following sub-questions:

1. Can adult L2 learners locate VP idioms when reading texts that contain them? Specifically, what textual "cues" do they use to identify them?
2. How do adult L2 learners decode VP idioms once they have been located in a text, and what particular reading strategies do they employ to comprehend and interpret them?
3. What are the processing constraints that adult L2 learners are likely to exhibit during VP idiom comprehension and interpretation?

RESEARCH DESIGN

Materials

Given the specific contextual design of this study, an investigation was launched to find paragraph-length target texts containing VP idioms. First, various dictionaries and stand-alone books were consulted. The search for naturally written texts finally came to an end with the discovery of a book series entitled *101 American English Idioms: Understanding and Speaking English Like an American*. The series is published by Passport Books (as is the *Guide to English Idioms*), a division of NTC Publishing group, and is also available in English, Spanish, French, and Japanese (see Cassagne & Cassagne, 1995a, 1995b; Collis & Risso, 1985). The *101 Idioms* series presents conversational exchanges and narrative texts of paragraph length but includes only *one* idiom per text. Even more importantly, the texts are written with the natural tone of the target language in mind, and idioms are presented in a natural context to clarify further their actual meanings and uses in everyday speech. While it is unclear whether or not these texts are taken from authentic sources, they nevertheless follow established conventions of human discourse in believable contexts supporting idiom use. Unfortunately, the series is not available in German. In order to maintain a consistent character among all texts used in this study, therefore, the English texts from *101 Idioms* were translated into German, and English idioms were replaced with culturally appropriate German idioms. This intervention ensured similarity across texts in all three languages and, furthermore, controlled for confounding variables that may have surfaced had the texts been of different natures (see sample of texts in Appendix).

All Spanish, French, and German idioms (to be used) were then entered into a computer in both English and the target language. Only those idioms that met the strict sub-categorization criteria of VP idioms were entered into the final sample corpus. Because this resulted in an inadequate number of LL, SLL, and PLL idioms for the study, some texts that did not contain idioms conforming to the three subcategories were translated from English into German, French, and Spanish. Again, English idioms were replaced with the culturally appropriate German, French, and Spanish idioms.

In the end, a random sample of 10 texts within each idiom subcategory was chosen for the purposes of this study: a total of 30 idioms for each of the three language groups. Within each language, 15 texts were once again randomly chosen for the *Idiom Detection Task* (IDT) for a total of 45 texts. These texts, accompanied by illustrative examples, were entered into a specially designed Macintosh *VP Idioms HyperCard* computer program for the study's participants, referred to in this study as the *That's All Greek to Me!* program. Table 1 presents the final 45 VP idioms chosen for this study in the order in which they were presented to the participants of this study. The table notes each particular idiom and its subtype, its literal translation into English, and the idiomatic meaning of the idiom in English.

Setting and Participants

Three hundred students, who had enrolled in thirty-five sections of third-year German, French, and Spanish courses at the University of Arizona during the Spring 1999 semester, served as the study's target population. Of these students, 53 volunteers formed the first group of students studied. This sample was equivalent to 17.66% of the total number of students enrolled in the above-mentioned courses for that semester.

Procedures: Idiom Detection Task (IDT)

All participants within a language group were exposed to the same number of idioms and idiomatic texts the same number of times in trial practice and testing. In order to mix all three subtypes of VP idioms—LL, SLL, and PLL—throughout the experiment, the order of presentation was distributed semirandomly. Each session lasted approximately 60 minutes,

Table 1. Overview of IDT Idioms

			Idiom Detection Task	
No.	Spanish Idioms	Type	Literal Translation	Idiomatic Meaning
1	colgando de un hilo	LL	to hang by a thread	to hang by a thread
2	coger a alguien con las manos en la masa	SLL	to catch someone with his or her hands in the dough	to get caught red-handed
3	andar pisando huevos	PLL	to walk stepping on eggs	to tread on thin ice
4	seguir los pasos de alguien	LL	to follow in someone's footsteps	to follow in someone's footsteps
5	largar a otro el mochuelo	SLL	to pass the owl to someone else	to pass the buck
6	no oír ni el vuelo de una mosca	PLL	to not even hear the flight of a fly	you could hear a pin drop
7	tener algo debajo de la manga	LL	to have something up one's sleeve	to have something up one's sleeve
8	estar entre la espada y la pared	SLL	to be between the sword and the wall	to be caught between a rock and a hard place
9	tener telarañas en los ojos	PLL	to have cobwebs in one's eyes	to be blind
10	tener al mundo agarrado por la cola	LL	to have the world by the tail	to have the world by the tail
11	¿Te comieron la lengua los ratones?	SLL	Did the mice eat your tongue?	Cat got your tongue?
12	empezar la casa por el tejado	PLL	to start building the house at the roof	to put the cart before the horse
13	buscar una aguja en un pajar	LL	to look for a needle in a haystack	to look for a needle in a haystack
14	quemarse las pestañas	SLL	to burn one's eyelashes	to burn the midnight oil
15	caundo las ranas críen pelo	PLL	when frogs grow hair	when pigs fly

Table 1. Overview of IDT Idioms (Cont.)

Idiom Detection Task

No.	French Idioms	Type	Literal Translation	Idiomatic Meaning
1	joindre les deux bouts	LL	to make ends meet	to make ends meet
2	se lever du mauvais pied	SLL	to get up on the wrong foot	to get up on the wrong side of the bed
3	avoir le coeur sur la main	PLL	to have one's heart on one's hand	to give the shirt off one's back
4	mordre la poussière	LL	to bite the dust	to bite the dust
5	ne pas réveiller le chat qui dort	SLL	do not wake up the sleeping cat	let sleeping dogs lie
6	tourner autour du pot	PLL	to circle around the pot	to beat around the bush
7	se tourner les pouces	LL	to twiddle one's thumbs	to twiddle one's thumbs
8	couper l'herbe sous le pied de quelqu'un	SLL	to cut the grass under someone's feet	to cut the ground from under somebody's feet
9	il tombe des hallebardes	PLL	halberds are falling	it's raining cats and dogs
10	aller à contre-courant	LL	to go against the stream	to go against the stream
11	appeler un chat un chat	SLL	to call a cat a cat	to call a spade a spade
12	c'est la goutte d'eau qui fait déborder le vase	PLL	it's the water drop that makes the vase over-flow	the straw that broke the camel's back
13	ne tenir qu'à un fil	LL	to hang by a thread	to hang by a thread
14	être sous les verrous	SLL	to be under the bolts	to be under lock and key
15	tirer les plans sur la comète	PLL	to draw up plans on the comet	to count one's chickens before they've hatched

Table 1.   Overview of IDT Idioms (Cont.)

		Idiom Detection Task	
No.	German Idioms	Type	Literal Translation	Idiomatic Meaning
1	Öl ins Feuer gießen	LL	to pour oil in the fire	to add fuel to the fire
2	Hunde, die bellen, beißen nicht	SLL	dogs that bark don't bite	his bark is worse than his bite
3	das Fell verkaufen, ehe man den Bären erledigt hat	PLL	to sell the hide before one kills the bear	to count your chickens before they've hatched
4	hinter dem Rücken sprechen	LL	to talk behind someone's back	to talk behind someone's back
5	Wem die Jacke passt, der zieht sie an	SLL	whomever the jacket fits, he or she shall wear it	if the shoe fits, wear it
6	wie die Katze um den heißen Brei herumreden	PLL	to walk like a cat around hot porridge	to beat around the bush
7	den Stier bei den Hörnern packen	LL	to take the bull by the horns	to take the bull by the horns
8	in die Klemme kommen	SLL	to be in a tight spot	to be in the hole
9	eine Lanze brechen für	PLL	to break a spear for someone	to go to bat for someone
10	schlafende Hunde soll man nicht wecken	LL	one should not wake up sleeping dogs	let sleeping dogs lie
11	schwing das Tanzbein	SLL	swing your dancing leg	shake a leg
12	die Suppe, die man sich eingebrockt hat, auslöffeln	PLL	to spoon the soup one has crumbled into alone	to face the music
13	das Kriegsbeil begraben	LL	to bury the hatchet	to bury the hatchet
14	hinter Schloss und Riegel	SLL	behind bars	under lock and key
15	ein Haar in der Suppe finden	PLL	to find a hair in the soup	to split hairs

although no specified time limit was set. Following a practice trial, participants were presented with 15 experimental texts containing either an LL, SLL, or PLL idiom. For each trial, all task instructions appeared at the center of an Apple Macintosh computer screen in order to familiarize participants with the demands and procedures of the *Idiom Detection Task* (IDT). An illustrative practice trial followed the "instructions" card, and then a preselected narrative or dialogue text containing either an LL, SLL, or PLL idiom appeared. The bottom of the card made use of fields into which participants could type their responses. Participants were also able to select the words they believed made up the idiom in each text using the highlighting feature of the computer mouse. This built-in self-selection feature assured reliability and accuracy of data across all fifteen texts and across language groups in the IDT. In addition to a button that called the next card, each card containing an idiomatic text also had a button that participants could click in order to see the correct answer. This built-in "answer documentation" feature was integrated into the *That's All Greek to Me!* program to motivate participants to complete the program. At no point, however, did the program allow participants to go back to previous responses to make corrections or changes. Throughout the study, participants proceeded at their own pace and controlled the rate of program and answer presentation.

Task Description

The aim of the IDT was to determine how well L2 learners strategize when confronted with reading texts containing a range of VP idioms, and what context cues and principles of communication they employ in identifying these idioms. As mentioned above, participants were presented with 15 experimental texts exemplifying LL, SLL, and PLL idioms. Each text item was made up of either a short narrative six to ten sentences long or a short dialog between two speakers with three to seven interactional exchanges. Narratives and dialogs were randomly selected from a preselected corpus of 30 texts. Every narrative and dialog contained only one idiomatic expression. Participants were asked to select the words making up the idiomatic expression in each text. Once they had made a decision, they had to explain their choice by writing a brief report on the cognitive-psycholinguistic processes, reading strategies, and inferencing techniques that guided their selection, including a discussion of the difficulties of detecting the given VP idiom and how they attempted to resolve those difficulties. They were also instructed to report on the feelings they had experienced during the task.

Task Assumptions

This task predicted that in the "process of discovery," participants will compute separately both a literal and an idiomatic meaning for a given VP idiom. In the former case, the literal meaning of the idiom will be computed automatically during the decoding of the text (the general or greater level of context) or of the particular idiom (the specific or narrower level of context). In the latter case, idiomatic meaning will be understood only after recognition of the greater contextual influences (the syntactic, semantic, and pragmatic constraints) upon that meaning is achieved. Expressed differently, the introspection of the general assessment of the meaning of the text will lead participants to the identification and interpretation of the idiomatic expression precisely because such expressions are embedded in the broader context of human experience.

Scoring

The idiom selections were evaluated on the basis of their correctness using a three-point scale. A score of 2 was given for those expressions that were correctly located in the text for a total of 30 possible points. For expressions that were only partially located, a score of 1 was given. For those expressions that were missed entirely, a score of 0 was assigned.

Anticipated Outcomes

Using the "literal meaning of the VP idioms," "translation," and "context," participants in this idiom detection study will be in most cases capable of selecting the phrasal unit that comprises the VP idiom. Furthermore, L2 learners will use various kinds of reading strategies such as forward inferencing; process of elimination; and contextual lexical, grammatical, and syntactic cues to reach a decision such as improbability, literal translation, word arrangement and placement in text, context, and fantastic/metaphorical images.

Data Analysis

The dependent variable was the number of correct answers within the experimental task. The data were analyzed using two types of statistical tests: (a) one-way analysis of variance (ANOVA) tests to determine the significance of possible differences in means between idiom categories and tasks; (b) Tukey Multiple Comparison tests to compare the pairs of means in an effort to denote the minimum significant difference. This analysis was conducted using the SPSS for Windows program. Following this analysis, students' explanations of their phrase selections were analyzed for commonalities. Recurring thematic units present in these explanations were then classified on the basis of a number of conceptual categories based on how participants decided which given phrase was a VP idiom (e.g., "transla-tion," "context," "image," "literal meaning does not make sense," "it stands out," "prior knowledge"). These units were then pooled, given a single label and, finally, quantified in terms of percentages of each category against all responses. In the process, whenever emerging patterns were ambiguous, follow-up interviews with individual participants were con-ducted in order to triangulate and supplement understanding of the issues at hand.[2]

RESULTS AND DISCUSSION

The number of correct idiom detections between idiom categories and across languages was high: an 86.33% success rate for the entire language group. Tables 2, 3, and 4 present the results of the experiment for each of the 53 participants in their respective language groups. Each of the three tables depicts several pieces of task performance information that can be read both across and down, and this information is organized in columns and rows. A heading indicating the task under investigation, the type of idiom investigated, the individual participants' ID numbers, the score, and the percent of VP idioms correctly identified precedes each column. Each row presents information on a particular VP idiom, the classification of the numbered idiom into one of the previously established three subtypes of VP idioms (LL, SLL, or PLL), the individual's rate of successful detections for each of the fifteen texts using the three-point scale system described earlier, and the total numeric score obtained for each idiomatic text (also expressed as a percentage). The percent value given at the end of each row represents the success rate of the particular language group as a whole for that particular text. Separate from the main table are two summary rows that provide additional information on the total time in seconds spent by individuals completing the task as well as the total individual and group score for the task under investigation. The total percent performance of the IDT is highlighted in bold print.

A comparison between groups revealed that there were no significant differences across the three language groups in terms of performance nor significant differences between success rates for identifying the three sub-types of VP idioms. It must be noted, however, that PLL idioms were consis-tently detected more often than the other two subtypes of VP idioms—LL and SLL idioms—across all languages. The number of VP idioms detected correctly ranged from a low of 7 (2 participants or 3.77%) to a high of 15 idioms (9 participants or 16.98%). The participants' average correct rate of detection as a group was 13 out of 15 VP idioms, resulting in an overall suc-

Table 2.   Spanish IDT Data

IDT Spanish Idioms	Type	7571	2013	5587	6149	3177	0616	7492	4665	1110	1764	8318	2044	9585	7767	8294	9182
1 colgando de un hilo	LL	2	0	0	2	2	2	0	2	2	2	2	2	2	2	2	0
2 coger a alguien con las manos en la masa	SLL	2	2	0	0	2	0	0	2	0	0	2	2	2	2	2	2
3 andar pisando huevos	PLL	2	2	2	2	2	2	2	2	2	2	2	2	2	2	2	2
4 seguir los pasos de alguien	LL	2	2	0	2	2	2	2	2	2	2	2	0	2	2	0	0
5 largar a otro el mochuelo	SLL	2	2	2	0	1	2	0	2	2	2	2	0	2	2	2	2
6 no oír ni el vuelo de una mosca	PLL	2	2	2	2	0	2	2	2	2	2	2	2	2	2	2	2
7 tener algo debajo de la manga	LL	2	2	2	2	1	2	2	2	2	0	2	2	2	2	2	2
8 estar entre la espada y la pared	SLL	0	0	2	2	2	2	2	2	2	2	2	2	2	2	0	2
9 tener telarañas en los ojos	PLL	2	2	2	2	2	2	2	2	2	2	2	2	2	2	2	2
10 tener al mundo agarrado por la cola	LL	2	2	2	2	2	2	2	2	2	2	2	2	2	2	2	2
11 ¿Te comieron la lengua los ratones?	SLL	2	2	2	2	2	2	2	2	2	2	2	2	2	2	2	2
12 empezar la casa por el tejado	PLL	2	2	2	2	2	2	2	2	2	2	2	2	2	2	2	2
13 buscar una aguja en un pajar	LL	2	2	2	2	0	2	2	2	2	2	2	2	2	2	2	2
14 quemarse las pestañas	SLL	2	2	0	2	2	2	2	2	2	2	2	2	2	2	2	2
15 caundo las ranas críen pelo	PLL	2	2	2	2	2	2	0	2	2	2	2	2	2	2	2	2
Total Time (sec)		763	786	731	1096	699	2406	1572	1313	993	914	612	1228	1415	1208	1094	1660
Total Score		28	26	22	26	24	28	22	30	28	26	30	26	30	28	26	26

Table 2. Spanish IDT Data (Continued)

IDT Spanish Idioms	Type	4693	9666	6643	5724	9288	0351	8833	9987	3094	3427	2169	9438	Score	Percent
1 colgando de un hilo	LL	2	2	2	2	2	2	2	2	2	2	2	2	48	85.71
2 coger a alguien con las manos en la masa	SLL	0	2	2	2	2	2	2	2	2	2	2	2	42	75.00
3 andar pisando huevos	PLL	2	2	2	2	2	2	2	2	2	2	2	2	56	100.00
4 seguir los pasos de alguien	LL	2	2	0	2	2	0	2	2	2	2	2	2	42	75.00
5 largar a otro el mochuelo	SLL	2	0	2	0	2	2	2	0	0	0	2	2	39	69.64
6 no oír ni el vuelo de una mosca	PLL	2	2	2	2	2	2	2	2	2	2	2	2	54	96.43
7 tener algo debajo de la manga	LL	2	2	2	2	2	2	2	2	0	2	2	2	51	91.07
8 estar entre la espada y la pared	SLL	2	2	2	2	2	2	2	2	0	2	2	2	48	85.71
9 tener telarañas en los ojos	PLL	2	2	2	2	2	2	2	2	2	2	2	2	56	100.00
10 tener al mundo agarrado por la cola	LL	2	2	2	2	2	2	2	2	2	2	2	2	56	100.00
11 ¿Te comieron la lengua los ratones?	SLL	2	2	2	0	2	2	2	2	2	2	2	2	54	96.43
12 empezar la casa por el tejado	PLL	0	2	2	2	2	2	2	2	2	2	2	2	54	96.43
13 buscar una aguja en un pajar	LL	2	2	2	2	2	2	2	2	2	2	2	2	54	96.43
14 quemarse las pestañas	SLL	2	2	2	2	2	2	2	2	2	2	0	2	52	92.86
15 caundo las ranas crien pelo	PLL	2	2	0	2	0	2	2	2	2	2	2	2	50	89.29
Total Time (sec)		1858	1775	1348	2810	1253	1735	2045	2221	2002	1956	1325	1786		
Total Score		26	28	26	26	28	28	30	28	24	28	28	30	756	**90.00**

Table 3.   French IDT Data

IDT French Idioms	Type	5483	9114	9686	5133	0178	7886	1440	5803	5263	6153	9820	8002	Score	Percent
1 joindre les deux bouts	LL	2	2	2	0	0	2	2	2	0	2	0	2	16	66.67
2 se lever du mauvais pied	SLL	2	2	2	0	0	0	2	2	0	2	2	0	14	58.33
3 avoir le coeur sur la main	PLL	2	2	2	2	2	2	2	2	0	2	2	2	22	91.67
4 mordre la poussière	LL	2	2	2	2	2	0	2	2	2	2	2	2	22	91.67
5 ne pas réveiller le chat qui dort	SLL	2	0	2	0	0	2	2	2	2	2	0	2	16	66.67
6 tourner autour du port	PLL	2	0	2	0	2	2	2	2	2	2	2	2	20	83.33
7 se tourner les pouces	LL	2	0	2	0	2	2	2	2	2	2	0	0	16	66.67
8 couper l'herbe sous le pied de quelqu'un	SLL	2	2	2	2	0	2	2	2	2	2	2	2	22	91.67
9 il tombe des hallebardes	PLL	2	2	2	2	2	2	2	2	2	2	2	0	22	91.67
10 aller à contre-courant	LL	2	0	2	0	2	2	2	2	2	2	2	2	20	83.33
11 appeler un chat un chat	SLL	2	0	0	2	2	2	2	2	2	2	2	2	20	83.33
12 c'est la goutte d'eau qui fait déborder le vase	PLL	2	2	0	2	2	2	2	0	2	2	2	1	19	79.17
13 ne tenir qu'à un fil	LL	2	0	2	0	2	0	2	2	2	2	2	2	18	75.00
14 être sous les verrous	SLL														
15 tirer les plans sur la comète	PLL	2	0	2	2	2	2	2	2	0	2	2	2	20	83.33
Total Time (sec)		2089	1419	889	1464	1464	1211	1243	867	1615	897	864	1495		
Total Score		28	14	24	14	20	22	28	26	20	28	22	21	267	**79.46**

Table 4. German IDT Data

IDT German Idioms	Type	3725	5620	1779	4733	1513	1234	1936	4601	4325	6879	9260	0408	1943	Score	Percent
1 Öl ins Feuer gießen	LL	0	0	2	2	0	2	2	0	2	2	2	2	2	18	69.23
2 Hunde, die bellen, beißen nicht	SLL	2	2	2	2	2	2	2	2	2	2	2	2	2	26	100.00
3 das Fell verkaufen, eheman den Bären erledigt hat	PLL	1	2	2	2	2	2	2	2	2	2	2	1	2	24	92.31
4 hinter dem Rücken sprechen	LL	2	2	2	2	2	2	2	0	2	2	2	2	2	24	92.31
5 Wem die Jacke passt, der zieht sie an	SLL	2	2	2	2	2	2	2	0	2	2	0	2	2	22	84.62
6 wie die Katze um den heißen Brei herumreden	PLL	2	2	2	2	2	2	2	2	2	2	2	2	2	26	100.00
7 den Stier bei den Hörnern packen	LL	2	2	2	2	2	2	2	2	2	2	2	2	2	26	100.00
8 in die Klemme kommen	SLL	2	2	2	2	0	0	2	0	2	2	2	2	2	20	76.92
9 eine Lanze brechen für	PLL	2	0	2	2	0	2	2	2	0	2	0	2	2	18	69.23
10 schlafende Hunde soll man nicht wecken	LL	2	2	2	2	2	2	2	0	2	2	2	2	2	24	92.31
11 schwing das Tanzbein	SLL	2	2	2	2	2	2	2	0	2	2	2	2	2	24	92.31
12 die Suppe, die man eingebrockt hat, auslöffeln	PLL	2	0	2	2	0	2	2	2	2	2	2	2	2	22	84.62
13 das Kriegsbeil begraben	LL	2	2	2	0	2	2	2	2	2	2	0	2	2	22	84.62
14 hinter Schloss und Riegel	SLL	2	2	2	2	2	2	2	2	2	2	2	2	2	26	100.00
15 ein Haar in der Suppe finden	PLL	2	2	2	2	2	2	2	2	2	2	2	2	2	26	100.00
Total Time (sec)		4464	3150	3297	5050	2035	1646	2963	1514	1233	1033	1891	1919	1115		
Total Score		27	24	30	28	22	28	30	18	28	30	24	29	30	**348**	**89.23**

cess rate of 86.33%. Individually, participants' performance ranged from a low of 58.33% to a high of 100%.

Table 5 presents the summary of all IDT data. Columns in the table identify the particular task under investigation, the individual languages investigated and, finally, the summary of IDT data for all languages combined. Rows, on the other hand, present the collective performance for each of the three subtypes of VP idioms across all languages and, finally, the row marked "Group Total" summarizes task performance for each individual language and for the languages as a whole. The final performance value is highlighted in bold print. All numeric values given are percentages of correct idiom detection. Performance was calculated by dividing the actual number of points achieved by the maximum number of points possible in each of the three idiom categories.

Table 5.   Summary of IDT Data

IDT	Spanish	French	German	Languages
LL	89.64	76.67	87.69	84.67
SLL	83.93	75.00	90.77	83.82
PLL	96.43	85.83	89.23	90.50
Group Total	**90.00**	**79.17**	**89.23**	**86.33**

A closer inspection of the PLL detection performance across the three languages reveals that while there is, on average, a 10% difference between LL and PLL, and between SLL and PLL for Spanish and French, the difference among VP idiom subtypes for German is almost nonexistent. This result, albeit interesting in many ways, may be attributed to the fact that L2 PLL idioms are the most striking of the three VP idiom subtypes perhaps because of the large gap between their literal and idiomatic meanings. If one keeps in mind that nearly half of all PLL idiom phrases used in this study have an animal or a body part as the key word, it is clear why these phrases do not make sense if taken literally. The following two comments highlight this point:

> They [idioms] were easy to spot if they contained animal expressions or were complete nonsense outside of the paragraph (for ex: to find a hair in the soup). If the idiom was present in the text, it helped me to figure out what the idiom may be referring to.

> Idioms with animals or other completely random words were the easiest to pick out, as they didn't fit the context.

Another point worth noting here is that of the eight VP idioms for which participants achieved a perfect score (i.e., a 100-percent success rate in idiom detection), four were of the PLL type, two were of the LL type, and another two were of the SLL type. Within these eight VP idioms then, the ratio of accurate VP idiom detection is a 2 to 1 ratio for PLL versus LL and SLL idioms combined. Tables 6, 7, and 8 display the results of the one-way ANOVA and Tukey analyses for all IDT data, along with other relevant descriptive statistics.

The results of the ANOVA and Tukey analyses show that there is sufficient evidence to support the notion that (1) the observed differences among the three idiom categories within a language group, (2) the observed differences across the three languages, and (3) the observed differences for all three languages may be the product of chance. Therefore, there are no significant differences among idiom categories or across languages in the ways in which L2 learners detect VP idioms. Significant findings to the contrary would have suggested: (1) that within a language group, a particular idiom type would be more likely to be detected than another type, (2) that VP idioms of one language are more or less difficult to detect than those of another language, and (3) that observed differences in means are consistent among idiom types and across languages. This is not to suggest that there are no differences either among idiom types or across the second languages here investigated, especially when the focus of investigation shifts from idiom detection to idiom understanding (i.e., the combined comprehension and interpretation process of VP idioms).

The study's use of Transactional Idiom Analysis (TIA)—an examination of how well L2 learners strategize and transact idiomatic meaning when confronted with VP idioms in a variety of reading tasks—reveals specific kinds of techniques used that the detection scores alone do not show. Analysis of participants' metacognitive protocols for VP idiom selection revealed a host of helpful information for both theory development and pedagogy. Tables 9, 10, and 11 present the reading strategies uncovered through such a qualitative inventory. Each of the three language-specific tables captures information on an individual's choice of contextual aids as well as the choice rate of the group as a whole. The farthest to the right column in each table, marked "Percent of Total Responses," indicates the percentage each category occupies within all other categories. In turn, each category is followed by the number of instances this particular category was mentioned in each participant's response, followed by a total score of coded instances for individual participants and the group as whole. The area marked "Total Tally" indicates the richness of data per participant, which in all cases surpassed the performance information obtained solely from the three-point scale system present in Tables 2, 3, and 4.

Table 6.   IDT Statistical Analyses Between Idiom Categories

Spanish

Performance per Idiom Type

Type	Score	Score	Score	Score	Score	Sum	Average	Variance	Difference in Types
LL	85.71	75.00	91.07	100.00	96.43	448.21	89.642	96.31327	5.714 LL-SLL
SLL	75.00	69.64	85.71	96.43	92.86	419.64	83.928	130.77810	6.788 PLL-LL
PLL	100.00	96.43	100.00	96.43	89.29	482.15	96.430	19.11735	12.502 PLL-SLL

ANOVA (One-Factor)

Source of Variation	SS	df	MS	Fobs	P-value	Fcrit	Q	W
Between Groups	391.711	2	195.85500	2.386459	0.134102	3.88529	3.77	15.2738
Within Groups	984.834	12	82.06956					
Total	1376.540	14						

French

Performance per Idiom Type

Type	Score	Score	Score	Score	Score	Sum	Average	Variance	Difference in Types
LL	66.67	91.67	66.67	83.33	75.00	383.34	76.668	118.03610	1.668 LL-SLL
SLL	58.33	66.67	91.67	83.33	N/A	300.00	75.000	231.51850	9.166 PLL-LL
PLL	91.67	83.33	91.67	79.17	83.33	429.17	85.834	31.26668	10.834 PLL-SLL

ANOVA (One-Factor)

Source of Variation	SS	df	MS	Fobs	P-value	Fcrit	Q	W
Between Groups	321.681	2	160.8409	1.369635	0.294347	3.98230	3.82	18.51288
Within Groups	1291.760	11	117.4333					
Total	1613.440	13						

German

Performance per Idiom Type

Type	Score	Score	Score	Score	Score	Sum	Average	Variance	Difference in Types
LL	69.23	100.00	92.31	84.62	92.31	438.47	87.694	136.1053	3.076 SLL-LL
SLL	100.00	76.92	92.31	100.00	84.62	453.85	90.770	100.6006	1.538 PLL-LL
PLL	92.31	69.23	84.62	100.00	100.00	446.16	89.232	165.6811	1.538 SLL-PLL

ANOVA (One-Factor)

Source of Variation	SS	df	MS	Fobs	P-value	Fcrit	Q	W
Between Groups	23.6544	2	11.82722	0.088178	0.916186	3.88529	3.77	19.5262
Within Groups	1609.5480	12	134.12900					
Total	1633.2020	14						

Table 7. IDT Statistical Analyses Across Languages

LL Idioms

Performance per Language

Language	Score	Score	Score	Score	Score	Sum	Average	Variance	Difference in Types
SPA	85.71	75.00	91.07	100.00	96.43	448.21	89.642	96.31327	12.974 SPA-FRE
FRE	66.67	91.67	66.67	83.33	75.00	383.34	76.668	118.03610	1.948 SPA-GER
GER	69.23	92.31	100.00	92.31	84.62	438.47	87.694	136.1053	11.026 GER-FRE

ANOVA (One-Factor)

Source of Variation	SS	df	MS	F_{obs}	P-value	F_{crit}	Q	W
Between Groups	489.4868	2	244.7434	2.095078	0.165799	3.88529	3.77	18.22266
Within Groups	1401.8910	12	116.8182					
Total	1891.3060	14						

SLL Idioms

Performance per Language

Type	Score	Score	Score	Score	Score	Sum	Average	Variance	Difference in Types
SPA	75.00	85.71	96.43	69.64	92.86	419.64	83.928	130.7781	8.928 SPA-FRE
FRE	58.33	91.67	83.33	66.67	N/A	300.00	75.000	231.5185	6.842 GER-SPA
GER	100.00	76.92	92.31	84.62	100.00	453.85	90.770	100.6006	15.770 GER-FRE

ANOVA (One-Factor)

Source of Variation	SS	df	MS	Fobs	P-value	Fcrit	Q	W
Between Groups	552.7404	2	276.3702	1.876506	0.198983	3.98230	3.82	20.73237
Within Groups	1620.0700	11	147.2791					
Total	2172.8110	13						

PLL Idioms

Performance per Language

Type	Score	Score	Score	Score	Sum	Average	Variance	Difference in Types
SPA	100.00	100.00	96.43	89.29	482.15	96.430	19.11735	10.596 SPA-FRE
FRE	91.67	91.67	79.17	83.33	429.17	85.834	31.26668	7.198 SPA-GER
GER	92.31	69.23	84.62	100.00	446.16	89.232	165.68110	3.398 GER-FRE

ANOVA (One-Factor)

Source of Variation	SS	df	MS	Fobs	P-value	Fcrit	Q	W
Between Groups	292.7214	2	146.3607	2.032175	0.173744	3.88529	3.77	14.3083
Within Groups	864.2604	12	72.0217					
Total	1156.9820	14						

Table 8.   IDT Statistical Analysis for All Languages

Spanish, French, German

Performance per Idiom Type

Type	Count	Sum	Average	Variance	Averages Difference in Idiom Types
LL	15	1270.02	84.668	135.0933	0.8472857 LL-SLL
SLL	14	1173.49	83.82071	167.1393	5.8306667 PLL-LL
PLL	15	1357.48	90.49867	82.64156	6.6779524 PLL-SLL

ANOVA (One-Factor)

Source of Variation	SS	df	MS	Fobs	P-value	Fcrit	Q	W
Between Groups	390.1129	2	195.0565	1.53173	0.228275	3.22567	3.438	10.017267
Within Groups	5221.0980	41	127.3439					
Total	5611.2110	43						

Table 9.   Spanish IDT Strategies

IDT Spanish Idioms	7571	2013	5587	6149	3177	0616	7492	4665	1110	1764	8318	2044	9585	7767	8294	9182
1 Translation					1				3	5	4		1			1
2 Literal meaning makes no sense					1		4	6	3	2			10	2		13
3 Contextual support						1	4	4	4	8			4	3		4
4 Similar to/reminds me of							3		3	5	4		1	5	3	
5 Process of elimination						1		4	5	3	3		4	1		11
6 Prior knowledge						1		5	3	3	7	15	1	2	10	
7 Graphophonics/arrangement					2	5			3			1	2			
8 Sounds/seems/looks like				2			1			2				4		
9 Guessing							1	1						1		
10 Comparison to other idiom														1		2
11 I have no idea/I do not know							1		1							
12 Placement in text																
13 No information given	15	15	15	13	13	8	3						1			
Total Tally	15	15	15	15	17	16	15	20	23	28	19	16	24	19	15	31

Table 9. Spanish IDT Strategies (continued)

IDT Spanish Idioms	4693	9666	6643	5724	9288	0351	8833	9987	3094	3427	2169	9438	Total	Percent of Total Responses
1 Translation	5	9	2	5	10	7	3	9	7	6	3	12	93	14.62
2 Literal meaning makes no sense	2	6	3	3	2	7	7	1	3	2		10	84	13.21
3 Contextual support	2	2	3	7	4	8	10	2	4	4	5	3	82	12.89
4 Similar to/reminds me of	6	5	2	5	7	1	3	4	7	6	3	3	76	11.95
5 Process of elimination	2			1	4	10				3	3	7	62	9.75
6 Prior knowledge	1	1	6		2				1	2	1	1	59	9.28
7 Graphophonics/arrangement	1	2	1	5		1	3			2	6	1	35	5.50
8 Sounds/seems/looks like		2										2	17	2.67
9 Guessing	3							4			1		11	1.73
10 Comparison to other idiom	3		1				2		1				10	1.57
11 I have no idea/I do not know			1					3			1		7	1.10
12 Placement in text		2	2										4	0.63
13 No information given	4	2	1					1		1	3	3	96	15.09
Total Tally	29	31	19	26	29	34	28	24	23	26	25	39	636	100.00

Table 10.   French IDT Standards

IDT French Strategies	5483	9114	9686	5133	0178	7886	1440	5803	5263	6153	9820	8002	Total	Percent of Total Responses
1 Translation			1		2		5		2	2		1	13	5.53
2 Literal Meaning Makes No Sense	13		2	3	6		9	1		1		1	36	15.32
3 Contextual Support	11		2		2		10					1	26	11.06
4 Similar to/Reminds me of							3			1			4	1.70
5 Process of Elimination							1						1	.43
6 Prior Knowledge	2		1				4		1	7		2	17	7.23
7 Graphophonics/Arrangement	2				1								3	1.28
8 Sounds/Seems/Looks Like			1	2	1		7		2	2			15	6.38
9 Guessing				3	6		1			5		3	18	7.66
10 Comparison of Other Idioms													0	0.00
11 I Have No Idea/I Do Not Know							1	1				10	12	5.11
12 Placement in Text													0	0.00
13 No Information Given		14	10	11	2	14		13	12		14		90	38.30
Total Tally	28	14	17	19	20	14	41	15	17	18	14	18	235	100.00

Table 11.   German IDT Strategies

IDT German Strategies	3725	5620	1779	4733	1513	1234	1936	4601	4325	6879	9260	0408	1943	Total	Percent of Total Responses
1 Translation	5	13	15	7	3	11	15	6	12	4	8	10	13	122	25.15
2 Literal Meaning Makes No Sense	9	8	1	5			2	4			3	6	2	40	8.25
3 Contextual Support	14	12	13	11	5	7	10	4	5		5	8	2	91	18.76
4 Similar to/Reminds me of		2	3		3	5	6	1	5	8	1	3	6	43	8.87
5 Process of Elimination				3	3		2	6		2		3		19	3.92
6 Prior Knowledge	1	6		4	2	4	4	1			2	2	2	28	5.77
7 Graphophonics/Arrangement	1	1		3		2		2			2	2	3	16	3.30
8 Sounds/Seems/Looks Like	14	13	15	11	8			2	8	4	1	6	7	89	18.35
9 Guessing			1			1	2	2	1	5	5	1		18	3.71
10 Comparison of Other Idioms														0	0.00
11 I Have No Idea/I Do Not Know											2		3	6	1.24
12 Placement in Text	1		1		1						1		1	5	1.03
13 No Information Given								5	3					8	1.65
Total Tally	45	55	49	44	25	31	41	33	29	23	30	41	39	485	100.00

Table 12 presents a final summary of all IDT strategies uncovered through the TIA qualitative procedure. All data are given first as numeric total tallies, then as a total percent of responses that each strategy occupies within all other strategies. Figure 1 graphically displays the strategies.

An analysis of strategies reveals that learners of Spanish, French, and German use predominately translation, contextual support, literal meaning of the idiom, and similarity between target and domain idioms as their main means of detecting VP idioms in reading texts. This is closely followed by knowledge of graphophonics and sentence arrangement, prior cultural and background knowledge, process of elimination, and guessing. Moreover, Table 12 reveals that the location of an idiom within a text was the lowest-occurring criterion for idiom selection: 0.66%. This observation is consistent throughout all languages tested. Only slightly higher (by eight-tenths of 1%) is the occurrence of "Comparison to Other Idioms."

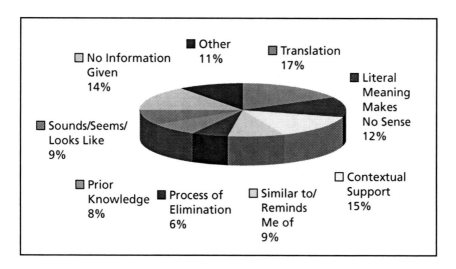

Figure 1.

A more pointed inspection of the three languages reveals that only participants in the Spanish group (6 individuals out of 28) used this latter strategy and, furthermore, that a third of that 1.57% is attributable to only one participant. The fact that this strategy is absent in both French and German groups is in all likelihood the direct result of the IDT task instructions given to all participants, which did not require them to compare the target idiom (once found) with the domain idiom. Of interest here is the observation that the first four reading strategies listed in Table 12 account for more than half of all reader activity than the remaining eight strategies

Table 12.   Summary of IDt Strategies

IDT German Strategies	Spanish	Spanish Percent	French	French Percent	German	German Percent	Total	Percent of Total Responses
1 Translation	93	14.62	13	5.58	122	25.15	228	16.81
2 Literal Meaning Makes No Sense	84	13.21	36	15.32	40	8.25	160	11.80
3 Contextual Support	82	12.89	26	11.06	91	18.76	199	14.68
4 Similar to/Reminds me of	76	11.95	4	1.70	43	8.87	123	9.07
5 Process of Elimination	62	9.75	1	0.43	19	3.92	82	6.05
6 Prior Knowledge	59	9.28	17	7.23	28	5.77	104	7.67
7 Graphophonics/Arrangement	35	5.50	3	1.28	16	3.30	54	3.98
8 Sounds/Seems/Looks Like	17	2.67	15	6.38	89	18.35	121	8.92
9 Guessing	11	1.73	18	7.66	18	3.71	47	3.47
10 Comparison of Other Idioms	10	1.57	0	0.00	0	0.00	10	0.74
11 I Have No Idea/I Do Not Know	7	1.10	12	5.11	6	1.24	25	1.84
12 Placement in Text	4	0.63	0	0.00	5	1.03	9	0.66
13 No Information Given	96	15.09	90	38.30	8	1.65	194	14.31
Total Tally	636	100.00	235	100.00	485	100.00	1356	100.00

combined (excluding the "No Information Given" category). The combined reader activity is 52.36% and 33.33% respectively.

This observation is further corroborated by the broad range of comments offered by participants. Only the most notable comments will be analyzed next. Table 13 presents an overview of all data collected from participants taking part in the IDT. This table provides a clear picture of the different types and amounts of information available for qualitative analysis. Under each column, rows indicate how many lines of comment were available for analysis, the amount of comment that each language group wrote as a whole (expressed in quantity of pages) and, finally, the total number of answers requested by the participants in each language group on the *That's All Greek to Me!* computer program, expressed both in total frequency and in percent.[3]

Table 13.   Summary Analysis of All *That's All Greek to Me! HyperCard* Output IDT Data

IDT	Spanish	French	German	Languages
Lines	400	103	409	912
Pages	43.25	15.5	18	76.75
Answers	346 or 82.38%	151 or 83.88%	171 or 87.69%	668 or 84.65%

Participants' retrospective comments revealed a host of contextual factors affecting the participants' decision process. Table 14 presents the most representative comments made by participants regarding their selections. Table 14 uses three columns to present information: Column 1 presents the Language ID (i.e., the specific language and the particular idiom in the task with regard to which the participant was making a metacognitive comment); Column 2 presents the main strategy or combination of strategies employed for that particular idiom; and finally, Column 3 presents the metacognitive comment supporting the inference or inferences drawn from each of the comments made.

Table 14.   IDT Metacognitive Comments

LAN	Strategy	Supporting Metacognitive Comment
F11	Similarity/Familiarity	We have this expression in English, so it was easy to pick out.
F03	Literalness Text reference	It is obvious that Pierre does not really have his heart on his hand, but from the previous description of his generosity one can conclude that this is an idiom for that.
F03	Literalness Personal background	Le coeur sur la main... as holding one's heart in one's hand, literally, would involve open heart surgery. I chose this as the idiom.

Table 14.   IDT Metacognitive Comments (Cont.)

LAN	Strategy	Supporting Metacognitive Comment
F05	Literalness Pragmatic knowledge	The phrase does not fit in with the rest of the paragraph if taken literally. Also 'Il ne faut pas…' sets it up as being a piece of advice in the rest of the paragraph that is using the 'tu' form.
F04	Literalness/Guessing	One cannot really bite the dust… that's why I guessed this would be the idiom.
G01	Literalness	I didn't use a strategy, the idiom was screaming to be recognized.
F07	Literalness	I doubt she is actually twisting her thumbs around.
F12	Graphophonics Arrangement	Sounds like words that aren't translated word for word.
F10	Graphophonics Arrangement	Seems the most out of place in the paragraph.
S09	Graphophonics Arrangement Semantics/Syntax	It is a group of words that all together do not make sense to me. Individually they do.
G10	Graphophonics Sounds/Looks like	It just, once again, looks and sounds out of place.
G12	Graphophonics Personal background	When I saw this, I didn't exactly know what it meant, but from the tone of the first sentence, I figured it was a saying 'for now you have to deal with it yourself,' which I related to 'now you have to spoon the soup yourself.'
F03	Graphophonics Semantics/Syntax	The words individually make sense, but you can see that the group of words is a concept. To me it reads 'the heart on the hand,' but that wouldn't make sense. So, it must be an idiom.
F10	Semantics/Syntax Lexical association	Since I know that 'contre' means 'against' and 'courant' is something 'that kind of flows along,' it was fairly easy to piece the two together and discover the idiom.
G13	Context	I didn't read through twice this time. I found it the first time I saw it. Of course I had to finish the paragraph to make sure there wasn't something else that seemed like an idiom.
F09	Context Process of elimination	I don't know what 'hallebardes' are, but it seems to be the only expression which could be an idiom.
G06	Context Personalizing situation	Don't beat around the bush. I was able to figure the idiom out by using the context, and pretending to put myself in the same situation.
F01	Context Literalness/Image Personal background	Read all of text, looked for something that does not make sense literally, but evokes an image that represents an emotion.

Table 14.   IDT Metacognitive Comments (Cont.)

LAN	Strategy	Supporting Metacognitive Comment
G15	Pragmatic knowledge	Hair and soup are out of strict context. 'B' is making an evaluative statement about 'A' that is not relevant to cars.
G06	Pragmatic knowledge	I chose this one because it again has a reference to an animal. I also believe from the context of the paragraph, that it may mean 'to beat around the bush.'
F10	Pragmatic knowledge	It is common to find idioms at the end of the paragraph.
G06	Pragmatic knowledge Context	I chose this one because it again has a reference to an animal. I also believe from the context of the paragraph, that it may mean 'to beat around the bush.'
G06	Pragmatic knowledge Personal background Context	Don't beat around the bush, say what you mean, instead of hinting at it, or talking around it. This is a common idiom for me again, it stood out like a sore thumb. Once again, this phrase had nothing to do with the text. Also, often when an idiom is coming, there are usually signal words like 'wie,' 'anstatt': like, instead of, and then an impossible happening.
G02	Pragmatic knowledge Context/Graphophonics Comparison/Contrast Sounds like	I chose this segment because it talks about 'dogs who bark don't bite,' which didn't seem to fit the context of the teacher who is very strict. It sounded like an idiom to me, because it seemed to describe a strict person in some sort of an analogy.
F06	Translation/Context	I chose this because I didn't know what it meant. It seems to have something to do with 'dancing around the subject,' but I do not know its specific meaning.
F03	Translation/Context Literalness	I translated the expression as written and it did not fully make sense based on the context of the paragraph.
G12	Translation Pragmatic knowledge	The idiom is something about 'eating your soup alone and suffering the consequences by yourself...' idioms are usually found near the end of a saying or phrase, as a result of something else.
G11	Image	The phrase gives a good visual image, so it is easy to understand.
G13	Image	I have never heard this expression before, but it gives a good image.
G15	Image	That's funny. It was easy to find because it is figurative.
G06	Image Paragraph organization	The expression gives me a funny image in my head (a whole bunch of cats around cheese) that just doesn't quite fit with the girl trying to go swimming.
S14	Process of elimination	Everything makes sense to me except that phrase.

Table 14.   IDT Metacognitive Comments (Cont.)

LAN	Strategy	Supporting Metacognitive Comment
G13	Process of elimination	Although I am not familiar with the word 'Kriegsbeil,' I chose this phrase because it is reinforcing the statement 'we solved the problem.'
F03	Process of elimination	I simply look for something which may not be physically possible. Somewhat of a 'moral' to the story here.
G15	Process of elimination Literalness	This expression is easy to spot because the clerk is all of a sudden talking about a hair in the soup, and this does not go along with the rest of the context.
F09	Process of elimination Literalness	Seems to stand apart from the normal flow of conversation.
F13	Process of elimination Literalness/Guessing	I didn't know exactly what 'ne tient qu'un fil' means, but process of elimination makes it the only part which might not be able to be taken literally. Similar to 'hanging by a thread,' I'm guessing.
F05	Process of elimination Context/Literalness Guessing	The text has nothing to do with cats, therefore I chose that expression. It corresponds to 'letting sleeping dogs lie' in English.

These metacognitive comments cited above show that literal translation of the lexical items comprising the idiomatic expression is omnipresent in the ways participants transact textual meaning. This suggests that lexical access is obligatory for individual words even when they are part of a VP idiom. While some lexical chunks were easily identified as idioms, others had to be computed first literally and then figuratively within a given text. Furthermore, the transaction of idiomatic meaning was not independent of the context in which the idiom was found. More often than not, knowledge of graphophonics, semantics, and syntax helped in the detection and comprehension of an idiom, but this did not necessarily result in its correct interpretation. In the words of one participant, "It was easier for me to pinpoint which phrase was an idiom, but it was more difficult to know what it said." To achieve the latter, a great many participants found it necessary to resort to their own pragmatic and cultural background knowledge in transacting idiomatic meaning, while others tried to envision how they would use the idiom in English in a similar situation. One participant phrased it this way:

I think the greatest challenge I faced was thinking of idioms in English. I guess, I just am not aware of the expressions in English. I just thought of what I would say in English. Most of the time the context and meaning of the words helped. I didn't know all the words, which hindered the process.

Scrutinizing participants' comments even more closely, it becomes clear that a major obstacle in the accomplishment of the IDT was lack of a familiarity with target vocabulary. This is particularly true for those participants who felt that they had limited vocabulary. As one participant said:

> I looked for phrases in the first part that did not make sense if taken literally and assumed that they were idioms. In figuring them out, I looked for key words that I knew from idioms. My biggest challenge was lack of vocabulary. Many of the idioms had the same feel as English idioms but with a different twist.

Another participant noted feelings of discouragement and frustration:

> I have no idea what this one means ... maybe something like 'it's good to the last drop...' I have no idea, this is so frustrating when it isn't a direct meaning.

One should note, however, that many participants did manage to work through such feelings and allowed context to help them understand the idiomatic expression, using a variety of contextual strategies and schematic inferences. Through a more pointed analysis of the summative entries, it becomes apparent that participants felt that their reading comprehension was greatly enhanced when they could (1) recognize the meaning of the individual words of an idiom, (2) distinguish between literal and figurative meaning, (3) identify the textual cues and communicative intents that supported the use of a particular idiom, (4) connect the L2 idiom to its equivalent L1 idiom, and (5) realize that in certain contexts their own pragmatic and cultural background knowledge can have a direct bearing on the accurate comprehension and interpretation of an idiom. In the end, more than 86% of participants succeeded at the Idiom Detection Task, a rather high percentage of success by any account.

In sum, it is clear from the variety of participants' comments noted above and from the discussion of the findings thus far that L2 learners employ a variety of (meta)cognitive strategies to identify VP idioms. Context cues influence the reader's interpretation of text in a variety of ways. Not only do cross-taxonomic elements become related, but intra-taxonomic relationships also become apparent. While there is no one linear path to understanding texts and the idioms contained in them, the emerging reading pattern of these 53 adult third-year learners of Spanish, French, and German seems to suggest that learner behavior is highly systematic and universal with regard to the ways in which learners identify, decode, and understand L2 VP idioms in texts supporting their idiomatic meanings. In other words, L2 learners, regardless of target language studied, analyze input and interpret idioms in much the same way. One source that learners draw upon regularly to construct idiomatic interpretations is the L1 which, in turn, greatly influences the quantity and quality of target idiom interpretation, leading to both positive and negative transfer. This finding corroborates results found by Irujo (1986) and Liontas (1997, 2001), which suggest that the learner's native language plays an important role in idiom understanding and, more generally, that context influences and affects transfer of idiomatic knowledge.

CONCLUSION

The primary focus of this research study was on how VP idioms are detected, decoded, and understood within texts supporting their use. A second focus was upon ascertaining the reading strategies adult L2 learners employ in the comprehension and interpretation of VP idioms as well as the meaning-making processing constraints affecting idiom understanding. To achieve these aims, a hybrid quantitative and qualitative data analysis was implemented. Analysis of data confirmed the hypothesis made at the outset of this study, namely that L2 learners are indeed able to "sense" successfully where the L2 VP idiom is "hiding" in a given narrative or dialog using a number of context cues such as syntax, semantics, and pragmatics. As seen, syntactic, semantic, and pragmatic analysis is necessary for L2 VP idiom comprehension. The data obtained also revealed the affective state of many participants, which ranged from a sense of accomplishment to complete frustration. As seen, not everyone had an easy time detecting the idioms in this study: indeed, some participants had considerable difficulty doing so, while others could not decide among phrases that could be the idiom for that particular text, and while still others were not able to verbalize how they picked out the idiom from the text or what their selection meant. Results also showed that both idiom type and the target language studied do not significantly affect the number of correct VP idiom detections made, that many kinds of reading strategies and inferencing techniques are used profitably in the selection of VP idioms and, finally, that the gap between L2 and L1 idioms, interaction between L1 and L2 idiomatic competence, and lack of a familiarity with target vocabulary greatly influence the accurate comprehension and interpretation of VP idioms across second languages.

The findings of this study underscore the notion that there may well be a universal *modus operandi* in the comprehension and interpretation of VP idioms in second languages and that, furthermore, the process of VP idiom comprehension and interpretation does not depend on the specific target language being learned. In addition, the findings suggest that L2 learners do compute literal and idiomatic meanings separately, yielding two alternative interpretations—a literal and an idiomatic meaning. "Idiomatic" sense is considered *only after* the literal interpretation has been transacted and rejected. This observation is grounded on participants' metacognitive comments and the researcher's discussions with them following completion of the Idiom Detection Task. Combined, these findings have important implications for both idiom theory development and language pedagogy. The most important implications are summarized below:

- It appears that, for the most part, VP idioms are detected with ease by learners at this general proficiency level given the strong concrete, imageable, and literal referential meaning of these idioms.
- While VP idioms may be easily detected in contexts supporting their use, their institutionalized figurative, metaphorical meanings are neither always predictable nor logically deducible in their entirety from either the graphophonic/syntactic or semantic character of their individual constituent elements.
- Comprehension and interpretation of VP idioms depend largely on the gap between L2 and their L1 counterparts.
- The closer the gap between L2 and L1 idioms and the more lexical items that are recognized within the L2 idiom, the higher the likelihood that such VP idioms will be understood accurately.
- Bridging the gap between L2 and L1 idioms is mediated by a variety of factors such as exposure to and knowledge of a wide variety of L1 idioms, but primarily by reading strategies such as forward-inferencing; process of elimination; and contextual graphophonic, syntactic, semantic, and pragmatic cues in which a given L2 idiom is found.
- Knowledge of target vocabulary appears to be a confounding variable affecting the comprehension and interpretation of a VP idiom in context.
- Interaction between L2 and L1 idiomatic competence appears to be omnipresent when VP idioms are being comprehended and interpreted.
- The process of comprehending and interpreting VP idioms in second languages during reading appears to be universal, at least with regard to German, French, and Spanish. The understanding of VP idioms is achieved because readers transact and produce meaning from a text and from what readers bring to the dynamic act of reading by way of their prior personal and cultural background knowledge, experience, interests, values, and societal paradigms. This meaning transaction is both continuous and interactive/integrative in nature, and is based on the simultaneous computation of the meaning-carrying systems available to readers (i.e., the graphophonic, lexico-grammatical, and semantic-pragmatic information

present in a text). This finding supports K. Goodman's (1992, 1994, 1996) *socio-psycholinguistic transactional reading model.*

- Regardless of the subtype of VP idiom used, the idiom's literal meaning is computed automatically during the decoding of the idiom or the text. Only when the literal meaning fails to yield a meaningful interpretation is the figurative meaning formulated within the greater context (involving syntactic, semantic, and pragmatic constraints) of the idiom in question. This finding clearly supports Bobrow and Bell's (1973) *literal first hypothesis,* although not without some modifications of the assumptions underlying their model.

- *Transactional Idiom Analysis* (TIA), when coupled with written protocols, holds much promise for research and pedagogy because it reveals how readers make sense of VP idioms in context (i.e., it gives a bird's-eye view of the readers' active thought processes leading to the construction of idiomatic meaning). In the process, patterns of contextual influence are revealed as well as the amount of language information L2 readers bring to the act of reading in general and to the comprehension and interpretation of VP idioms in particular.

Each of the findings above, if investigated further, will lead to a more complete model of the skills required for fluent idiom recognition and understanding in second and foreign languages. The precise workings of this model, including its limitations, remain the subject of further investigation. Perhaps in the not-so-distant future the profession will begin to formulate a systematic program for developing *idiomatic competence* (i.e., the ability to understand and use idioms appropriately and accurately in a variety of sociocultural contexts with the least amount of mental effort, and to use them in a cultural manner similar to that of a native speaker) in second and foreign languages, helping learners to read between the lines.

NOTES

1.   This study is based on the author's dissertation study with sixty adult third-year university learners of Spanish, French, and German (Liontas, 1999). Due to space constraints, only the Spanish, French, and German data for the IDT experiment are presented here.

2.   Fetterman (1989, p. 89) highlighted a key point about triangulation when he said, "Triangulation is basic in ethnographic research. It is at the heart of ethnographic validity, testing one source of information against another to strip away alternative explanations and prove a hypothesis" and that "Triangulation works with any topic, in any setting, and on any level ... The trick is to compare comparable items and levels during analysis." These are precisely the specific objectives of the detection task employed in this study.

3. A quick look at the data reveals that the Spanish group as a whole did considerably more work than the French group, which did the least amount of work in terms of lines and pages written. This discrepancy is quite understandable, however, given the fact that the Spanish ($n = 28$) group had more than twice as many students participating in the study than did the French ($n = 12$) and the German ($n = 13$) groups combined.

REFERENCES

Arnold, K. M., & Hornett, D. (1990). Teaching idioms to children who are deaf. *Teaching Exceptional Children, 22* (4), 14–17.

Bobrow, S. A., & Bell, S. M. (1973). On catching on to idiomatic expressions. *Memory and Cognition, 1,* 343–346.

Botelho da Silva, T., & Cutler, A. (1993). Ill-formedness and transformability in Portuguese idioms. In C. Cacciari & P. Tabossi (Eds.), *Idioms: Processing, structure, and interpretation* (pp. 27–55). Hillsdale, NJ: Erlbaum.

Cassagne, J. M., & Cassagne, L. N. (1995a). *101 French idioms: Understanding French language and culture through popular phrases.* Chicago: NTC Publishing Group.

Cassagne, J. M., & Cassagne, L. N. (1995b). *101 Spanish idioms: Understanding Spanish language and culture through popular phrases.* Chicago: NTC Publishing Group.

Collis, H., & Risso, M. (1985). *101 American English idioms: Understanding and speaking English like an American.* Chicago: NTC Publishing Group.

Colombo, L. (1993). The comprehension of ambiguous idioms in context. In C. Cacciari & P. Tabossi (Eds.), *Idioms: Processing, structure, and interpretation* (pp. 163–200). Hillsdale, NJ: Erlbaum.

Cronk, B. C., & Schweigert, W. A. (1992). The comprehension of idioms: The effects of familiarity, literalness, and usage. *Applied Linguistics, 13* (2), 131–146.

Fetterman, D. M. (1989). *Ethnography step by step.* Newbury Park, CA: Sage.

Gibbs, R. W., Jr. (1980). Spilling the beans on understanding and memory for idioms in conversation. *Memory and Cognition, 8,* 149–156.

Gibbs, R. W., Jr. (1984). Literal meaning and psychological theory. *Cognitive Science, 8,* 275–304.

Gibbs, R. W., Jr. (1995). Idiomaticity and human cognition. In M. Everaert, E. van der Linden, A. Schenk, & R. Schreuder (Eds.), *Idioms: Structural and psychological perspectives* (pp. 97–116). Hillsdale, NJ: Erlbaum.

Goodman, K. S. (1992). *Reading, writing, and written texts: A transactional sociopsycholinguistic view.* Tucson, AZ: Literacy and Learning Center, University of Arizona.

Goodman, K. S. (1994). Reading, writing, and written texts: A transactional sociopsycholinguistic view. In R. B. Ruddell, M. R. Ruddell, & H. Singer (Eds.), *Theoretical models and processes of reading* (4th ed.) (pp. 1057–1092). Newark, DE: International Reading Association.

Goodman, K. S. (1996). *Ken Goodman on reading.* Portsmouth, NH: Heinemann.

Irujo, S. (1986). Don't put your leg in your mouth: Transfer in the acquisition of idioms in a second language. *TESOL Quarterly, 20,* 287–304.

Levorato, M. C., & Cacciari, C. (1992). Children's comprehension and production of idioms: The role of context and familiarity. *Journal of Child Language, 19* (2), 415–433.

Levorato, M. C., & Cacciari, C. (1995). The effects of different tasks on the comprehension and production of idioms in children. *Journal of Experimental Child Psychology, 60* (2), 261–283.

Liontas, J. I. (1997, November). "Building castles in the air": The comprehension processes of modern Greek idioms. Paper presented at the 15th International Symposium on Modern Greece, Kent State University, Kent, OH.

Liontas, J. I. (1999). *Developing a pragmatic methodology of idiomaticity: The comprehension and interpretation of SL vivid phrasal idioms during reading.* Unpublished doctoral dissertation, The University of Arizona, Tucson, AZ. (University Microfilms No. 9946784).

Liontas, J. I. (2001). That's All Greek To Me! The comprehension and interpretation of modern Greek phrasal idioms, *The Reading Matrix: An International Online Journal, 1* (1), 1–32. Available: http://www.readingmatrix.com/articles/john_liontas/article.pdf

McGlone, M. S., Glucksberg, S., & Cacciari, C. (1994). Semantic productivity and idiom comprehension. *Discourse Processes, 17* (2), 167–190.

Nippold, M. A., & Rudzinski, M. (1993). Familiarity and transparency in idiom explanation: A developmental study of children and adolescents. *Journal of Speech and Hearing Research, 36* (4), 728–737.

Swinney, D. A., & Cutler, A. (1979). The access and processing of idiomatic expressions. *Journal of Verbal Learning and Verbal Behavior, 18,* 523–534.

Titone, D. A. (1994). Descriptive norms for 171 idiomatic expressions: Familiarity, compositionality, predictability, and literality. *Metaphor and Symbolic Activity, 9* (4), 247–270.

APPENDIX
SAMPLE OF SPANISH, FRENCH, AND GERMAN IDT TEXTS

Task: IDT, Number: 6, Idiom Type: PLL, Words: 55

Spanish Idiom: *no oír ni el vuelo de una mosca*
Les dije a los nuevos estudiantes que no hablaran durante el examen, pero no esperaba el absoluto silencio que mantuvieron durante los 50 minutos del examen. **No se oía ni el vuelo de una mosca.** Quedé bien impresionada y decidí decirles que estudiaran español tres horas diarias a ver si eso tendría el mismo resultado.

Translation: *you could hear a pin drop*
I told the new students not to talk during the exam, but I didn't expect the absolute silence they maintained for the 50 minutes of the exam. **You could have heard a pin drop**. I was very impressed and decided to tell them to study their Spanish for three hours a day to see if that would bring the same result.

Task: IDT, Number: 10, Idiom Type: LL, Words: 77

French Idiom: *aller à contre-courant*
Robert est un nouvel enseignant à l'université de Nancy. Il a beaucoup d'idées au sujet de l'enseignement pratique des langues et l'utilisation des technologies, mais, malgré tout, il a beaucoup de mal à convaincre ses collègues des avantages d'une telle approche de l'enseignement et de l'apprentissage des langues. Certains d'entre eux le trouvent même un peu trop radical. Cependant, Robert ne se préoccupe pas de leurs critiques: il a toujours été du genre à **aller à contre-courant**.

Translation: *to go against the stream*
Robert is new at the University of Arizona. He has lots of ideas about communicative language teaching and the use of technology. Nevertheless, he has a hard time convincing his colleagues of the benefits of such an approach to language learning and teaching. Some of his colleagues even consider him to be a bit too radical about the whole thing. Robert, however, does not mind their criticism since he has always been one to **go against the stream**.

Task: IDT, Number: 11, Idiom Type: SLL, Words: 36

German Idiom: *das Tanzbein schwingen*

A: Gisela, immer brauchst du so lange um dein Make-up aufzutragen. Komm' schon, **schwing das Tanzbein!**

B: Ich bin in einer Minute fertig. Hab' Geduld.

A: Du mußt dich beeilen, sonst sind wir nicht rechtzeitig zur letzten Vorführung da.

Translation: *shake a leg*

A: Gisela, you always take so long to put on your make-up. Come on, **shake a leg!**

B: I'll be ready in one minute. Be patient.

A: You have to hurry up, otherwise we will not make the last showing.

CHAPTER 10

ADVANCED FOREIGN LANGUAGE READERS' INFERENCING

JoAnn Hammadou Sullivan

ABSTRACT

Reading comprehension is believed to be an active process involving build-ing models of understanding in the mind of the reader. This study investi-gated whether successful foreign language readers at the advanced levels of university coursework are aware of their inferencing activity when attempting to recall accurately the writer's original text. The differences in outcome when using a recall protocol and open-ended comprehension questions were also investigated using a case study qualitative analysis. Ten advanced stu-dents of French read an authentic French text. Their written recalls revealed few examples of inferencing, primarily within-text inferences that summa-rized segments of the original. The open-ended questions produced consid-erably more inferences, mostly elaborative inferences, from the readers' own prior knowledge. Participants also reported their strategies for successful recall, which may be helpful models for less successful readers.

INTRODUCTION

Comprehending another language is a complex process that occurs without many external signs along the way. Recent research supports the notion that comprehension is not just understanding words, sentences, or even texts, but involves building a model within the mind of the comprehender. Today, models of comprehension are interactive and attempt to describe features of language (e.g., lexical items, syntax, topic) and features of the comprehender (e.g., goals, prior knowledge, intelligence, proficiencies) and the ways in which all of these features may interact in the process that we call comprehension (Bernhardt, 1986, 1991; Swaffar, 1988).

Because of the many contributing features of comprehension and because of the internal, nearly invisible nature of the process, comprehension has been notoriously difficult to capture and describe in all of its complexities. Researchers must continually attempt to unravel small pieces of the fabric of comprehension at a time in hopes of making our understanding of the whole more complete. Second language researchers sometimes turn to the longer tradition of first language research for guidance or direction. Unfortunately, first language comprehension research has been marred by bitter debates such as the "paradigm wars" making it more difficult for second language researchers to build on what has gone before (Kamil, 1995; Strauss, 2001).

In reading comprehension research, two features that do have a growing body of research and a seemingly compelling role are background knowledge and inferencing. These features are studied for both how they influence reading comprehension and what they tell us about the model-building process that comprehension is hypothesized to be.

Prior Knowledge Studies

A plethora of first language (L1) studies document the influence of prior knowledge on reading comprehension. Anderson and colleagues (1984) gave an ambiguous reading passage to music and physical education majors. With a text that could have been describing a woodwind quartet or a card game and another that could have been a wrestler's hold or a prison escape, the special background of the readers guided their understanding of the piece. Stahl, Hare, Sinatra, and Gregory (1991) studied the effect of both prior topic knowledge and vocabulary knowledge on recall of a text on baseball. They found that vocabulary knowledge tended to affect the number of units recalled overall and that prior knowledge tended to influence which units were recalled.

In second language (L2) research, background knowledge has also been proven to play a significant role in comprehension (e.g., Bransford & Johnson, 1972; McNamara, Kintsch, Songer, & Kintsch, 1996). Johnson (1982) gave ESL readers a passage on Halloween and demonstrated that cultural familiarity had a greater impact on comprehension than did the preteaching of vocabulary. In a study primarily of the effect of analogy on reading comprehension, Hammadou (2000) found prior topic knowledge as tested by a 12-item multiple choice test to be the most powerful factor affecting recall (p. 42).

Inference Studies

The second feature, inference, appears to be a cognitive process used to construct meaning. Inference is, in other words, a thinking process that involves reasoning a step beyond the text, using generalization, synthesis, and/or explanation. For example, when reading the text: *She saw the doctor yesterday and is now taking antibiotics*, the reader usually reasons a step beyond the words on the page and surmises both what may have brought her to the doctor's office and the conclusions that the doctor most likely came to. To do so, the reader uses generalizations of typical events and the explanatory reasoning of how those typical events would apply to the text at hand.

The significance of inferencing to L1 comprehension continues as an ongoing, open-ended investigation. The interpretation of the research findings remains problematic due to competing research paradigms, varying experimental tasks, and different types of inferences studied (Fincher-Kiefer, 1992; Perfetti, 1993; van den Broek, Fletcher, & Risden, 1993). Nevertheless, first language researchers have found inferences to be a fruitful source of clues about both the types of mental models or situational models that readers build and the possible route that readers take toward comprehension (Zwaan & Brown, 1996). First language readers are believed, in general, to construct and retain mental models of texts that contain information explicitly stated in the text as well as inferences used to bind the text together and/ or to link the text to the reader's prior knowledge. Much overlap may be found in the last two elements (links within the text and links to readers' background knowledge) such as might occur with the doctor/antibiotics example above. Inferencing within this frame of reference can be viewed as one of the key cognitive processes by which readers formulate and refine their own model of the text (Collins, Brown, & Larkin, 1980).

The topic of inference in second language reading studies is shedding light on the nature of reading comprehension in a new language as well. Hammadou (1991) investigated the differences in L2 readers' inferencing according to topic familiarity and language proficiency. Using written recall protocols to capture comprehension of L2 texts by 166 beginning and advanced L2 readers, Hammadou found a greater amount of inferencing done by beginners. Advanced readers not only wrote fewer inferences, those that reported greater familiarity with the passage topic showed a decline in illogical inferences (inferences that had no direct support in the original text). The inferencing that did occur in the written recalls of advanced readers showed a tendency to increase in logic with increased background knowledge of the topic.

Barry and Lazarte (1998) studied the amount and type of inferencing activity by L2 readers of Spanish depending on level of syntactic complexity of the passage and on amount of prior knowledge of the passage topic. Studying written recall protocols, they found, as did Hammadou (1991), that decreased prior knowledge produced greater inaccuracies in the readers' inferences, even though they eliminated from their study any inference that did not relate to ideas presented in the reading passage (Barry & Lazarte, 1998, p. 182). In addition, their study revealed that inferences in the written recalls increased with the syntactical complexity of the passage read. Unlike Hammadou (1991), Barry and Lazarte (1998) found that inferencing increased for high knowledge readers over those with little prior knowledge of the topic.

Horiba (1996) looked at narrative, not expository texts, with a focus on story line inferences. Her participants were L1 and L2 readers of Japanese and English who were asked to verbalize their thinking at the end of each sentence of a story while reading either more or less coherent stories. She found that L1 readers made fewer elaborative inferences for more coherent texts than for less coherent ones. Second language readers did not process the more and less coherent texts differently. In general, L2 advanced readers did not report as many elaborative inferences and "general knowledge associations" as L1 readers (Horiba, 1996, p. 442). It is difficult to know from Horiba's study the reason for the large number of elaborative inferences from the L1 readers. Perhaps the simple short story required only the most automatic and largely unconscious processing from them so that when asked to say something at the end of each sentence, they provided comments such as "This reminds me of..." (Horiba, 1996, p. 471). A more challenging text may have produced more similar data to the advanced L2 readers who commented extensively on issues of sentence coherence (45% to 48%) and somewhat on elaborative inferences (11% to 20%) (Horiba, 1996, p. 445). Advanced L2 readers were probably demonstrating the comprehension process during a moderate challenge—making some elaborative inferences but commenting mostly on issues of sentence coherence.

Measurement Tools

The influence of the type of measurement task used as a dependent variable (typically recall protocols, think-aloud procedures, or comprehension questions) on the results found is not yet clear in L2 reading research. Because comprehension is an internal, and normally invisible, process, researchers always have trouble finding ways to make the invisible visible without unduly disrupting the process. Some of the measures used by first language researchers are very problematic for second language researchers. For example, L1 researchers may measure self-paced reading time or speed of response to a word meant to prompt an inference, or they use word naming latencies for test words that are interspersed in the text (Graesser, Swamer, & Hu, 1997). Such measures are particularly untenable for L2 research given the interferences caused by gaps in learners' semantic and syntactic repertoires (Barry & Lazarte, 1998; Koda, 1993). L1 studies have found that differing research tasks are likely to produce differing results and may be better suited for specific types of research questions (van den Broek et al., 1993). It is necessary to investigate the effect that the research task has on the information gleaned about L2 reading comprehension.

THE STUDY

Purpose

A study was undertaken in order to: (a) investigate the differences in outcome of using a recall protocol and open-ended questions for information about L2 readers' inferencing and (b) determine successful advanced L2 readers' awareness of their inferencing when attempting to recall accurately the ideas of a writer. It was hypothesized that successful advanced L2 readers would be aware of the inferences that they have generated to bind the text to their prior knowledge and that the different tasks would produce different types of recall data.

Participants

Ten participants were selected among French majors at a major New England university. The participants were solicited based on teacher recommendation and grade-point average. Subjects were sought who were strong readers in their L1 as evidenced by teacher recommendation and self-reported success with L1 verbal testing, good French students as evidenced by their grade point average, and successful overall students as evidenced by their overall grade point average. All ten were native speakers of English who had recently completed or were near completion of a BA degree in French. These French students were labeled as "advanced" language learners for the preceding characteristics. Official ACTFL oral proficiency ratings were not available for them and the term "advanced" should be interpreted in a more general sense. From the original ten participants, eight were retained for the study. Two were eliminated as outliers on a measure of background knowledge of the reading text's topic: AIDS. These two readers with the highest and lowest score on the background knowledge test (2 and 8 out of 10 respectively) were eliminated leaving good readers with an average, hopefully typical, background knowledge of the topic in question. The remaining eight participants scored between 4 and 7 with a mean score of 5.125 and a mode of 5 for prior knowledge.

Instrumentation and Procedures

The target reading passage used was a 378 word French news article widely distributed on the Internet by the news agency *Agence France Presse* and therefore probably intended for a general (French-speaking) audience (see Appendix). A naturally occurring passage was chosen instead of a research-contrived passage since such a passage might differ from a naturally occurring one in unintended ways. Also, views of what constitutes good writing have been shown to differ for newspaper writers from those of university researchers (Graves et al., 1988). Finally, a topic was sought that would reflect the type of expository reading that many second language learners might encounter and an article on the AIDS epidemic in Africa was selected. The intent was to search for insights into the reading process on texts most likely to resemble texts typically read by American L2 readers.

Participants were first given the passage, titled *L'Afrique après 20 ans: la saignée déjà, le réveil peut-être* (Africa after 20 years: blood letting first, wake up call perhaps[1]) to read as often as they needed until they felt they understood it. Then, they were instructed to put the passage aside and try to recall the passage in writing as much as possible in their native language. After they had written their recalls, I identified the inferences that they made in the recall protocol. Those inferences were randomly listed with an equal number of accurate representations from the text and were read to the subjects. They were instructed to rank their certainty that the phrase was an accurate representation of an idea directly from the original text from 10 (most certain) to 1 (least certain). Participants then were asked a series of open-ended comprehension questions about the text and their replies were audiotaped. They were given a 10-item multiple-choice test that measured their additional knowledge of AIDS and its problems in

Africa. Finally, they were asked to describe the strategies they used to accomplish the tasks and the difficulties they had.

Participants' recall protocols were analyzed, first by counting idea units and mapping them for main ideas. Their inferences were categorized according to three categories: within-text, elaborative, or incorrect. Within-text inferences were those that summarized or synthesized ideas found in the original text. Elaborative inferences were those that combined concepts from the text with a reader's prior knowledge to add information to the original text. Incorrect inferences were those that either contradicted the text, overgeneralized or resulted from misreading (Barry & Lazarte, 1998, p. 177). The participants' open-ended answers and discussions were transcribed. These were analyzed for number of inferences and those inferences were also categorized. Finally, individual cases were analyzed for their similarities and unique qualities. The audiotaped data were searched for patterns of responses.

Group Results

There were numerous similarities among the work of these successful readers as they tackled the tasks given to them. The average number of idea units recalled was 33.25 or 43% of the original text. The range of scores was narrow—from a low of 37% of the original to a high of 49%. All eight of the participants recalled all five main ideas of the passage.[2] They all followed the basic structure of the text by commenting on each of the five main ideas in the order they were originally presented. They all (but one) abandoned examples or details that they were uncertain of, which will be discussed in greater detail later. Table 1 provides some summary data from the individuals' recalls.

Table 1.   Content of Individuals' Recall Protocols

Reader	Number of Idea Units Recalled from Original	Total Number of Words	Total Number of Inferences
Brad	41	253	2
Elaine	38	345	10
Laura	33	191	3
Margaret	28	200	4
Mary	28	265	7
Nick	37	130	2
Susan	29	251	4
Sarah	32	278	6

Inferencing and the Recall Protocol

The group wrote few inferences in their written recalls. There were a total of 19 within-text inferences, 12 elaborative, and 7 incorrect inferences. All but one participant had at least one within-text inference and only three participants had any incorrect inferences. As shown in Figure 1, most of the readers had more within-text inferences than any other kind, but the overall mean was less than 5 inferences per text. If these readers were doing much inferencing as they read, the recall protocols were not revealing them.

What was more revealing in the recall protocols was what was missing. After all of the readers had successfully reproduced the five main ideas of the passage, their reporting of supporting detail showed the most divergence in their recalls. But even this divergence was often a simple question of quantity of detail. As supporting detail to the idea that AIDS is pandemic in Africa, the original article offered overall statistics and specific numbers from Botswana. Five of the eight readers recalled the overall statistics (one incorrectly) and seven of the eight provided the Botswana example (one incorrectly). Other supporting details caused greater problems and produced greater diversity. Seven of the eight participants left out the detail

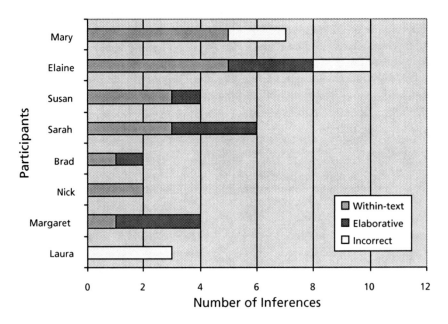

Figure 1. Type of inferences in recall protocols.

that South Africa has the worse situation. And five left out any reference to a quote by the Namibian president. These omissions might suggest that readers did not recall these details or considered them unimportant. The open-ended comprehension questions revealed a different reality, however, and will be discussed later.

Certainty Ratings

Would successful advanced readers express greater certainty about accurate representations and recognize when propositions from their own background knowledge appeared in their written recalls? It was hypothesized that they would recognize ideas that they had generated to connect the text's propositions to their own prior knowledge or to other ideas in the passage as their own. On average, the readers did rank the accurate representations with their highest certainty of 8.35 out of 10. Figure 2 shows the ratings of each type of recall.

The seven readers who made within-text inferences rated those nearly as highly as the accurate propositions. Most of these inferences were summaries that reduced the number of propositions in the textbase through synthesis. For example, one reader reduced two sentences on AIDS drugs to "pharmaceutical companies are players in the fight against AIDS." Another reduced the consequences of a government official's discussion of AIDS that, in the original, was "a public 'first' acknowledged as a turning point in the recognition of AIDS in the heart of the ruling class of the country" to "this made a big impact on the country."

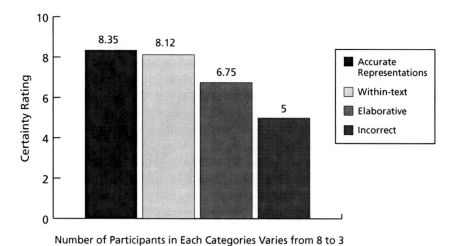

Number of Participants in Each Categories Varies from 8 to 3

Figure 2.   Readers' certainty about inferences v. accurate representations.

Elaborative inferences in the recall protocols got more varied reactions from participants. Whereas within-text inferences received ratings from seven to ten, elaborative inferences received ratings ranging from ten down to one. One participant rated her elaboration that "some pharmacies have begun to spring up in certain African countries" with a ten, but another of her elaborations "there is hope that the lower classes as well as the government officials and upper class are waking up and trying to battle against AIDS" with a six. The article makes no mention of "lower classes." There was an overall group tendency to recognize elaborative inferences as coming from one's own prior knowledge or at least to doubt their position in the original, but individuals differed in their ability to have that insight. Finally, there was a clear tendency with the handful of incorrect inferences (total $n = 7$) to doubt their existence in the article.

Inferencing and Open-Ended Questions

The first obvious difference between the recall protocol measure and the open-ended questions was the increased quantity of inferencing that occurred. Compared to 38 inferences in the written recalls, the corpus of data now included 60 inferences. Not only was there an increase in the overall amount of inferences, there was also a switch from mostly synthesis, within-text inferences to the more expansive, elaborative inferences. During the open-ended questions, two important patterns emerged—(a) readers were pushed to display what they did not fully understand and successfully had masked in the written recall and (b) most readers shared their elaborative inferences more readily and spontaneously.

The elaborative inferences that appeared frequently in the open-ended questions were supporting details to the argument of the passage, but they had not appeared in the original text. Readers explained that AIDS victims "are getting AIDS sooner" or that "drug companies are in the business to make money and not necessarily just save people's lives." Several of the readers signaled their inferencing while answering (e.g., "Because, it doesn't say in the article why, but you assume, it's implied, because of AIDS.").

As stated earlier, recall protocols usually left out several supporting details from the passage. One might conclude that readers forgot those details or dismissed them as unimportant. Several of the questions revealed other reasons for the omissions. The clearest examples are the answers to the question: "Why were some pharmaceutical companies originally suing?" One reader replied: "Oh, that's what they were doing? Is it possibly because they were bringing generic drugs and not the ones associated with what was needed? Or maybe, I'm not positive on that." Another stated: "I don't think that it said that they were actually suing. It said they didn't want generic drugs to be brought in instead of their own products, or something like that."

In the original, the final two sentences read: "But here and there, some false notes continue to disturb the wakening conscious of the continent. Such as when the Namibian president Sam Nujoma declares in June 2000, Africa as the 'victim' of AIDS, which 'started up in certain countries that produced this biological war.'" Readers demonstrated the most confusion over this detail of the text. One reader described the sentence as "very strange" and thought there was "something wrong with it." Another said, "'...*demarré*', [started up] I'm not sure of the word, ravaged almost, certain states which have produced this war. Its biological war really because its something that they can't fight with bullets." Yet another reader said, "I have managed to make no sense out of it. I thought that it was ... this president said that Africa was the victim ... I don't know if he is saying that the states produced the biological war. Because the 'qui' I don't know what that is in reference to because there are two of them, one before and one in the quote."

In general, these good readers were aware, or at least suspected, when they were "outside" the original text. They approached the two comprehension tasks in slightly different ways. All of the readers tried to be as faithful as possible to the author's original ideas in writing their recall protocols. Most, but not all, continued to try to stay within the bounds of the author's original ideas when answering the open-ended questions. Most inserted much more of their own background knowledge into those answers, however.

A detailed profile of several different readers brings to light the diversity within the very similar responses of the advanced L2 readers studied here. Although the group results show considerable similarities, the individuals each created unique responses. Their struggles as well as their successes can enlighten educators.

THREE PROFILES OF INDIVIDUAL SUCCESSFUL READERS' INFERENCING

Brad

Brad was a successful reader whose recall was noteworthy for its near complete accuracy. Brad's recall stayed more closely to the original text than any other and his written recall contained only two inferences, which consisted of 5% of the total number of idea units. The first was a summary statement (within-text inference) that Brad added to the final paragraph stating that improvements had occurred "in terms of social prejudice." The original stated that pharmaceutical companies had "renounced suing over the importation of copies of generic drugs." Brad added the elaborative inference "generic copies of *patented anti-AIDS* drugs." His addition of "patented" from his own background knowledge further clarified the original sentence. He was completely unaware of this inference, ranking it 10 in his certainty rating. Beyond these two relatively minor points, Brad did not deviate from the original text content or structure. When asked to describe his approach to the comprehension task, he explained that he visualized the original text's paragraph structure and "liked" to remember the numbers used, that recalling numbers was an "easy" habit of his.

Brad stayed just as close to the original text in his response to the open-ended questions. The good studenting behavior of staying close to what the teacher (or the researcher) is believed to want seemed to be at work here. The original text stated that "Africa has buried 3/4 of the 20 million dead since the beginning of the epidemic." When asked: "What killed 15 million people in Africa?", Brad displayed explicitly his understanding of the question by answering, "Oh, I guess that would be AIDS because it killed 3/4 of the 20 million that died of AIDS."

When asked "Why does South Africa have the greatest number of AIDS cases in the world?" Brad (unlike six of the other seven participants) was reluctant to make a global inference beyond what the text stated. "I don't know. It didn't give an actual reason. I think they mentioned that it was hard because of the climate of ignorance and poverty, but that's imposed by developed countries, but poverty does explain a lot how disease will spread."

Brad had been actively engaged with the text as he read it as witnessed by his personal commentary about developed countries above. As he wrote his recall protocol, he asked: "You want the author's point of view, not mine, right?" Halfway through his written protocol he added as an aside: "This article reeks of racism." Although Brad scored only a 5 out of 10 on the background knowledge test for prior knowledge, he conveyed a keen interest in the political situation in Africa that the AIDS article alluded to. This interest may be, in part, responsible for his superior recall result. Brad reported 53% of the original idea units, more than any of the other readers. He had strong opinions on the broader topic of politics in Africa and consciously restrained from incorporating his personal thoughts into his recall of the text. He signaled frequently his intent to stay reliable to, but separate from, the text with asides such as "they seem to think" and "I think they were saying" during the open-ended questions. He also signaled his opposition to the slant of the article by saying "their solution is not mine, right?" and adding his own beliefs as asides ("but that's imposed," "only after thousands of Africans protested"). Therefore, not only might his engagement with the article's topic be a facilitating factor, but his conscious strategy to stay faithful to the text's content and structure may also have been important. His interest in numbers may also have added some additional details to his recall beyond the top main ideas that all readers reported. Finally, in the follow-up review of the text with me, Brad confirmed that he had not encountered unknown vocabulary in the text with the possible exception of the word "*percées*" [here: "breakthrough"] that he reported recognizing only from weather reports about moving warm and cold fronts.

Nick

Unlike Brad, a second reader demonstrated dramatically different approaches to the written recall task versus the open-ended comprehension questions. Nick, with slightly less French coursework than the other French majors (still 9 more credits of French to go), did encounter segments of the text that were unfamiliar to him. However, he still managed to recall the third highest number of idea units and did so in the shortest and most concise of the written protocols. Nick's protocol was only 130 words compared to the average of 239 words among recalls that ranged up to 345 words. But he managed to make each phrase count, staying very faithful to the text. In fact, Nick wrote no elaborative or incorrect inferences and only two within-text inferences that reduced the number of propositions in the text through synthesis. The original stated: "The worse is yet to come ... the continent is promised a dramatic mortality rate for years." Nick wrote: "Obviously, the mortality rate will grow." Nick's second within-text inference was: "The president of Namibia has called Africa a victim of AIDS and compared its spread to biological weaponry." The original stated: "...The Namibian president, Sam Nujoma, declares in June, 2000, that Africa was a 'victim' of AIDS, which 'started up in certain countries that produced this biological war.'" Neither inference strays far from the original text and demonstrates only a slight amount of synthesis. Like all of the participants, Nick wrote all of the major points of the article in his recall.

Nick demonstrated an entirely different approach to the open-ended comprehension questions. In response to this task, Nick began to make a large number of elaborative inferences. He made 15 inferences compared to an average of 7 each by the others. For example, in response to the question "Why has life expectancy dropped in Botswana?" Nick responded:

Without sufficient medication, rarely will you live to sixty, even in the US, with AIDS if you catch it at a young age. And what is happening in Africa is most of the children are catching AIDS, either through birth, because they don't have most of the preventative medication, or very early on as soon as they become sexually mature ... And then there are the older people who are still living, and they die out possibly because of natural causes. The older generations with these massive infections are just sitting ducks. Their days are numbered.

Nick's background knowledge test score was the lowest of those retained, 4 out of 10. He did not have an overwhelming amount of prior knowledge to include. He did, however, approach the open-ended questions in a manner different from all the others. When asked why South Africa has the greatest number of cases of the disease (which is not answered in the text) he did not say that the text did not tell us like all of the others did. Rather, he readily speculated: "South Africa, being the form of government it has, may have actually studied the problem more than countries out there that don't have a reported number ... so the number is a bit suspect as being the most." On one question, Nick's answer stayed faithful to the text: "What are the solutions to the AIDS epidemic in Africa?" He answered: "According to the article, action, education, and a lot of public recognition of AIDS from the higher up government." His other answers contained numerous elaborations about tribal people's lack of vocabulary for modern medical conditions, copyrights for generic drugs, and access to AIDS testing.

Nick's reactions to the two different tasks highlight the differences that a researcher may find when choosing one assessment task over another. His recall protocol is the shortest, most concise of the eight. His comprehension answers are the longest. His recall protocol ties Brad's for the fewest number of inferences. His open-ended answers have more than twice the number of inferences than any other. His recall protocol contains no incorrect or elaborative inferences at all. His eleven open-ended answers contain eleven elaborative inferences, triple that of any others. When discussing these results with me afterward, Nick believed that he had had many of these thoughts as he read but put them aside to write the recall protocol.

Nick described reading the text three times. The first "at a pace to get through it," the second for "themes" and "points of sentences" and a final time "to memorize numbers, divide the text into different paragraphs with different points. I tried to remember the points." He explained that "problematic areas" seemed linked to problem words. When he read that children were left (*livrés*) on their own he said "that translates to they don't have books (*livres*) to call their own, but that doesn't make any sense." When he encountered the word *dirigeants* he wondered "I think something said or something of that nature from *dire* [to say]. It's unclear, but that's all right. The rest was clear." Nick, like most of the others, had trouble with the text segment "But the tide is turning perhaps. Some relative breakthroughs are being noted." He explained: "In English that would be, 'but

the tide is beginning to turn, some relatives are' ... I'm not sure what that
second sentence is ... *enregistrer* is to log onto a network but ... Many large
pharmaceutical firms are offering medications free or at cost, others have
renounced that they will no longer prosecute the companies for the importation of the generic medications that they hold the international copyrights of." Nick recognized that the text signaled a new concept, could not
fully understand the signal due to gaps in vocabulary knowledge, but
retained the important concept that followed. He believed his gaps in comprehension were caused by gaps in vocabulary knowledge and he could
point out those words and explain how he struggled with them.

Margaret

Like most the successful readers, Margaret also tried to stay close to the
text in both her recall protocol and her answers to the open-ended questions. When asked why South Africa has the greatest number of AIDS cases
she replied: "Gee, that's something I don't remember." And, in fact, the
article does not give a reason. Like both Brad and Nick, Margaret made no
incorrect inferences in her recall protocol. Like Nick, she attempted to
maintain the five paragraph structure of the article and ended up with four
of the five paragraphs. The reason for this shortage reflects one of the
most common strategies used by all of the successful readers—when in
doubt about the accuracy of a point that you belief to be less important,
leave it out.

Margaret's recall protocol did not refer to the pharmaceutical companies suing. It was Margaret who first reported incorrectly in the open-
ended section that the pharmaceutical companies were not actually suing.
"It said they didn't want generic drugs to be brought in instead of their
own products or something like that." After having heard the question
about *why* companies were suing, she tried to explain the paragraph this
way in our final discussion: "It says, 'but perhaps the wind is turning. Relatives have been registered'. I'm thinking if you have AIDS you have to register so that its known in your family ... 'several large pharmaceutical firms
are offering medicine either free or at a reduced price, others are', oh,
maybe *renonce* means suing?"

Margaret described her approach to the passage as follows:

> I read it through once pretty quickly. Then I went back and I just tried to pick
> up the major points. When there were a few words I wasn't clear about I
> would reread the sentence to try to get an understanding. Like the part
> about the drug companies not wanting to import generic drugs. That one
> sentence I had to read a couple of times and I am still not sure that I got the

angle of it. I didn't pay too much attention to numbers, details. Just the main points in each paragraph. I tried to remember them. I tried to follow the story line in my head. The progress of the story. Then they have this synopsis at the end.

THE WRITTEN RECALL PROTOCOL TASK

Conciseness

Among these good readers' written recalls, a tendency toward written conciseness seems connected to successful comprehension. Researchers should beware of a possible confounding of writing style with the variable they are trying to view, comprehension. Of the eight participants, the two with the longest written recalls also had the fewest idea units from the original text. None of these readers were unsuccessful, but the most successful at retaining the largest number of idea units did so with the fewest words. Precision of writing or conciseness of thoughts seems somehow related to these readers' ability to recall, as measured by a written recall protocol.

Topic Level Structures

All of these successful readers recalled the main theme and the five central ideas of the news article. They all reported looking for main ideas and using paragraph structure to guide their recalls. All readers reported reading first for gist and then rereading for the text's structure of main ideas. They varied on their approach to supporting details. Some made a conscious effort to retain them, others reported not focusing on them. Several reported questioning themselves over whether something "made sense" before including it in their recall.

Signaling

The most common signal that readers reported using to help their comprehension were the beginnings of a new paragraph. Signals at the sentence level in this particular passage happened to contain vocabulary that most of the readers were unsure of (e.g., *percées relatives* in "Some relative breakthroughs are being noted"). Text signals at the word or phrase level such as "especially," "here and there," and "as when" were almost never reproduced in the recall protocols or mentioned in the open-ended answers. When questioned about them, readers reported recognizing that these expressions were meant to signal a new idea and that they therefore gave their attention to the idea that followed.

Incorrect Inferences

These propositions were a very small part of the advanced readers' interpretation of this text. They agreed that they used their sense of certainty about an idea to either report it or leave it out of their text recall. In earlier studies (e.g., Hammadou, 1991) beginner readers' incorrect inferences play a much larger role in their attempt to recall a passage. Some L2 reading researchers discard those propositions in a subject's recall that are not in the original reading text (e.g., Barry & Lazarte, p. 182). However, in this qualitative study *everything* that a learner chose to label as "recall" from a text was analyzed with input from the reader on his/her intent. When responding to specific questions, the reader would report inferences that were incorrect but when left to produce a written recall, the reader could suppress nearly all such incorrect inferences.

DISCUSSION

Assessment Tool Effect

Investigators should note that the outcomes that they find will be profoundly affected by the assessment tool that they choose. Readers here tried to recreate the text structure with their written recall. They made no such effort in response to open-ended questions. In response to open-ended questions, they revealed what they did not understand. In recall protocols, successful readers masked or deleted what they were unclear about. In answering comprehension questions, successful readers sometimes discovered clues to the content of the text that they had not fully understood.

For investigators interested particularly in inferences, the manner in which learners responded to the same text will produce very different types and amounts of inferences. Horiba (1996) found large numbers of inferences using a think-aloud method of data collection. This researcher also found large number of inferences using open-ended questions, but found much fewer inferences using learners' written recalls. Not only were the numbers greater, the inferences were also of a different nature. Recall protocols gave rise to within-text inferences, whereas comprehension questions gave rise to many more elaborative inferences. It appears that recall protocols show fewer inferences than think-aloud protocol studies, but think-aloud procedures interrupt the very process that they are meant to study. Open-ended questions immediately after the reading prompted readers to regenerate many of their inferences without interrupting the reading process. Within these overall group tendencies were also idiosyncratic differences.

For educators using the results of reading research, attention should be paid to the manner in which each assessment tool is used and the manner of data analysis. In the current study, all inferences were included in the analysis, correct or far-fetched. If some data are not included in subsequent analyses, then results are likely to differ. The type of question asked, the tools used to collect answers and the methods used to analyze data are all likely to influence the results. Educators need to use vigilance when comparing studies and use caution when drawing conclusions across studies.

Readers' Awareness

These successful readers reported holding back on ideas of their own as they wrote their recall protocols. They reported mentally questioning the distant, unknown author. Most of the readers readily reported elaborative inferences in response to open-ended questions. All readers reported paying attention to text structure and rhetorical signals to assist their recalls.

We have growing evidence that inferencing provides a window into a reader's comprehension processes. Successful advanced L2 readers did recognize when their ideas were from outside the text. They reported engaging in a sort of mental dialogue with the author during which they tracked the writer's ideas, their judgments of their significance and their certainty of their understanding of them. These successful readers were even able to identify the source of their confusion as coming from either vocabulary or syntax. Several pointed out words that they knew hindered their understanding and others pointed out referents that puzzled them.

CONCLUSION

The good readers profiled here offer an encouraging picture of what foreign language readers can and do achieve. Their approaches to the comprehension tasks presented to them were successful at gleaning and reporting all main ideas of the authentic text. They all reported seeking the text's main ideas, using the text's structure and rhetorical signals successfully to help them (even when some gaps in their L2 were a hindrance). Most relevant to the current study, they all showed considerable awareness of their thought processes in general and their inferencing in particular. All of the readers accessed their (albeit limited) prior knowledge of the text topic and all showed evidence of monitoring its use. These results can provide support and encouragement to foreign language educators that their learners can attain the goal of being independent readers who are capable of reading in their second language for new meaning and new information beyond that which they bring to the text already in prior knowledge.

The assessment procedures profiled here show that results will vary considerably depending on the assessment tools used. Educators should always take into account the assessment tasks used when interpreting or applying research results. Think-aloud protocols, oral comprehension questions, written multiple-choice questions, recall protocols (either written or oral) may all inspire learners to produce very different responses. More study is needed to guide L2 researchers in the consequences of selecting each tool.

The current study suggests several additional avenues for productive further research. Reading comprehension, in all its complexity, is still only a part of second language literacy. The different results from oral comprehension questions vs. written recalls here highlight the importance of studying the links between reading and writing. The apparent link between conciseness of written expression and quality of recall should be investigated further. How do these two abilities interact? How can they best be influenced through instruction to maximize benefits to students? Studies such as the research reported here could be embedded into more realistic contexts (e.g., reading a news article in order to enter an international online discussion of the topic). L2 readers as well as native speakers could be observed in such naturalistic settings in order to describe the mental models they create as they read for realistic purposes and the monitoring strategies that serve them best. Second language literacy, the ability to use text to communicate ideas in writing, understand information and make interpretations, is an important goal of many language learners and their teachers.

NOTES

1. All translations here are mine.
2. There were five main topics: (a) Africa has an AIDS epidemic. (b) The epidemic is getting worse. (c) Many children are affected. (d) Africa has not done enough to stop AIDS because of poverty, ignorance and societal taboos. (e) There is some hope for improvement.

REFERENCES

Anderson, R.C., Reynolds, R.E., Schallert, D., & Goetz, E.T. (1984). Frameworks for comprehending discourse. *American Educational Research Journal, 14*, 367–82.

Bernhardt, E.B. (1986). Cognitive processes in L2: An examination of reading behaviors. In J. Lantolf & A. Labarca (Eds.). *Research in second language acquisition in the classroom setting.* Norwood, NJ: Ablex.

Bernhardt, E.B. (1991). *Reading development in a second language: Theoretical, empirical and classroom perspectives.* Norwood, NJ: Ablex.

Bransford, J.D., & Johnson, M.K. (1972). Contextual prerequisites for understanding: Some investigations of comprehension and recall. *Journal of Verbal Learning and Verbal Behavior, 11*, 717–26.

Collins, A., Brown, J.S., & Larkin, K.M. (1980). Inference in text understanding. In R.J. Spiro, B.C. Bruce, & W.F. Brewer (Eds.), *Theoretical issues in reading comprehension: Perspectives from cognitive psychology, linguistics, artificial intelligence, and education* (pp. 385–407). Hillsdale, NJ: Erlbaum.

Fincher-Kiefer, R. (1992). The role of prior knowledge in inferential processing. *Journal of Research in Reading, 15*, 12–27.

Graesser, A.C., Swamer, S.S., & Hu, X. (1997). Quantitative discourse psychology. *Discourse Processes, 23*, 229–263.

Hammadou, J.A. (1991). Interrelationships among prior knowledge, inference, and language proficiency in foreign language reading. *Modern Language Journal, 75*, 27–38.

Hammadou, J.A. (2000). The impact of analogy and content knowledge on reading comprehension: What helps, what hurts. *Modern Language Journal, 84*, 38–50.

Horiba, Y. (1996). Comprehension processes in L2 reading: Language competence, textual coherence, and inferences. *Studies in Second Language Acquisition, 18*, 433–473.

Johnson, P. (1982). Effects of reading comprehension on building background knowledge. *TESOL Quarterly, 16*, 503–16.

Koda, K. (1993). Transferred L1 strategies and L2 syntactic structure in L2 sentence comprehension. *Modern Language Journal, 77*, 490–500.

McNamara, D.S., Kintsch, E., Songer, N.B., & Kintsch, W. (1996). Are good texts always better? Text coherence, background knowledge, and levels of understanding in learning from text. *Cognition and Instruction, 14*, 1–43.

Perfetti, C.A. (1993). Why inferences might be restricted. *Discourse Processes, 16*, 181–192.

Stahl, S.A., Hare, V.C., Sinatra, R., & Gregory, J.F. (1991). Defining the role of prior knowledge and vocabulary in reading comprehension: The retiring of number 41. *Journal of Reading Behavior 23*, 487–508.

Strauss, S.L. (2001). An open letter to Reid Lyon. *Educational Researcher, 30* (5), 26–33.

Swaffar, J.K. (1988). Readers, texts, and second languages: The interactive process. *Modern Language Journal, 72*, 123–49.

van den Broek, P., Fletcher, C.R., & Risden, K. (1993). Investigations of inferential processes in reading: A theoretical and methodological integration. *Discourse Processes, 16*, 169–180.

Zwaan, R.A., & Brown, C.M. (1996). The influence of language proficiency and comprehension skill on situation-model construction. *Discourse Processes, 21,* 289–327.

APPENDIX

Passage Read by Participants

L'Afrique après 20 ans de sida: la saignée déjà, le réveil peut-être

JOHANNESBURG, 3 juin (AFP)—En 20 ans, le sida a causé en Afrique des ravages pires que les guerres ou les catastrophes naturelles, il annonce une terrible saignée avec 25 millions de gens infectés, mais semble enfin pousser Etats et dirigeants à s'éveiller et réagir à la pandémie. L'Afrique a enterré les trois-quarts de 20 millions de morts depuis le début de l'épidémie. Dans certains pays comme le Botswana (où un adulte sur trois séropositif), l'espérance de vie, de 60 ans en 1995, devrait chuter à 36 ans sur 2000-05.

Le pire est sans doute à venir. Avec 12 millions d'orphelins du sida, avec la naissance de 70.000 bébés séropositifs par an dans un pays comme l'Afrique du Sud (pays le plus touché au monde), le continent est promis à une mortalité dramatique pour des années et a un impact socio-économique cauchemardesque. Car au-delà des chiffres, l'impact social du sida en Afrique se lit sur le terrain, dans ces foyers où le "chef de famille" survivant est parfois âgé de 10 ans, à travers ces enfants sans attaches ni espérance de vie, livrés aujourd'hui à eux-mêmes, demain à la rue ou au crime.

L'Afrique n'a pas réagi assez tôt face au sida. Un environnement fait d'ignorance et de pauvreté rend difficile de s'attaquer au problème. Les dirigeants sont importants, l'engagement doit être important, tout comme la capacité de parler d'amour et de sexe et des tabous de la société.

Mais le vent tourne peut-être. Des percées (relatives) sont enregistrées. Plusieurs grandes firmes pharmaceutiques offrent des médicaments gratuits ou à prix cassés. D'autres ont renoncé à combattre en justice l'importation de copies de médicaments génériques.

Surtout, des tabous continuent de tomber. En avril, la député sud-africaine (ANC) Ruth Bhengu a fait au Parlement le poignant récit de la séropositivité de sa fille, une "première" publique saluée comme un tournant dans la reconnaissance du sida au sein de la classe dirigeante du pays. Mais ici et là, des fausses notes continuent d'inquiéter sur la prise de conscience du continent. Comme lorsque le président namibien Sam Nujoma qualifie en juin 2000 l'Afrique de "victime" du sida, qui "a démarré dans certains Etats qui ont produit cette guerre biologique."

CHAPTER 11

WHEN PHONOLOGICAL LIMITATIONS COMPROMISE LITERACY:

A CONNECTIONIST APPROACH TO ENHANCING THE PHONOLOGICAL COMPETENCE OF HERITAGE LANGUAGE SPEAKERS OF SPANISH

María M. Carreira

ABSTRACT

Heritage language students of Spanish experience significant difficulties mastering the orthographic rules of Spanish stress. This study reveals that this difficulty does not stem from a systemic inability on their part to hear the phonetic cues of Spanish stress, but rather from their inability to access these cues for purposes of making explicit linguistic judgements. Research in applied neuroscience suggests that training with amplified phonetic cues can render sound differences more salient for children with language-based learning disabilities (Tallal et al., 1996). In keeping with this line of work, we trained thirteen heritage language students of Spanish to identify the location of stress in words whose stressed syllables they heard with exaggerated pitch, loudness, and duration. A control group listened to the same words uttered without any exaggeration. Posttest scores reveal that the experimental group improved significantly in its ability to identify the location of the stressed syllable in words rendered without exaggeration. In contrast, the control group registered a much more modest improvement. These results indicate that training with amplified phonetic cues can render the phonetic cues of Spanish stress more accessible for heritage language speakers of Spanish.

TEACHING SPANISH AS A HERITAGE LANGUAGE: GENERAL ISSUES

According to the U.S. Census, Latinos now number approximately 35 million, or 12.5 percent of this country's population. This rate is considerably higher in large urban areas that have been traditional hubs of Hispanic immigration such as Southern California (35%), New York (27%), Chicago (26%), and Miami (66%) (www.census.gov/pubinfo/www/hisphot1.htm). While many of the discussions related to the education of young Latinos have focused on the teaching of English literacy skills, a growing body of research reveals that there are significant challenges inherent in teaching Spanish as a heritage language to this population of students. Specifically, the fields of sociolinguistics and Spanish for native speakers (henceforth SNS) point to particular affective, ethnocultural, and academic needs of U.S. Hispanics that are not met in traditional Spanish-language courses for anglophone students.

Regarding the affective needs of SNS students, research reveals that U.S. Hispanics approach the learning of Spanish with ostensible insecurities about their linguistic abilities (Rodríguez Pino, 1997; Villa & Villa, 1998). These insecurities stem not only from the limited exposure that many of these students have to the prestige varieties of Spanish, but also from the severe criticism that they often encounter when they attempt to speak the language. Fishman (1997, p. xiii) notes, "(n)ot all Spanish-speaking students arrive in such classes with positive attitudes toward either using or improving their Spanish. If the larger society is so structured as not to reward them appropriately for any excellence that they might evidence in connection with their mastery of English, then it is even less inclined to be appreciative of their mastery of Spanish. Likewise, even their more intimate intracultural (i.e., intra-Hispanic) interaction networks are unlikely to be entirely appreciative in this regard." Accordingly, the past decade has witnessed a proliferation of pedagogical materials aimed at boosting the linguistic self-esteem of Latino students learning Spanish and of validating varieties of U.S. Spanish (Carreira, 2000; Hidalgo, 1997). Similarly, a significant number of professional development programs during this time have sought to instruct SNS teachers on the linguistic validity of U.S. Spanish and on the nonlinguistic basis of language prejudice (Rodríguez Pino, 1997; University of California, Los Angeles, 2001).

Research also points to the crucial role of ethnocultural topics in the SNS classroom in enhancing students' awareness of their linguistic and cultural legacy. Indeed, Fishman (1994) states that "language and ethnocultural identity and existence are inextricably linked" (p. 5). Hernández Chávez (2000) echoes this sentiment, as he asserts that linguistic preservation cannot take place outside the boundaries of the notion of community:

> Para el mantenimiento de un idioma, es la integridad de la comunidad y de su cultura la que tiene prioridad. Si no se integra la lengua a la vida comunitaria para formar parte de la tradición del pueblo, permanece como una lengua auxiliar, usándose sólo de vez en cuando para ejercer funciones particulares." (p. 6)

As far as the preservation of a language, it is the integrity of the community and of its culture that must have priority. If language is not integrated with the daily life of the community so as to form part of the people's tradition, it remains an auxiliary language, used on occasion and with only particular functions (translation by Carreira).

Berman (1992) identifies cultural validation as one of several key attributes of exemplary schools. According to this study, validation involves incorporating materials and fostering discussions that focus on the linguistic and cultural roots of students. In light of these and other findings, Fantini (1997) calls for a redefinition of the instructional materials of SNS to include culture/language as inextricable components of instruction.

The interweaving of language and culture in SNS courses has resulted in a curriculum that goes beyond the mere presentation and practice of grammar and vocabulary. SNS courses are rich in literature, history, and culturally authentic materials. The linguistic demands placed on students by such a curriculum have put a higher premium than ever on the acquisition of literacy skills and the development of proficiency in academic Spanish. Furthermore, the recent proliferation of professional opportunities for Spanish-English bilinguals in this country and in the global market, make such skills a highly valuable commodity for heritage speakers of Spanish (Carreira & Armengol, 2001).

While there is considerable debate among specialists regarding which spoken variety of Spanish should constitute the focus of SNS courses, when it comes to writing, there is a high degree of consensus about the literacy needs of U.S. Hispanics. At the textual level, the research literature and SNS textbooks evidence the importance of teaching organizational and interpretive skills. At the grammatical level, these materials emphasize the importance of teaching a written variety of Spanish that conforms in its vocabulary, morphology, syntax, and orthography to the language of educated society. Apropos this topic, Villa (1996) argues that "...there are certain stylistic norms used for different types of writing, be it for student papers in the university environment, technical manuals, newspapers, journal articles, memoranda, advertising, or public information literature, among other . . . Any spoken community variety can serve as a passageway to the use of a corresponding formal written variety. The transition from the former to the latter requires training in the norms established by the context of the written variety" (p. 197).

When it comes to teaching these norms, certain assumptions regarding the linguistic competence of SNS students underlie the inclusion of some grammatical topics and the exclusion of others. One assumption is that, by and large, heritage language students are fairly proficient speakers of an *informal* variety of Spanish. However, because of their limited explosion to the written registers of Spanish, they lack general academic skills in this language. For this reason, SNS courses generally devote a considerable amount of time to presenting the main linguistic conventions that differentiate the written varieties of Spanish from the more informal varieties of this language represented in the classroom. Moreover, because Latino students often use a rural or stigmatized variety of Spanish, SNS instruction has traditionally focused on sensitizing students to linguistic registers, as well as to validating the students' vernacular.

Another assumption is that, by and large, Latinos bring to the Spanish classroom a basic mastery of the core grammar rules of Spanish. As such, the role of SNS instruction is that of adding details and complexity to the solid linguistic scaffolding that SNS students possess. Thus, unlike anglophone students of Spanish, heritage language students generally don't have to be taught the basic differences between *ser* and *estar* or the preterit and the imperfect, two of the standard grammar topics of traditional Spanish courses. They may however, have to be instructed on semantic nuances that fall outside the scope of everyday usage, on conjugational and orthographic idiosyncrasies of these forms, and on patterns of usage particular to U.S. varieties of Spanish that do not conform to the general conventions of the standard language.

PHONOLOGY: THE OVERLOOKED COMPONENT IN SNS COURSES

Not all parts of this grammatical scaffolding however, have been heretofore considered to be in equal need of intervention. Typically, the lexical module has received the greatest amount of attention, followed by the syntactic, semantic, and morphological modules of grammar. When it comes to phonology, the linguistic scaffolding of SNS students has been assumed to be particularly solid, if not identical to that of monolingual speakers of Spanish. Undoubtedly, this assumption has been based on the observation that but for the most extreme cases, SNS students speak Spanish without a foreign accent, and they do not show any particular difficulty understanding the spoken language, as used in informal settings. For this reason, the field of SNS has all but ignored the phonological competence of heritage language speakers as an area of research, as well as a topic of pedagogical innovation.

This is not to say that phonology has been entirely absent from SNS classes. Pronunciation, as it relates to the use of register in the *spoken* language and as it serves to mark membership in a social or dialectal class, figures prominently in the SNS research literature (Lipski, 1997). The same is true of SNS textbooks, though to a lesser extent. However, when it comes to the teaching of writing, phonological issues have played a very limited role in SNS classes. By and large, the contributions of this module of grammar have been confined to pointing out those aspects of pronunciation that have been found to interfere with students' ability to spell correctly. This is the case, for example in dialects of Spanish where syllable-final /s/ is deleted or aspirated. Outside of this, the field of SNS has failed to identify any need for phonological instruction, as it pertains to the acquisition of literacy skills.

This state of affairs has served to frame the teaching of the orthographic rules of accentuation, a notoriously problematic task for students, as strictly a literacy issue, rather than an matter of phonological competence. Given the relative simplicity of the rules of Spanish accentuation, the difficulties experienced with this topic by SNS students, have confounded and frustrated instructors. In light of the failure of many heritage language students to acquire a mastery of these rules, (despite repeated instruction on the topic), many instructors have simply thrown up their arms and concluded that students "just can't do accents," a proclamation widely echoed by SNS students. Regrettably, since orthographic accent in Spanish is as much a part of correct writing as is accurate spelling, this conclusion is tantamount to a capitulation on the part of SNS teachers and students with regard to a basic rule of literacy.

Admittedly, the absence of orthographic accents rarely, if ever, compromises the comprehensibility of a text. Because of this, and because of the extensive array of other linguistic challenges encountered by SNS students, accentuation has yet to enjoy any prominence as an area of research or pedagogical innovation. However, a number of compelling arguments suggests that this topic indeed deserves the special attention of SNS specialists. The first such argument is that, as previously noted, conformance to the rules of accentuation is a characteristic feature of the writing of educated Spanish-speakers. As such, failure to adhere to this convention generally marks a writer as lacking in academic preparation.

Secondly, students that intend to make professional use of their Spanish-language skills in areas such as the media, marketing, advertising, and translation and interpretation, can effectively diminish their employment opportunities in this country, as well as abroad, if they cannot demonstrate mastery of this topic. Case in point, Olga Navarrete, Section chief of Translation Services at the FBI, asserts "heritage language speakers that cannot do accents cannot be employed as language specialists at the FBI" (personal communication).

Thirdly, students themselves identify accentuation as one of their most glaring deficiencies in Spanish. Acquiring a mastery of this topic is also one of their primary goals with regard to SNS courses. All too often, these students interpret their failure to acquire competency in this area to signal a constitutional or systemic incapacity on their part to master formal Spanish. Conversely, success in this area frequently breeds feelings of linguistic confidence and accomplishment on the part of students, and serves to propel further linguistic explorations both within and beyond the classroom setting. Therefore, although accent placement does not usually interfere with communication, the subjective importance of this topic to learners and to educated society in general should serve to elevate the importance of this topic within the SNS curriculum.

Finally, from a purely academic perspective, the pedagogical challenges inherent in teaching accentuation to SNS students raise a number of theoretically interesting questions:

- Are the challenges inherent in acquiring the rules of accentuation borne out of a failure on the part of students to learn the written conventions of accent placement or do they point to a deeper phonological limitation?
- If they represent a phonological limitation, what is the nature of this limitation? Specifically, does it reflect a systemic incapacity to perceive stress or rather an inability to explicitly identify the location of perceived stress?
- Are there training exercises that improve the ability of heritage language students to deal with the problem(s) represented by stress?

These are the questions that will occupy us for the remainder of this paper.

IS ACCENTUATION AN ISSUE OF PHONOLOGICAL COMPETENCE?

The Pretest

If the problems with accentuation stem from a phonological limitation, we predict that SNS students will have trouble identifying the location of the stressed syllable, whether or not they know the orthographic rules of accentuation. In order to test this hypothesis, we designed an experiment consisting of two tasks. For the first such task (henceforth, the reading task) SNS students looked at list of words and circled the location of the stressed syllable in each word based on their own silent reading of the list. The sixty-two words comprising this list were at least three syllables long, and represented all the possible stress patterns of Spanish, namely final, penultimate, and antepenultimate (see List I in the Appendix). Some of these words were cognates; others were words that were deemed to be familiar to bilingual students (e.g., sábado, número); still others were chosen to be unknown to students (e.g., chécheres, cáñamo).

For the second task (henceforth, the reading + listening task), students received a different list of 66 words which was designed to match the first list along the variables of syllabic constitution, word structure, stress patterns, and levels of familiarity (see List 2 in the Appendix). This time, they listened twice to an audio taped reading of the words as they circled the location of the stressed syllable in each word on the list. The words were read by a native speaker of Peruvian Spanish who was not informed of the purpose of the experiment until all of the results reported in this paper were analyzed.

We checked for inattention or defective hearing as possible sources of low scores in the reading + listening task by interspersing the names of seven cities or countries at random intervals in the reading of the words. Students were asked to write these down as they heard them. All subjects succeeded in correctly identifying all seven items, suggesting to us that neither inattention nor hearing difficulty played a role in students' ability to perform the listening task.

In order to eliminate certain complexities inherent in the system of verbal accentuation, only nouns and adjectives comprised both lists, a fact that was made known to the subjects. For each of the two tasks, students were encouraged to guess the correct answer in cases where they were uncertain, and to mark no more than one answer per word and to circle no more than one syllable per word. In addition, they were instructed to disregard orthographic accentuation and to focus only locating spoken stress. At no point did students receive feedback on the correctness of their answers on either task.

The Subjects

Twenty-five heritage language speakers of Spanish (HLSS) participated in this study.[1] These were students who enrolled in Spanish 250 (Spanish for Native Speakers) in the Spring semester of 2001 at California State University, Long Beach. Spanish 250 is an introductory language course for heritage language speakers of Spanish that covers a range of grammatical topics and engages students in extensive reading and writing activities. In order to qualify for this class, students must meet four criteria in a rigorous assessment process that takes place during the first week of the semester and involves an oral interview and a written test. First, they must demonstrate the ability to understand informal spoken Spanish by listening to a short reading and answering questions. Second, they must be able to engage in an informal conversation in Spanish with the instructor for five minutes on a current event topic. Third, they must be able to read a newspaper article in Spanish and answer short questions about its contents. Fourth, they must be able to express themselves in writing, albeit with grammatical flaws or limited vocabulary.

All of the students in the class filled out a personal background questionnaire, which included the following information:

- Place of birth. If born abroad, age of arrival in the United States
- Age
- Highest level of education achieved in a Spanish-speaking country (if any)
- Amount of formal training in Spanish in the United States. This included years of bilingual education, Spanish language courses at the primary, secondary, or post-secondary levels, and religious education in Spanish.
- Experiences traveling or vacationing in a Spanish-speaking country.

Of the twenty-five students participating in the study, all but three were born in the United States. Of these four, one arrived in this country at the age of two, another at the age of 6, and a third arrived at age 10. The latter completed fourth grade in a Spanish-speaking country. The former two received all of their education in the United States, as did all of the U.S.-born subjects. The amount of formal instruction in Spanish received by the U.S.-educated subjects varied widely, ranging from none at all, to up to four years of formal education in bilingual education classes and/or Spanish language classes at the secondary level.

Six native (non-heritage) Spanish-dominant speakers (henceforth, NSDS) also completed the reading and reading+listening tasks. In addition, these six speakers completed a different listening + reading task in which they identified the location of stress in 12 nonce or made-up words (see List 3, Appendix). The purpose of this task was to determine if NSDS could rely strictly on phonetic cues to identify the location of stress, as opposed to relying on other factors such as their knowledge of vocabulary or of Spanish morphology to provide essential information as to the location of stress.

From the point of view of their background, HLSS and NSDS differ from each other in number of significant ways. First, all NSDS were born in a Spanish-speaking country and did not arrive in the United States until after the age of twenty-one. HLSS, on the other hand, were either born in this country, or if born abroad arrived in the United States before the age of 11. Secondly, while the NSDS completed their high school preparation in a Spanish-speaking country, HLSS completed at least a portion of their grammar school education and all of their high school years in the United States. Thirdly, unlike the heritage language students, NSDS have medium to heavily accented English and are clearly Spanish dominant.

Despite our efforts to clearly demarcate two separate populations of Spanish speakers for purposes of this study, it is important to point out that, in general, the linguistic borders between heritage language speakers and native speakers can overlap considerably. For example, a native monolingual speaker of Spanish with little formal education, may exhibit many of the same difficulties with the written and formal registers of Spanish found among certain heritage language speakers. By the same token, a highly educated heritage language speaker may have linguistic abilities that closely match those of many educated monolingual speakers of Spanish.

Results

As shown in Table 1, HLSS experienced tremendous difficulty identifying the location of the stressed syllable, averaging error rates of more than 50% for each task. These scores contrast sharply with the low-error rates of the NSDS group.

Table 1.   Average Error Rates in the Silent-Reading and Listening Tasks

Group	Reading	Reading+listening	Nonce
HLSS	53.5%	53.6%	–
NSDS	8.2%	1.3%	2.2%

Two significant findings bear notice. First, there is a remarkable difference between HLSS and NSDS with respect to their ability to correctly identify the location of the stressed syllable in the reading task (53.5% v. 8.2%, respectively). These results suggest that HLSS lack strategies for (a) explicitly identifying stress in familiar words in print and (b) for predicting the location of stress in unfamiliar words in print. NSDS, on the other hand, can clearly identify stress in familiar words in print. Whether or not they possess the ability to guess with any accuracy the location of stress in unfamiliar words in print, remains outside the scope of this experiment. Phonological research however, suggests that native Spanish speakers are indeed able to make predictions and grammaticality judgements about stress in made-up words (Harris, 1983).[2]

Second, HLSS differ greatly from NSDS with regard to their ability to benefit from aural input. A comparison of HLSS scores in the reading and reading + listening tasks reveals the astonishing fact that listening to the words made no statistically significant difference in students' ability to correctly identify the location of the stressed syllable in the words in the list. On the other hand, NSDS show strong evidence of benefitting from aural input, as evidenced by a) the improvement in the listening task relative to the silent-reading task, and b) by the low error rates in the nonce task.

These findings raise two possibilities. One possibility is that what differentiates NSDS from HLSS, is that the former are able to hear the cues associated with Spanish stress, while the latter are not. The other possibility is that like NSDS, HLSS have the ability to hear stress. However, unlike NSDS, they lack the ability to explicitly identify its location. This last situation is analogous to the difference between trained musicians and non-musicians with respect to their ability to identify whether a musical note is in a minor or major key. Though non-musicians are likely to perceive a difference between a major and minor note, it is not certain that they would be capable of labeling the difference correctly. Trained musicians, on the other hand, would have no difficulty with this task. In the next section, we explore these two possibilities.

WHAT IS THE NATURE OF THE PHONOLOGICAL LIMITATION EXHIBITED BY HLSS?

Acknowledging the difficulty associated with learning the rules of Spanish accentuation, Barrutia and Schwegler (1994) add: "...somos conscientes de que los estudiantes no colocan siempre el acento primario en la sílaba correcta; son, sin embargo, relativamente pocas las palabras mal articuladas" (p. 32). (We are aware that students don't always place the primary accent on the correct syllable, however, mispronounced words are relatively few in number. My translation). The fact that HLSS generally do not mispronounce stress in normal conversation suggests that they are indeed capable of hearing stress, and that their fundamental difficulty with this topic resides in having to explicitly identify stress.

To investigate this hypothesis, we designed two additional tests. First, we asked HLSS to read aloud a list of 12 words that were familiar to them (see List 4, Appendix). Subsequently, we asked them to repeat 12 nonce words, one at a time, as they heard them in an audio taped recording. These were the same words as used previously in the nonce task with NSDS. However, unlike NSDS, HLSS did not have access to a printed list of the nonce words as they heard and repeated them. Students' performance in both tasks was recorded and analyzed by three native speakers of Spanish who determined whether the pronunciation of each item was correct.[3]

As shown in Table 2, HLSS performed extremely well in both of these tasks. Astonishingly, in the Reading-aloud task, these subjects consistently succeeded at pronouncing three-syllable words that were very similar in structure to those for which that they had failed to locate stress earlier in the silent-reading task. The Nonce-repeating task fared equally well, indicating that HLSS can accurately interpret the phonological cues of stress for purposes of reproducing words. Interestingly, they can do so with a rate of success that is just slightly below that of NSDS in the reading+listening and nonce tasks (1.3% and 2.2%, respectively).

Table 2.   HLSS Error Rates in the Reading-aloud and Nonce-repeating Tasks (in percentage)

Reading-aloud Task	Nonce-repeating Task
2.9%	2.6%

In light of these findings, the hypothesis that HLSS are unable to hear the phonetic clues of Spanish stress must be rejected as untenable. In fact, rather than lacking the ability to perceive stress, what HLSS appears to lack is the ability to explicitly identify the location of stress in Spanish words. Crucially, HLLS seem unable to access their implicit knowledge of Spanish stress for purposes of making explicit linguistic judgements.

A review of the literature suggests that the challenges inherent in analyzing stress stem both from the general nature of this phonological feature, as well as from the specific properties of Spanish accentuation. Kenstowicz (1993) notes: "…it is well known that stress is the most phonetically elusive phonological feature. It has no invariant phonetic cues. Rather, stress is realized through the offices of other phonetic features, typical choices being the pitch contour of an intonation pattern or vowel/consonant length" (p. 549).

Languages differ from each other in terms of the number of phonetic features that they employ to mark the location of the tonic syllable. English makes use of four phonetic cues: loudness, length (quantity), pitch, and articulation (quality). For example, in a word like *consideration*, the syllable that bears primary stress (ra) is louder, carries a higher pitch, and has a longer duration than the rest of the syllables. In addition, while the vowels in the unstressed syllables (con, de, tion) are reduced to schwa, those in the penultimate (ra) and pre-antepenultimate syllable (si) retain their full articulation, by virtue of the fact that they carry primary and secondary stress, respectively (Barrutia & Schwegler, 1994; Kenstowicz, 1993; Whitley, 1986). Together, these cues make English stress particularly salient.

Unlike English, Spanish offers little in the way of phonetic cues to mark the location of stress, using only loudness as its regular correlate (Barrutia & Schwegler, 1994; Whitley, 1986). Notably, stressed and unstressed vowels in Spanish do not differ from each other significantly in quality, quantity, or pitch. This is not to say that stressed syllables in Spanish are never pronounced with a longer duration or a raised pitch. However, in contrast to English, lengthening the duration of a stressed syllable and raising its pitch are exceptional devices in Spanish that signal strong emphasis (Bull, 1965, p. 78).

CAN TRAINING HELP HLSS ACCESS THE CUES ASSOCIATED WITH SPANISH STRESS?

Because of their emphatic value, conventional pedagogical wisdom has held that length and pitch should never be exaggerated as a way to teach stress, as such a practice might lead students to adopt aberrant prosodic patterns when speaking Spanish. The argument has also been made that it might render students incapable of hearing Spanish stress in non-emphatic speech.

Contrary to this position, recent advances in applied neuroscience suggest that training with amplified speech may indeed render linguistic distinctions more audible under normal circumstances. This kind of training assumes a connectionist view of the human brain, according to which learning consists of adjusting the connections between the simple processing units in neural networks so that a given input is mapped onto a desired output. The relative frequency of the input/output patterns determines the strength of the connections. That is, the more salient and frequent the presentation of the pattern, the more likely it is that learning will take place (McClelland, 1989; Pinker & Prince, 1989; Omaggio Hadley, 2001).

In keeping with this paradigm, Tallal et al. (1996) designed a computer algorithm that extended and amplified the acoustic cues of speech, in order to train 500 children with a variety of language-based learning disabilities to discriminate between different English sounds (e.g., /ba/ v. /da/). The children trained for one hour and forty minutes per day, five days a week, for an average of 6–8 weeks, using a variety of computer games and listening exercises designed to adaptively change acoustic cues in speech and non-speech cues. Overall, the children improved significantly in both their receptive and expressive language skills, as determined by pre-training and post training tests. Specifically, as a result of this training, they appeared to have been able to set up distinct phonological representations for each phoneme in their language.

To investigate whether this type of training can render Spanish stress more accessible for explicit manipulation, we divided our HLSS's into two subgroups, an experimental group and a control group. These were closely matched with respect to three different measures of performance on the reading and reading + listening tasks in the pretest: (a) average error rate in percent, (b) median error rate in percent, and c) standard deviation of error scores. These scores are listed below in Table 3.

Table 3. Error Rates (%), Median Error Rate (%), and Standard Deviation of Error Scores for the Experimental and Control Groups In the Reading and Reading + Listening Tasks In the Pre-Test

	Experimental Group (13)	Control Group (12)
Error rate in reading	57.07%	57.39%
Error rate in read + listen	55.70%	55.77%
Median error rate in reading	46.77%	45.16%
Median error in read+listen	45.165%	42.93%
Std of reading scores	9.02	9.77
Std of read + listen scores	10.03	8.63

Both groups underwent five training sessions over a period of two-and-a-half weeks. Each training session engaged students in a reading+listening task similar where students were asked to identify the location of the stressed syllable as they listened to and looked at a list of words. Both groups trained with identical printed lists of words (for a sample list, see List 5 in the Appendix). However, the experimental group listened to audio-taped readings of these words in which the tonic syllables were rendered with amplified pitch, length and loudness. By contrast, the control group listened to audio-taped readings in which the tonic syllables were uttered with normal (non-exaggerated) phonetic cues.

A few details regarding the execution of the training sessions bear pointing out. First, all lists consisted of exactly 25 words, each three or more syllables in length. Accordingly, a total of 125 words were used over the five sessions that comprised the training period. Second, the total time per training session was approximately seven minutes. The first two minutes of the session were spent reviewing the rules of the task and giving students the opportunity to look at the words on their own. For the remainder of the time, students listened twice to a reading of the words and circled the location of the stressed syllable on their printed list of the words. Altogether, the total training period included approximately twenty-five minutes of aural input and five to ten minutes of silent reading of the words. Third, the amplified phonetic cues heard by the experimental group were not generated by a computer, but came about from the reader's attempt at uttering the words with the highest level of emphasis or exaggeration, as instructed by this investigator. In an effort to keep loudness constant in all training sessions for both groups, all recordings were made with the same setting of the volume knob in the tape recorder. Finally, although students turned in their completed lists at the end of each training session, they did not receive any feedback regarding the correctness of their answers. In fact, all answers to student questions regarding the point of these and other tasks were deferred until all work pertaining to this project was finished.

THE POSTTEST

After the completion of the training period, all students were tested under conditions very similar to those employed in the pretest. First, students were asked to identify the stressed syllable in a reading task that made use of the same list of words as used in the reading+listening portion of the pretest (i.e., List 2, Appendix). Subsequently, students were asked to identify the stressed syllable in a reading+listening task where the words were rendered without emphasis or exaggeration. The list of words used for this portion of the posttest task was the same as used earlier in the reading task (i.e., List 1 in Appendix).

In order to render the pretest and the posttest as similar to each other as possible, the audio portions of both tests were made by the same Peruvian speaker at the development stage of this project, prior to commencing all work with students. Furthermore, both recordings were made using the same equipment at the same setting of the volume knob. Both recordings were also carefully timed to last approximately three minutes. As was the case in the reading + listening portion of the pretest, the names of seven cities and countries were interspersed in the reading of the words in the posttest, as a way to control for inattention or hearing difficulties as a source of low scores. All students properly identified these cities, writing them down as they heard them. This indicated to us that they were indeed paying attention to the task and that the input that they received was audible.

RESULTS

While the experimental and control groups had nearly identical error rates in the pretest, they performed very differently with regard to the post-test. As shown in Table 4, after training with amplified input, the experimental group registered an error rate of 30.65% in the reading task and 27.29% in the reading+listening task. In contrast, the control group registered error rates of 52.55% and 48.65% in the reading and reading+listening tasks, respectively.

If the posttest scores for the reading and the reading + listening tasks are averaged together, the experimental group demonstrates an overall error rate of approximately 29%. This means that subsequent to training with amplified input, these students are able to guess the location of stress with a 71% success rate. By contrast, the control group's error rate stands at approximately 50%. Translated into an academic scale, this difference corresponds to a passing grade (C) for the students in the experimental group, and a failing grade (F), for students in the experimental group.

Table 4.   Pre-test v. Posttest Error Rates (in percent) for the Experimental and Control Groups

Group	Pre/post Error Rates in Reading	Pre/Post Error Rates In Read + Listen
Experimental	57.07/30.65	55.70/27.29
Control	57.39/52.55	55.77/48.65

Table 5.   Pre-test v. Posttest Error Rates (in percent) for the Experimental and Control Groups

Group	Pre/post Error Rates in Reading	Pre/Post Error Rates In Read + Listen
Experimental	57.07/30.65	55.70/27.29
Control	57.39/52.55	55.77/48.65

The drop in error rate for the experimental group was statistically significant (Wilcoxon's Sum of Ranks test) for both testing conditions (from 57% to 31% errors for the reading task, $p < 0.002$; from 56% to 27% errors for the reading plus listening task, $p < 0.01$). The slight decrease in error rate seen for the control group was not statistically significant for either testing condition (from 57% to 53% errors for the reading task and from 56% to 49% errors for reading + listening, $p > 0.1$).

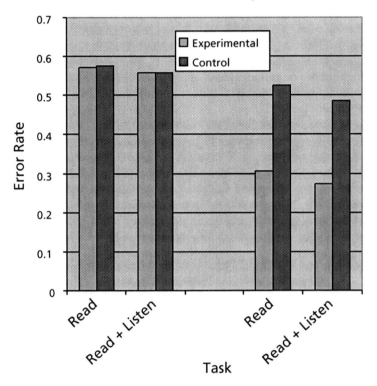

Figure 1.   Effect of training mode.

DISCUSSION

The results obtained strongly suggest that training with amplified phonetic cues represents an effective way to teach SNS speakers to identify the location of stress. A comparative analysis of the scores for the reading and the reading + listening tasks in the pre- and posttests provide some insight as to how this kind of training might work. As noted earlier, the pretest scores of HLSS revealed that simultaneously reading and listening to a list of words offered no significant advantage for purposes of identifying the location of stress over simply reading the words. We hypothesized that this situation stemmed from students' inability to hear the phonetic cues associated with stress. However, the Reading-aloud and Nonce-repeating tasks amply demonstrated that HLSS were indeed capable of hearing the phonetic cues associated with stress. This led us to the conclusion that what these students lacked was the ability to access their implicit knowledge of Spanish stress for tasks that involve explicit manipulation or analysis of linguistic data.

Now, a comparison of pretest scores to posttest scores, leaves little doubt that the experimental group radically improved its ability to identify the location of word stress in both the reading and the reading+listening tasks, as a result of training with amplified input. However, the narrow margin of difference between the experimental group's reading and reading+listening scores in the posttest, suggests that the aural input provided in the second task was of little value to students in locating stress. Indeed, when it comes to identifying the location of stress, this input appears to be a redundant cue with respect to students' own silent reading of the words.

This is not at all surprising, given HLSS' ability to perceive and reproduce stress, as demonstrated in the Reading-aloud and Nonce-repeating tasks. As such, in the majority of cases, the external aural input in the listening task provides little more than a confirmation of students' own correct silent pronunciation of the words.[4] This is not to say, of course, that listening to external aural input is never beneficial. In fact, with unknown words, this is often the only way to determine the position of word stress. However, when it comes to identifying stress in familiar words, external aural input adds no relevant information beyond that which is already available in students' own pronunciation of the words.

Crucially, training with amplified input appears to have improved the reading + listening scores by raising the baseline score of the reading task. That is, training with amplified input seems to have given students in the experimental group access to their own inner voice as the primary mechanism for determining the location of word stress. Of course, this is the very mechanism that guides the collocation of orthographic accents in most writing situations. In fact, the conditions of the reading+listening task are, at best, highly artificial, as most people do not have access to an aural rendition of written text as they seek to place accents.

In sum, as this study demonstrates, the way to train heritage language students to identify Spanish stress, is to give them the ability to pick out the information present in their own rendition of words. Our findings indicate that training with amplified input represents an effective way to achieve this goal.

CONCLUSIONS AND IMPLICATIONS FOR THE CLASSROOM

Though heritage language speakers of Spanish generally have no overt phonological deficiencies when speaking and listening to their language, this work amply demonstrates the necessity of phonological instruction in the SNS classroom. When it comes to stress, this need does not stem from an inability on the part of such students to perceive and reproduce the phonetic cues associated with Spanish stress, but rather from an inability to make explicit use of these cues in tasks that involve explicit manipulation of language.

Of course, many of the skills underlying higher order reading and writing skills call precisely for explicit manipulation of units of language, be they of a phonological, morphological, or syntactic structure. While our conclusions must be confined to the realm of phonology, and more precisely to stress, our findings raise the tantalizing possibility that other areas of the linguistic competence of heritage language speakers may also be inaccessible for the kind of explicit manipulation found in the classroom.[5] For example, there may be grammatical constructions and morphological rules that students may be able to use correctly when speaking, but that they may not be able to fully manipulate or control when writing. If further research reveals that is indeed the case, then pedagogical innovations that can release this knowledge for explicit use can greatly enhance the acquisition of literacy skills by heritage language speakers.

NOTES

1.   Though twenty-seven students were enrolled in Spanish 250, two students have been excluded from this report because their absences prevented them from completing the entire training regimen.

2.   While word stress is not entirely predictable in Spanish, there are patterns that make stress fairly predictable. For example, consonant-final words generally bear stress on the final syllable, while vowel-final words tend to exhibit penultimate stress. Antepenultimate stress is relatively uncommon, and it is only possible in words that have final and penultimate syllables that do not contain a diphthong and are not closed by a consonant (i.e., that are light syllables).

3.   Evaluators were instructed to disregard any phonemic errors (i.e., saying [b] for [p]), and to focus only on stress.

4.   This situation may be likened to listening to two similar readings of the same material. In the case of the experimental group, one such reading is internally generated by each student as he or she looks at the words, while the other one comes from the audio-recording. Given that both readings are very similar to each other, there is no reason why the second reading should offer any additional advantage over the first one.

5.   One potential example of this in the area of syntax concerns the use of articles by SNS students. Though students rarely make a mistake with the placement of the article when speaking, when writing they frequently omit this item in places where they shouldn't.

APPENDIX

List 1

elite	romance	embolo
natural	checheres	fabrica
cantaro	hispanico	mascara
musical	manipulador	cañamo
sabana	Margarita	microfon
puritano	revolver	polvora
solido	articulo	chimenea
Salvador	semaforo	fragmento
berrinche	imbecil	genesis
elegante	baldragas	reforma
esteril	original	diploma
canibal	disimil	ignorante
neurosis	America	penoso
cascabel	Africa	corrupto
lodazal	saliva	literatura
telegrafo	mediterraneo	cicatriz
acustico	cartabon	Fernandez
basilica	alfiler	ofensa
holgachon	Jupiter	gratitud
gramatical	incorrecto	marroqui
Jerusalem	carmesi	brujula
tajada	elami	digital

List 2

telefono	contrabando	Malinche
pragmatico	nispero	capital
libelula	Hernandez	democrata
elefante	busilis	regimen
verosimil	examen	adjunto
famulo	Israel	tornado
directo	miscelaneo	cabañal
planeta	mizcalo	molecula
silaba	caracter	bacalao
paralisis	placebo	sabado
fugitivo	longitud	inutil
tamesis	elevador	gramatical
satelite	reposo	eclipse

estrangul	perfecto	versatil
instructor	cibicon	departamento
capiller	hipnosis	profundo
directo	reciproco	algodon
metrico	canesu	mineral
hospital	economico	feligres
camara	deposito	tragico
capuchino	maniqui	osigrago
sebillo	tayuya	singular

List 3

Caniso	pastinad	iscalpan
Septago	berenol	gesupia
Piesala	tierprino	nelgozor
Tantarmo	derona	tenesis

List 4

Mariposa	división	teatro
espejo	animal	libreta
estuche	caliente	dinamita
calentador	emperador	periodico

List 5

Milenio	correo	introduccion	terapia
Especialista	pizarra	diferencia	hectarea
Psicologia	escolar	circulo	periodo
Publico	astronauta	declaracion	destino
Inocente	poblacion	organismo	
Ecologia	cementerio	alivia	
Incomodidad	alternativa	horoscopo	

REFERENCES

Barrutia, R., & Schwegler, A. (1994). *Fonética y fonología españolas.* New York: Wiley.
Berman, P. (1992). *The status of bilingual education in California.* Berkeley, CA: Paul Berman.

Bull, W. (1965). *Spanish for teachers: Applied linguistics.* New York: Ronald Press.

Carreira, M.M. (2000). Validating and promoting Spanish in the U.S.: Lessons from linguistic science. *Bilingual Research Journal, 24*(4), 423–42.

Carreira, M.M., & Armengol, R. (2001). Professional opportunities for heritage language speakers. In J.K. Peyton, S. McGinnis, & D. Ranard (Eds.), *Heritage languages in America: Preserving a national resource* (pp. 109–142). Washington, DC and McHenry, IL: Center for Applied Linguistics and Delta Systems. Manuscript submitted for publication.

Fantini, A. (1997). El desarrollo de la competencia intercultural: Una meta para todos. In M.C. Colombi & F.X. Alarcón (Eds.), *La enseñanza del español a hispanohablantes* (pp. 206–221). Boston: Houghton Mifflin.

Fishman, J. (1994). *In praise of the beloved language: A comparative view of positive ethnolinguistic consciousness.* Berlin: Mouton de Gruyer.

Harris, J. (1983). *Syllable structure and stress in Spanish: A nonlinear analysis.* Cambridge MA: MIT Press.

Hernandez Chávez, E. (2000, October). *La lucha para el mantenimiento del español frente a la hegemonía del inglés.* Paper presented at Romance Languages and Linguistic Communities in the United States. The University of Maryland at College Park.

Hidalgo, M. (1997). Criterios normativos e ideología lingüística: aceptación y rechazo del español de los Estados Unidos. In C. Colobi & F. Alarcón (Eds.), *La enseñza del español a hispanohablantes* (pp. 109–120). Boston: Houghton Mifflin.

Kenstowicz, M. (1993). *Phonology in generative grammar.* Cambridge MA: Blackwell.

Lipski, J.M. (1997). En busca de normas fonéticas del español. In M.C. Colombi & F.X.Alarcón (Eds.), *La enseñanza del español a hispanohablantes* (pp. 121–132). Boston: Houghton Mifflin.

McClelland, J.L. (1989). Parallel distributed processing: Implications for cognition and development. In R.G.M. Morris (Ed.), *Parallel distributed processing: Implications for psychology and neurobiology* (pp. 8–45). Oxford: Clarendon Press.

Omaggio Hadley, A. (2001). *Teaching language in context.* Boston: Heinle & Heinle.

Pinker, S., & Prince, A. (1989). Rules and connections in human language. In R.G.M. Morris (Ed.), *Parallel distributed processing: Implications for psychology and neurobiology* (pp. 182–99). Oxford: Clarendon Press.

Rodríguez Pino, C. (1997). La reconceptualización del programa de español para hispanohablantes: estrategias que reflejan la realidad sociolinguística de la clase. In C. Colombi & F. Alarcón (Eds.), *La enseñanza del español a hispanohablantes* (pp. 65–82). Boston: Houghton Mifflin.

Tallal, P., Miller, S., Bedi, G., Byma, G., Wang, X., Nagarajan, S.S., Screiner, C., Jenkins, W.M., & Merzenich, M. (1996, January). Language comprehension in language-learning impaired children improved with acoustically modified speech. *Science, 271,* 81–84.

University of California, Los Angeles. (2001). *Heritage language research priorities conference report.* Los Angeles: Author. Available: www.cal.org/heritage.

Villa, D.J. (1996). Choosing a "standard" variety of Spanish for the instruction of native speakers in the U. S. *Foreign Language Annals, 29,* 191–200.

Villa, D., & Villa, J. (1998). Identity labels and self-reported language use: Implications for Spanish language programs. *Foreign Language Annals, 31,* 505–516.

Whitley, M.S. (1986). *Spanish/English contrasts.* Washington, DC: Georgetown University Press.

CHAPTER 12

LITERACY IN DIGITAL ENVIRONMENTS:

CONNECTING COMMUNITIES OF LANGUAGE LEARNERS

Mary Ann Lyman-Hager, Ann Johns, Honorine Nocon, and James N. Davis

ABSTRACT

The purpose of this chapter is to highlight issues regarding the reading/writing connection in foreign language education and to describe several recent research and pedagogical initiatives at San Diego State University that have explored this connection. These initiatives and research programs have been partially funded by the United States Department of Education, International Programs, Title VI, and by the City Heights Project, sponsored by Price Charities and San Diego State University. The element that the initiatives have in common is a refocusing on new populations of speakers (writers) and listeners (readers) engendered by widespread use of internet technologies and pedagogical approaches derived from social constructivist theory, primarily Vygotsky-based approaches, and from a decade of research into L2 computerized hypertextual reading.

INTRODUCTION

> Writing has always been about making connections: between writer and read-
> ers, across time, and through space. (Eisenstein; Ong, cited in Johnson-
> Eilola, 1998, p. 17)

In many ways, the so-called digital revolution is not that very revolutionary,
in light of the above statement that underscores the functional relationship
between reading and writing. Writers and readers are now, just as they have
been in the past, inexorably linked in a mutual desire to speak and to be
heard, to write and to be read. However, literacy practices, primarily reading and writing, have experienced dramatic changes in confronting the
challenges of space and time in the digital age. Technologies (internet-and
web-based chat, discussion groups, etc.) provide new possibilities of linking
together communities who may never before have communicated with one
another in such an intimate and direct manner. The presence of new audiences and new speakers thus has the potential to dramatically impact the
quality and quantity of cross-cultural interactions.

THE CHALLENGE

The problem for the academy remains pedagogical rather than technological: transforming educational practices of the academy to take the new
medium into account and to appropriate it effectively for second language
acquisition is our biggest challenge as language teachers. How have the
computer and new proposed language pedagogies that enable reading and
writing across time and space influenced the academy? Are we teaching
foreign and second languages more effectively because of this so-called digital revolution? Are teachers adjusting foreign language curricula, and are
teacher training programs including instruction in the new digital media
as a pre-text to creating meaningful activities in reading and writing? Are
evolving literacy practices resulting in better intercultural communication
and increased multicultural understanding? Several literary research and
curricular experiments undertaken at San Diego State University attempt
to address these questions. Specific projects described in this chapter
include: the Fifth Dimension Spanish Program (Nocon 2001), the Human
Rituals and Migration Project (Johns, 2001a), and the Reconceptualizing
Reading in a Digital Age Project at LARC (the Language Acquisition
Resource Center) at San Diego State University (Davis, 2000).

READING/WRITING RESEARCH LINKS

Many researchers have concluded that computers might fundamentally change how we learn to read and write in a first (Meyer & Rose, 1998) or foreign/second (Davis, 2000) language. Prior to the late 1990s, descriptions of computers as "patient tutors" and as reading/writing "coaches" abound in the literature. Ample consideration has been given to the evolving role of the teacher as a "facilitator" of language learning rather than as its "director" or "choreographer." The possibilities of mediating an authentic foreign language text electronically and/or digitally to make it more comprehensible (with hypertextual links, for example) abound in research reports of the 1990s (see Davis & Lyman-Hager, 1997; Landow, 2000). In particular, great hopes have been placed in creating technology-assisted reading glosses to help foreign language learners increase limited lexical, cultural, and grammatical knowledge (Lyman-Hager, Davis, Burnett, & Chennault, 1993). Reading researchers in ESL and FL (Bernhardt, 1991) have used recall protocols, or summaries-texts written in L1, of a text just previously read by L2 learners. The protocols, once analyzed and broken down into logical thought groups, help to determine how L2 readers process and subsequently retain textual information. Thus, examining written output allows reading researchers a way to determine what is retained or "noticed" about the text.

"Noticing"

Irrespective of the delivery mode of the text (electronic or print), if students fail to notice lexical, grammatical, or other salient content-based features of a foreign language text, they will most assuredly fail to read, process, retain, and write cogently about a text they have read (Robinson, 1995; Schmidt, 1990). In other words, if they fail to care about the overall purpose and message of the text, or if it has no particular meaning to them, knowledge about the text will not be retained. It follows that designing reading/writing tasks that hold particular meaning to students, or allowing leeway in the selection of texts to be read or writing topics would be important considerations in curricular design.

Certain physical features of text impact readers' comprehension and intake, or the manner in which readers process linguistic "data." Leow (1997) explored the variables of text length and input enhancement with 84 college-level second semester students of Spanish. He found that for this population of learners, passage length alone had a significant effect on intake. Conversely, input enhancement (i.e., simplification of an authentic text, to make it more "comprehensible" to second language learners) appeared to Leow to have had little effect on learners' intake. He concluded that intake may not be affected by "external manipulation of written input to facilitate these learners' comprehension and further processing of linguistic forms in the input" (Leow, p. 151). Others have found that text length is not among the primary impediments to foreign language comprehension, but rather, background knowledge and signaling[1] play a more prominent role in determining text accessibility (Hauptman, 2000).

Audience

Increasingly language teachers are acknowledging the potential impact on second language literacy practices of the accessibility of broad global audiences of L2 speakers. Because of the Internet and web-based technologies, foreign language students can now interact much more directly with target language interlocutors in task-based reading and writing activities. The challenge to the pedagogy of foreign and second language literacy, then, is to create authentic, realistic cross-cultural learning opportunities that cause students to first notice and then interact with foreign language text (of an appropriate length), and then with others, in meaningful ways. These learning tasks cause readers/writers to care enough about the message of the text and to personalize the writing task in order to explore issues that the text brings to the reader. For example, if reading a section of text that discusses rites of initiation in adolescents, students might be asked to list similar rites of passage in their culture. They might then contrast and compare the expectations of native and target cultures regarding the rites of initiation. To gather detailed information about rites of passage into adulthood, for example, they might also contact people from the target culture or view a number of web sites.

If tasks required of learners do not adequately inspire them to acquire missing background knowledge of a particular topic by first reading about it and then sharing knowledge—or negotiating meaning by writing to others about what they have learned—active language learning may be compromised. Several elements are key to acquiring literacy: understanding the characteristics of the text to be read, the traits of the hypothesized reader for whom the text is intended, and finally, the nature of the interaction between reader and text. Underlying the three elements is the essentially social nature of literacy. Implicitly involved are producers/writers of authentic text and consumers/readers of these texts.

PROJECT I: FRESHMEN SUCCESS PROGRAM:
THE HUMAN RITUALS AND MIGRATION

San Diego State University is one of the West's largest public universities, with 32,000 students. Its incoming freshmen classes are increasingly diverse, due to its location near the Mexican border and near the "Ellis Island" area of San Diego. A growing number of freshmen come from this multiethnic, largely immigrant population immediately surrounding the campus (Johns, 2001). In an effort to retain students who may enter the university unprepared to read and write in a predominantly English-language academic setting, the University in 1991 established the Freshman Success Program (FSP). By fall 1999, the FSP served more than 1300 first time freshmen, a good number of whom were ESL or bilingual students and first generation college bound.

What are the distinguishing features of the eight unit program? The most unusual aspects of the program are the linked/adjunct arrangement and the portfolio program design in writing classes. Clustered around a required basic 3 unit General Education (commonly referred to as "gen ed" or "GE") class such as sociology, Africana studies, Chicano/a studies, anthropology, are study groups and composition/literacy classes. These study groups (1 unit) and composition classes (3 units) are required of students who do not achieve sufficiently high scores on the university placement exam.

A committed, active cohort of expert teachers designs the curricula for the composition/literacy classes. The primary goals of the literacy/composition classes are to create students who will be able to:

- Produce a variety of texts under varied circumstances.
- Develop an awareness of a range of discourse styles in public prose, including academic discourse.
- Increase their repertoire of strategies for approaching different kinds of reading and writing tasks.
- Demonstrate awareness of the possibilities for multiple interpretations of subject matter and texts by teachers and students.
- Develop a sense of power and motivation in relation to the language, contexts, topics, and texts of academic disciplines (Johns, 2001, p. 65).

Johns points to the importance of both the psycholinguistic (process) approach to literacy development as well as the social constructionist approach. Central to this multidimensional approach are the cultures and contexts for writing, encouraging students to "develop a variety of strategies for approaching rhetorical tasks in an unpredictable number of contexts" (p. 65). The portfolio is required of each student in the program and contains three types of required entries and three selected optional entries. The required entries include (1) a summary/abstract/précis or summary response (described above), (2) a timed writing completed in the classroom, and (3) a semester reflection. For the optimal entries students choose three of the following:

1. A paper for which students gather and analyze data (GE related).
2. A paper, including observation and report or critique.
3. An interview (GE discipline related).
4. A collaborative writing paper (GE related).
5. An intertextual project (in which students examine one text in relation to another).
6. An argumentative or persuasive essay.
7. A letter project, focusing on purpose and audience (using GE material).
8. A genre-based project, generally analytical (GE related) (Johns, 2001, p. 66).

Johns describes the two-hour final exam and the manner in which the composition teachers assist students in choosing material for inclusion in the individual portfolio and in preparing for the final. Other FSP teachers evaluate both the portfolio and the final examination to determine whether or not students will enroll in regular freshman-level composition courses or whether they will be required to enroll in a developmental class.

A Special FSP Program in Academic English Writing: The Hoover High Project of City Heights

A particular GE class (Cultural Anthropology) involved FSP students in an experimental collaborative approach with neighboring Hoover High, a City Heights school. As noted above, a good number of the City Heights students belong to newly arrived immigrant families. This community-based learning project was the most ambitious of all of the FSP projects at San Diego State, involving collaboration of eight instructors at secondary and college levels and students of thirty-some different native languages groups. Students from Hoover and SDSU visited each other's campuses and engaged in a mentoring process, whose ultimate product is a co-developed research paper. The project differed slightly from the FSP goals listed above. Students enrolled in FSP Cultural Anthropology will be able to:

1. Value the diverse experiences of their high school partners and their families, particularly those relating to issues of migration into and within the United States.

2. Develop more sophisticated research skills: interviewing techniques, use of the World Wide Web and the library, note taking, citing, paraphrasing, and other necessary abilities.
3. Complete increasingly difficult tasks, resulting in a complex, intertextual, research paper.
4. Provide academic and personal mentoring for diverse high school students.
5. Demonstrate their knowledge of subject matter and their own writing processes through speeches to the high school students and written reflection (Johns, 2001).

Challenges abound in this community-based service learning and academic writing project. Families in transit in the City Heights area created havoc with interviewing schedules between SDSU students and their Hoover High counterparts. The lack of consistently available Internet and e-mail facilities at Hoover High (see El-Wardi & Johns, 1997/8 for a discussion of these difficulties) made the ideal—a continuous distance-based collaboration and mentoring—difficult, if not impossible. Johns concludes that the benefits to the Freshman Success Program are many, even taking into account the difficulties inherent in working with a "diverse and complicated" school such as Hoover (Johns, 2001, p. 70). SDSU's so-called remedial (developmental) students appear to be "empowered by their opportunities to mentor younger students who are like themselves ... They and their Hoover counterparts are able to draw from their own experiences and those of their families to produce academic texts, a factor that is central to pedagogies in our multiliterate world..." (Johns, 2001, p. 70). Developing intertextual and technology-based abilities that standardized tests often cannot capture, SDSU students enrolled in the Hoover collaborative writing project nonetheless demonstrate very well written and edited final research. Because of the involvement of composition instructors inherent in the Freshmen Success Program, the range of genres available to these students, in reading and writing activities, is much larger.

This project was important to the students at both sites for a number of reasons, many of which relate to academic literacies in second languages. The final research report was organized, drafted, revised, and edited throughout the semester, and it was different in terms of both genre and intertextual demands than anything the students had experienced in the past (see Johns, 2002 for issues of genres at academic levels). Most of the students' experiences in reading had been with the genres of literature, and their writing had consisted of short essays and personal reflections. Yet in this project, they were required to read, take notes from, and evaluate WEB pages and to intertextually integrate the results of their student interviews, classroom readings, and WEB page notes into their final research reports. The genres in which they wrote were also different from what had been required in the past. The research reports modeled those in anthropology, using the IMRD (Introduction, Methodology, Results, and Discussion) format common to the sciences and social sciences. Particularly important to this discipline is the methodology section, which the students found very difficult to write. Also daunting were the discussions in which the results were analyzed. However, their efforts paid off: the anthropology instructor noted that she had never seen research of this quality among novice students.

Johns offers a variety of practical suggestions for L2 literacy teachers. The first involves student exposure to a number of genres that are not literacy, but appear in academic classes in a number of disciplines, such as the summary/abstract, the review/critique, and the research report. The FSP portfolio approach assures that students write in these genres for a number of audiences, using texts that are organized in different ways and that reflect different values and cultural assumptions. These texts should be meaningful to the learners and to the purposes of their course—but also demanding and reflective of academic requirements beyond the course itself. The university and secondary schools should do everything possible to ensure access to advanced technologies in order to develop technological literacies. Public speaking and interviewing skills should be considered along with reading and writing abilities when evaluating overall literacy in this type of course. Finally, students should be encouraged to draw from personal experiences (both cross cultural and linguistic) to enrich their writing research-based papers. Johns has found that, in this experience, those students with a heightened sense engagement in the task derive a positive image of self and often become better readers, speakers, and writers (Johns, 2001, p. 72).

PROJECT II: SPANISH FIFTH DIMENSION (5D) MODEL

A similar Vygotskian-based service learning approach was used in an experimental SDSU intermediate-level Spanish class taught by Honorine Nocon. The Fifth Dimension Model incorporates computer-mediated activities and games to encourage "intense interaction with academic content through collaborative, exploratory learning and play" (Nocon, 2001, p. 5). Developed by Peg Griffin, Michael Cole, and others at the Laboratory of Comparative Human Cognition, University of California, San Diego (UCSD), the Fifth Dimension was conceived as a community-based after-school program to link children with college age students, fostering learning through play activities (Cole, 1996). Groups of two or three, centered around a computer or other educational tools, focus on accomplishing specific game-like learning tasks.

More than 30 research sites in the United States (including all campuses of the University of California and several California State University campuses), Mexico, Sweden, and Australia have utilized the model. The 5D model's loose structure affords opportunities for diverse participants to play, learn, work, socialize, and conduct research across academic disciplines. Fifth Dimension sites draw on Vygotsky's (1978) notion of the *Zone of Proximal Development* and his methodology. He defines the *zone of proximal development* as "the distance between the actual developmental level as determined by independent problem solving and the level of potential development as determined through problem solving" (Vygotsky, 1978, p. 86). The Fifth Dimension applies certain cultural-historical theories of development and Vygotskian theories of pedagogy currently cited in language research and methodology (see Donato & McCormick, 1994; Lantolf, 1994; Warschauer 1997).

Nocon was motivated to apply the 5D methodology to the teaching of Spanish based on her observations of the impacts of the linguistically rich San Diego/Tijuana border culture on literacy practices in Hispanic populations and in her experiences teaching Spanish at San Diego State University. The Fifth Dimension model provides researchers a variety of opportunities to conduct both qualitative research through ethnography, participant observation, and quantitative research using specific performance measures. This "genetic methodology assumes that one will have the opportunity and take the time to watch development as it occurs over time, and also to consider the complexity of its sociocultural context" (Nocon, 2001, p. 11). Consequently, Fifth Dimension researchers most often use qualitative, ethnographic methodologies, as Nocon opted to do in the Spanish 5D Project. Consistent with ethnographic studies' methodologies, several research questions emerged:

> What would happen in a university Spanish class introduced to the Fifth Dimension model?
> Would diverse learners work together productively? Would they learn Spanish?
> What would be the effect on the affective environment and student motivation? (Nocon, 2001, p. 11)

The Principal Investigator, Nocon, functioned as teacher/researcher in the Fifth Dimension Second Language Project. An experimental section of Spanish 201 (Intermediate Spanish) at San Diego State University in the spring of 1998 was listed in the schedule of classes without special designation along with 34 other sections of Spanish 201.Students in this experimental section, located in the LARC multimedia language laboratory, used the same texts as students in other sections, with the same general requirements. Students were informed at the beginning of class that the approach would be different and that they could leave the section if they did not wish to participate in the experimental course. Students in the Intermediate 201 Spanish experimental course were told that they would be given new ways to practice language and literacy (reading and writing practices) within in the context of the standard intermediate level Spanish curriculum for San Diego State University.

The special approach used in the experimental section involved students working at computers within groups, using E-mail to communicate with college students in Mexico and accessing the World Wide Web to read about a bi-national educational research project called the Fifth Dimension. Sites consulted included: http://www.buap.mx (Benemérita Universidad Autónoma de Puebla) and http://communication.ucsd.edu/ Fifth.Dimension (Doorway to the Fifth Dimension.)

After gathering information, the students wrote brief reports based on their research. Students in the experimental section used their E-mail accounts and internet connections to contact researchers from Fifth Dimension sites in Puebla, Mexico, and Mexico, D.F. as well as the Looking Glass Neighborhood, a Fifth Dimension project run by SDSU in San Diego, and La Clase Mágica and the Magical Dimension, both run by UCSD in San Diego County.

They also used computer programs to produce written materials for Spanish-speaking children in these ongoing 5D projects. Groups of three worked collaboratively on various computer programs (*Hyper Studio*™, *Kid Pix Studio*™, and *Storybook Weaver Deluxe*™) designed to facilitate collaborative play at the various 5D sites involved in the project. These computer programs were useful for producing computer-based materials and were commonly used both by children and adults. These programs were all potentially useful in making presentations for the Spanish-speaking children in the bi-national Fifth Dimension projects. All three programs shared the capacity to produce text-based and graphic displays and included limited animation capacity as well as voice-record capability.

As in the other sections of Spanish 201, students in the experimental section produced three compositions: the first two were collaboratively created in the groups, using *Storybook Weaver* and covering the topics: "La Quinta Dimensión en SDSU y Puebla" and "El día que Juanito (de Puebla) visitó a Sarah (en San Diego)." Oral presentations during the last (fifteenth) week of classes were prepared within groups using *Story Book Weaver*, *Kid Pix*, or *Hyper Studio*. Student presentations could be collective and integrated or completed as a series of individual presentations, with each person speaking 5 minutes on the general theme of *An Aspect of Life in the United States*. Presentations were video-recorded as messages for the children and adults in the Spanish-speaking community of the bi-national Fifth Dimension.

The experimental class took the standard Spanish 201 tests, including five chapter tests, four quizzes, and a final exam. Similarly, as stated above, they produced three compositions and an oral presentation. In addition, as with the other sections of Spanish 201, they spend the required 50 minutes per chapter (for each of six chapters) in the language lab, in addition to normal class time. Students completed writing and listening activities in the language lab, using audiocassette tapes and a workbook. There was no control group, due to the nature of ethnographic research. The experimental class contained 28 adults, 19 females and 9 males, drawn from the general population of SDSU students enrolled in Spanish 201, representing several areas of study. There were no freshmen, and there was an even mix of second, third and fourth year students. Access to computers during most of the experimental class sessions was a key to being able to focus on telecommunication and collaborative production using the computer. In addition, LARC's lab configuration encouraged student collaborative group work.

During the E-mail exchanges, an obvious difficulty was the disparity in language registers the participants used. After having received various messages from the Spanish 201 students, one of the Mexican students asked innocently how old the children were. In contrast, the disparity in language levels did not affect the students in the 201 class, who remained enthusiastic about writing to the students in Mexico and did so quite unabashedly, disclosing likes and dislikes, their fears about upcoming exams, and inquiring about Mexico. Nocon notes that "the sign-offs or message closings that students used were surprising: Con amor, Escribanos por favor, Buena suerte, and adiosito" (p. 15). Throughout the course messages progressed in complexity, first asking typical "beginning level" questions about the weather, favorite colors, and what the Fifth Dimension site in Puebla was like, then pursuing more sophisticated topics like the correspondents' respective difficulties in gaining computer access. E-mail exchange was typically laborious for both the students in the class and the Mexican correspondents. The Mexican students' messages required time-consuming decoding by SDSU intermediate Spanish students, whose simple and somewhat redundant messages sometimes failed to inspire Mexican students to respond directly. More highly skilled SDSU Spanish language students (those with higher grades in Spanish at the end of the course) in the experimental section, however, were found to have sought out supplemental E-mail exchanges as an opportunity to engage in more complex communication.

For a more detailed account of the experimental results, see the full report in Nocon (2001). In general, using traditional grammar-based measures of achievement in place for Spanish 201, most of the twenty-seven students demonstrated improvement in reduction in errors. In response to a question about how the class could be improved, students frequently expressed concern about the tests and grammar. Some students suggested that more information on tests be given, that more specific reviewing for the tests take place, that the tests be shorter, and that there be fewer tests. A number of students expressed concern that the class was conducted almost entirely in Spanish and suggested more English. The most frequent positive response was that the students liked the computers and that the class was fun, mentioning *Storybook Weaver* specifically. For example, one student wrote: "when using the computers you don't realize you are using Spanish." In response to whether they felt they were learning Spanish, students responded that they were: ("I feel that I am learning more ... than in other classes.") Students described the experimental section as fun, good, interesting, comfortable, and "cool." It was also categorized as rigorous, rushed, and "better for an upper level" of Spanish instruction. There were contradictory recommendations for greater emphasis on grammar and less emphasis on grammar. A common theme was that the class was too much work. Individual responses called for easier assignments, less homework, and elimination of the lab requirement, which traditionally (until Spring 2001) the Spanish Department required of all students in beginning and intermediate language classes. The main advantage of the experimental section lies in the impact on students' desire to continue communicating in Spanish. Nocon (2001) summarizes that in the experimental section, students engaged in meaningful, if imperfect, communication with native speakers. The resulting affective environment allowed many students to become engaged in learning Spanish. An indication of that engagement is the moderate increase in the numbers of students who said, after having been in the experimental class, that they would—or maybe would—continue to study Spanish. Other evidence of an improved affective environment in the class is in the form of student comments indicating that they found friends in the class and that they found it to be a comfortable forum for expression in Spanish. The video data accumulated during the course of the semester shows students engaging in pleasant discourse while working on their Spanish. The classroom environment resembled the type of "productive interactive space" of a Fifth Dimension site more than a traditional teacher-centered language classroom. Student comments affirm that the use and presence of computers in the class was positive (p. 11, part 3). Comparing the results of the experimental and traditional students' equivalent departmental exams and on the common final exam showed that the experimental and "traditional" students learned equivalent amounts of

Spanish. The major difference between groups is the positive attitude about language learning and intercultural communication generated in the experimental section, as measured by the increase in percentages of students wishing to continue studying the language.

PROJECT III: READING IN A DIGITAL AGE

Research has shown that proficient native language (L1) readers do not simply transpose L1 skills into the second language (L2) (see Davis & Lyman-Hager, 1997). Most undergraduates in the United States stress oral "communicative" skills (i.e., speaking and listening) and spend limited time reading in a foreign language. As a result, these students confront a "literacy gap" as they continue in upper level classes where they must read on their own in the L2. (Shultz, 1981).

In the 1990s, Davis and Lyman-Hager authored a computer-annotated version of Ferdinand Oyono's 1956 *Une vie de boy*, an African reading in French whose historical context and vocabulary are quite unfamiliar to the neophyte L2 reader. The software included a tracker that supported a variety of theory-driven inquiries into the nature of reading, including a doctoral dissertation (Hayden, 1997). Research examining tracking data and written recall protocols indicated that students at lower proficiency levels did not make use of the culturally rich electronic annotations unless specifically required to do so. Student writing immediately following their computerized readings, in other words, contained inaccurate or highly fanciful interpretations of the story line. Students with higher levels of proficiency in French, on the other hand, tended to make better use of cultural and vocabulary aids, and their understanding of the text narrative was enhanced (see Hayden, 1997, pp. 190–224).

From the original *Une Vie de Boy* software, a reading template was developed from an existing authoring system (ToolBook for PC and Hypercard for Macintosh) to annotate other authentic language texts. Using the GALT (Glossing Authentic Language Text) template, a number of Francophone texts representing various genres of literary production were included in a CD ROM published by John Wiley & Sons, *A l'aventure* (Lyman-Hager & Fischer, 1998). The template, GALT, is available for download online at (http://larcnet.sdsu.edu). It has been used at LARC Summer Institutes and has been used to annotate foreign language text in a variety of foreign languages, including double byte languages with difficult font issues, such as Japanese and Chinese. The template has been recently modified to become more interactive and to be "web-able." This new version, entitled GEMINI, reflects intense collaboration with Robert

Fischer of Southwest Texas State University, who authored the popular LIBRA authoring system for the Macintosh computer.

The *Reading in a Digital Age* project incorporates findings of the decade of research involving the use of tracking devices and written recall protocols and considers L2 learners whose reading proficiency and background cultural knowledge are still developing. The use of annotated, electronically-mediated text was linked to enhanced comprehension when readers encountered certain types of L2 texts whose contexts were largely unfamiliar to American students. With the advent of the Internet, however, Lyman-Hager proposed to Davis to reexamine both the reading practices and the strategies readers use to gather information. Clearly missing from earlier research, for example, are dimensions of interactivity afforded by the newer authoring tools for the Internet, and the possibility of engaging online collaborators in asynchronous and synchronous dialogues. Davis took the challenge seriously and has created an "interactive" summary of new research on the topic to date. This interactive article serves as the beginning of an on-line, collaboratively created and evolving article, involving additional Reading/Second Language Acquisition experts and those interested researchers whose task will be to define the research agenda and parameters of this new area of inquiry. *Reconceptualizing L2 Reading in the Digital Age* (Davis, 2000) thus reframes the questions that have emerged from research-based inquiries into the nature of L2 reading and writing.

While Davis emphasizes reading in his article, he also shows how digitization actually blurs the distinction between reading and writing, principally because new communications technologies (most dramatically, the World Wide Web) "decenter" texts. That is, a text on a computer screen is not finished and complete in the way it is in print format. It can easily be rewritten and even reconfigured by its reader. Furthermore, non-print media (e.g., images and audio) may also be used to enhance or perhaps to overshadow the original text (or, of course, to create an entirely new one). The new technologies, then, not only diminish the writer's authority, which is a given in contemporary "book culture," but also subvert the prestige of print, which is decreasingly the primary (and most prestigious) transmission vehicle of knowledge.

Davis argues that these two characteristics of the new media, along with several others constitute a new phase in the history of literacy (the broader term "literacy" including, of course, reading AND writing). Citing Donato (Personal communication, June 18, 2000), he defines literacy as "a semiotic toolkit for communicating and constructing knowledge." The uniqueness of this new literacy requires special skills, which, in his view, should be systematically addressed in L2 instruction. That is, L2 digital literacy[2] should be taught just as L2 analog literacy has been.

In order to support his arguments, Davis, first, situates digital literacy in the history of literacy in the West; second, identifies special qualities of digital literacy; third, suggests ways to address the new media in curricula and instruction. Finally, in the spirit of digital literacy, he invites readers to download and revise his article and then to upload their version for inclusion at the Language Acquisition Resource Center (LARC) website. The article can be downloaded from (http://larcdma.sdsu.edu/larcnet/home.html) and discussion forum is located at (http://balrog.sdsu.edu/~lymanha).

CONCLUSIONS FROM THREE
LITERARY CURRICULAR INITIATIVES

A common theme to the three San Diego State University projects cited in this article is their emphasis on the necessarily symbiotic relationship between reading and writing, particularly when compelling interactions between reader and author are called into play by the particular curricular approaches and literary-focused design of the project. The three projects focus on three aspects of literacy that unite readers with writers in different types of social settings: academic literacy (Johns), multicultural literacy (Nocon), and digital literacy (Davis & Lyman-Hager).

Johns cites the effectiveness of personal involvement of the SDSU students with Hoover High students in the collaborative writing project. Mastering academic discourse for SDSU students enrolled in the writing-intensive Freshmen Success Program involves more than a sterile exercise in producing text that no one will care to read, but rather, creating a portfolio of text-based and media-enhanced readings that constitute shared meaning—products of a fruitful collaboration between multi-leveled an unequally paired peers.

For the Spanish 201 students, the creation of task-based learning tools for younger children's after school activities, as well as connecting to older, "more capable Spanish-speaking peers" through internet-based messaging, proved meaningful to readers and writers alike. Using linguistic and computer skills to create games and stories for a population of real (as opposed to hypothetical) readers enhanced the motivation of the intermediate level Spanish students and increased the likelihood of their continuing to study Spanish. Certainly their communications with Spanish speakers in Mexico were more carefully crafted because they were actually written to be read, for a specific purpose related to the authentic learning tasks in which they were engaged.

Both the Hoover High/Human Migration Freshman Success Program and the Fifth Dimension Spanish curricular projects made extensive use of internet and E-mail technologies and would have relied on them more even more extensively, were they universally available in each setting. However, one wonders if extensive use of technology to communicate would have drawn attention away from the engaging and very personalized human relationships that developed over the course of the semester in the LARC projects. In the case of the Hoover High students who had very limited access to networked computers and therefore could not readily e-mail their SDSU counterparts when a question came up about writing or about life in general, the lack of networked communications might have diminished the potential of the mentoring relationship. On the other hand, the personalized visits described in Johns (2001) at each respective location and the end of term open houses and group presentations that the Hoover High students and the SDSU students hosted for one another were critical to closure for each cohort. Replicating this highly visible and successful Freshman Success Program Cultural Anthropology Course in the fully networked environments that now exist at each location, conducting on-site ethnographic research with some quantitative descriptive studies of the populations, and following up with written evaluations would help answer questions about the appropriate and timely role that technology might play in reinforcing literacy skills. Similar to the 5D model, dyads or triads of students (SDSU students and Hoover High students) might work together on tasks requiring Internet connected computer access, either at a distance from one another, or at a predetermined "after school" setting.

With respect to the Fifth Dimension based Spanish project, the lack of networked communication capabilities seemed not to diminish the impact of the messages from native Spanish speakers. The adage of "less is better," particularly with respect to complexity and length of target-language messages read by less than fluent readers, appears to have some validity, particularly in the light of research by Leow (1997) who found that for low intermediate level Spanish learners, passage length affected intake. Because of adverse conditions (the Mexican interlocutors cited computer theft as one reason why communication had ceased for a certain time), fewer messages of a nonessential content were sent via E-mail. SDSU intermediate level Spanish students of higher ability, who sought more interaction from native language interlocutors, were able to obtain it by writing personalized, targeted messages to their Mexican counterparts. The messages received back were a rare, and therefore (arguably) more precious, gift. In other words, when received, they were perhaps "noticed" and more meaningful.

In the case of the Digital Age Reading project, technology assumes an essential role in the query. Finally, researcher J.N. Davis, through posting his call to researchers and language practitioners interested in exploring interactively the influence of the Internet on reading, attempts to engage colleagues in a lively debate on the very nature of reading and writing in digital environments. His goal, "to help our students, in very systematic ways, to become effective users of the Internet in their L2 . . . instead of treating the Internet as simply another teaching tool . . . [of teaching] L2 Internet literacy just as we have taught L2 print literacy" (Davis, 2000) seems an obvious yet rarely explored course of action in foreign language writing instruction (see Warshauer, 1997, 1999). An addendum to the Davis paper might read "to create curricular plans for strengthening socio- and cross-cultural communication between communities of learners by incorporating Internet and web-based technologies at strategic junctures where learning tasks rely on connectivity and communication to be accomplished." These technology-based curricular plans might be instantiated through the creation of software, or, more appropriately, courseware developed collaboratively for diffusion on the Internet, highlighting themes that have proven engaging and relevant to cross-cultural groups and composing searchable libraries of authentic texts that readers can use in writing their texts.

Second and foreign language students increasingly use technology to communicate with native writers via the Internet, to accomplish authentic communicative tasks involving reading and writing in a target language. Certain so-called "authentic" tasks are undoubtedly more meaningful than others to facilitate language acquisition and cross-cultural understanding by linking readers and writers. Davis calls for a sharing of successes from research-based reading (literacy) instruction and for a reexamination of the impact of digital technology on reading practices. The other San Diego State University projects encourage connections between readers and writers in a collaboratively shared work space, with specific purposes in mind. The meaningful nature of the communications where individuals team with more capable peers in task-oriented learning is the essence of the Vygotskian methodology. The work space, whether virtual or real, whether synchronous or asynchronous, is shared—the individuals sharing the richer because of it.

NOTES

1. Signalling is defined by Hauptman (2000, p. 623) as "increased redundancy," through use of icons (pictures, graphs, charts, maps) and through non-iconic means (blooding, margin notes, titles/subtitles, etc.)

2. Davis also identifies the following as unique characteristics of the new literacy as implied by the WWW: easy access to texts (but difficulty in locating the desired one); mechanics of use (e.g., the hypertextual link structure and the scrolling format); the (increasingly challenged) predominance of English and U.S.-inspired cultural and aesthetic values.

REFERENCES

Barthes, R. (1975). *The pleasure of the text*. (R. Miller, Trans.) New York: Hill and Wang.

Bernhardt, E. (1991). *Reading development in a second language: Theoretical, empirical, and classroom perspectives*. Norwood, NJ: Ablex.

Childers, J., & Hentzi, G. (1995). *Columbia dictionary of cultural criticism*. New York: Columbia University Press.

Cole, M. (1996). *Cultural psychology: A once and future discipline*. Cambridge, MA: Belknap/Harvard University.

Davis, J.N. (2000). San Diego, CA: LARC Press. [http://larcnet.sdsu.edu]. Note: See downloads section on left of screen.

Davis, J.N. (1998). If the Internet is the answer, what was the question? *French Review, 72*(2), 382–395.

Davis, J.N., & Lyman-Hager, M.A. (1997). Computers and L2 reading: Student performance, student attitudes. *Foreign Language Annals, 30*, 58–72.

Donato, R., & McCormick, D. (1994). A sociocultural perspective on language learning strategies: The role of mediation. *Modern Language Journal, 78*, 453–64.

Eisenstein, E. (1979). *The printing press as an agent of change: Communications and cultural transformations in early-modern Europe* (2 vols.) Cambridge: Cambridge University Press.

El-Wardi, R., & Johns, A.M. (1997/98). A high shool/university e-mail partnership project. *CATESOL Journal, 10*(1), 7–28.

Hauptman, P.C. (2000). Some hypotheses on the nature of difficulty and ease in second language reading: An application of schema theory. *Foreign Language Annals, 33*, 622–631.

Hayden, S. (1997). *An investigation into the effect and patterns of usage of a computer-mediated text in reading comprehension in French*. Unpublished doctoral dissertation, The Pennsylvania State University.

Hyper Studio™. (1993/1997). Roger Wagner Publishing.

Johns, A.M. (1988). On reading to summarize. *Reading in a Foreign Language, 4*(2), 79–90.

Johns, A.M. (2001). An interdisciplinary, interinstitutional, learning communities program: Student involvement and student success. In I. Leki (Ed.), *Academic writing programs* (pp. 61–72). Alexandria, VA: TESOL.

Johns, A.M. (2002). Destabilizing and enriching novice students' genre theories. In A.M. Johns (Ed.), *Genre in the classroom: Multiple perspectives* (pp. 237–248). Mahwah, NJ: Erlbaum.

Johnson-Eilola, J. (1998). Negative space. In T. Taylor & I. Ward (Eds.), *Literacy theory in the age of the Internet* (pp. 17–33). New York: Columbia University.

Kid Pix Studio™. (1995, 1996). Broderbund.

Lanham, R. (1989). The extraordinary convergence: Democracy, technology, theory and the university curriculum. *South Atlantic Quarterly, 20*, 265–290.

Landow, G. (2000). URL: http://landow.stg.brown.edu/cpace/ht/htov.html. [Hypertext.website.]

Lantolf, J.P. (1994). Sociocultural theory and second language learning: Introduction to the special issue. *Modern Language Journal, 78*, 418–420.

Leow, R.P. (1997). The effects of input enhancement and text length on adult L2 readers' comprehension and intake in second language acquisition. *Applied Language Learning, 8*, 151–182.

Lyman-Hager, M.A., Davis, J.N., Burnett, J., & Chennault, R. (1993). Une vie de boy: Interactive reading in French. In F.L. Borchardt & E.M.T. Johnson (Eds.), *Proceedings of the Computer Assisted Learning and Instruction Consortium Annual Symposium of "Assessment"* (pp. 93–97). Durham, NC: CALICO Press.

Lyman-Hager, M., & Fischer, R. (1998). *A l'aventure.* CD ROM. New York: Wiley. [Software/CD ROM].

McConkie, G.W., & Zola, D. (1987). Two examples of computer-based research on reading: Eye movement monitoring and computer-aided reading. In D. Reinking (Ed.), *Reading and computers: Issues for theory and practice* (pp. 147–166). New York: Teachers College Press.

Meyer, A., & Rose, D. H. (1998). *Learning to read in the computer age.* Cambridge, MA: Brookline Books.

Negroponte, N. (1999). *Being digital.* New York: Knopf.

Nocon, H. (2001). *Fifth dimension second language project: Strategies for language teaching/learning.* San Diego: LARC Press.

Ong, W. (1982*). Orality and literacy: The technologizing of the word.* London: Methuen.

Robinson, P. (1995). Attention, memory, and the "noticing" hypothesis. *Language Learning, 45*, 283–331.

Schmidt, R.W. (1990). The role of consciousness in second language learning. *Applied Linguistics, 11*, 129–58.

Schulz, R.A. (1981). Literature and readability: Bridging the gap in foreign language reading. *Modern Language Journal, 65*, 45–53.

Storybook Weaver Deluxe™. (1994/1996). MECC/The Learning Company.

Toon, T.E. (1991). Drypoint annotations in early English manuscripts: Understanding texts and establishing contexts. In S.A. Barney (Ed.), *Annotation and its text* (pp. 74–93). New York: Oxford University Press.

Tuman, M.C. (1992). *Word Perfect: Literacy in the computer age.* Pittsburgh: University of Pittsburgh Press.

Vygotsky, L. (1978). *Mind in society.* Cambridge, MA: Harvard University.

Warschauer, M. (1997). A sociocultural approach to literacy and its significance for CALL. In K.A. Murphy-Judy (Ed.), *Nexus: The convergence of language teaching and research using technology: CALICO Monograph Series, No. 4* (pp. 88–97). Durham, NC: CALICO Press.

Warschauer, M. (1999). *Electronic literacies: Language, culture, and power in online education.* Mahwah, NJ: Erlbaum.

Printed in the United States
57543LVS00001BA/3